AF531754

STATUS OF DALIT WOMEN

STATUS OF DALIT WOMEN

By

Dr. G. Samba Siva Rao

M.A.

Deptt. of Sociology & Social Work
Acharya Nagarjuna University
Guntur (Distt.), Andhra Pradesh
(INDIA)

and

Dr. Allu Gowri Sankar Rao

M.S.W., Ph.D.

Assistant Professor
Deptt. of Sociology & Social Work
Acharya Nagarjuna University
Nagarjuna Nagar - 522 510, Guntur (Distt.)
Andhra Pradesh
(INDIA)

D P H

DISCOVERY PUBLISHING HOUSE PVT. LTD.
NEW DELHI-110 002

Published by:

Tilak Wasan

DISCOVERY PUBLISHING HOUSE PVT. LTD.

4383/4B, Ansari Road, Darya Ganj

New Delhi - 110 002 (India)

Phone : +91-11-23279245, 43596064-65

Fax : +91-11-23253475

E-mail : discoverypublishinghouse@gmail.com

sales@discoverypublishinggroup.com

website : www.discoverypublishinggroup.com

***First Edition:* 2015**

ISBN: 978-93-5056-711-1

Status of Dalit Women

Printed at:

Infinity Imaging Systems

Delhi

Dedicated
to
My Parents
Sri. G. Lakshmaiah
Smt. G. Lakshmma

PREFACE

Caste is what determines a person's status and dignity in Hindu society. He/She is born into a caste and his/her social status is therefore pre-detrained and unchanged. M. K. Gandhi one of the staunchest supporters and advocates of caste systems said that: "Caste means the pre-dissemination of a man's profession Caste implies that a man must-practice one profession of his ancestor of the livelihood.

They are about 250 millions Dalits in India, there is meager improvement in the Socoi-Economic conditions of Dalits in the past 65 years which is not enough to compare to non-Dalits. Every fourth Indian is Dalit and there is no proper survey to give current number of Dalit women in India. They are generally scattered in villages and they are not monogamous groups.

Though India has all along been a male dominated society and women have never been given the equally status in Socio-Economic fields, the Scheduled Caste women have been tied the bottom of the hierarchy as sweepers and scavengers. The status of women in India has been a chequred one as its as seen many ups and downs. Women in India here subject to discrimination not just on the basis of gender but on the basis of names of other factors such as Caste, Community, Religious affiliation and Class.

– Authors

ACKNOWLEDGEMENTS

This work has been carried out under the guidance of Dr. Allu Gowri Sankar Rao, M. S. W., Ph.D., Assistant Professor and Assistant Co-ordinator of Gandhian Studies Centre, Department of Sociology and Social Work, Acharya Nagarjuna University, Nagarjuna Nagar. I am extremely thankful to him for his sustained encouragement and helpful guidance. But for his support this thesis would not have been a reality and he spared no pains in going through this work at different stages inspite of his tight schedule. I profusely thank him for his guidance in my work.

I express my heartfelt gratitude to Dr. V. Venkateswarlu, Co-ordinator, Dr. M. Trimurthi Rao, Assistant Professor and Assistant Co-ordinator Dr. Y. Ashok Kumar, Assistant Professor and Assistant Co-ordinator, Dr. Saraswati Raju Iyer, Assistant Professor, Dr. K. Dhana Lakshmi, Assistant Professor, Department of Sociology and Social Work, Acharya Nagarjuna University, for their co-operation and encouragement in completing my research work.

Further I am thank full Dr. Chenna Reddy, Assistant Professor, Department of English for his help during my research work. Dr. D. Sai Sujatha, Associate Professor Department of Population science and Social Work, Sri Venkatewhwara University, Tirupathi for her encouragement my research work. I express heartfelt gratitude to Dr. Ch. Swaroopa Rani, Associate Professor; Centre for Mahayana Buddhist Studies, Acharya Nagarjuna University for her encouragement my research work.

I have immense pleasure to express my gratitude to Prof. Chandan, Department of Statistics, Acharya Nagarjuna University and Dr. P. Venkata Rao, Assistant Professor, Department of Social Work, Acharya Nagarjuna University, P. G. Campus, Ongle, G. Samba Siva Rao, A. S. O Tenali Mandal, further their timely help in the research work.

I am grateful to Dr. Bala Severry, (late) M.A., Ph.D (JNU - New Delhi). Mr. K. Nagabushnam, Mr. P. Pothu Raju (Ret.), M. Chitti Babu, Mr. Ijack Syam, (Ret., H.M), Ms. P.S.S. Kiran, (Ph.D)., Miss. P. Yesodhamma (late), G. Vendatam, M.A., B.Ed, P.S.V. Chary, M.A., Mr. K. Sudharshan Babu, B.Tech. Mr. K. L. Srinivasa Rao, K. Anna Rose, M.A., K. Kiran, M.Tch., Mr. K. Nani for their encouragement and help in completion of my theses work.

I express my thanks to my friends and my Co-Scholars namely: B. K. Chaitanya, V. Ganga Raju, B. Srinivasu P. Venugopal Rao, K. Mohan Rao, M. Galaiah in completing my thesis.

I further thankful to other non-teaching staff like: B. Sankar Reddy, Ch. Venkataiah and Jhonsi, Department of Sociology and Social Work, Acharya Nagarjuna University.

Finally I am deeply grateful to my parents Sri G. Lakshmaiah and Smt. Lakshmma, my sisters and my family members and for their affection, co-operation during my work.

– Authors

CONTENTS

1 INTRODUCTION

In India and other countries in South Asia, people have been systematically discriminated against on the basis of their work and descent for centuries. Over 200 million people are Dalits, also known as untouchables or outcastes. They experience violence, discrimination, and social exclusion on a daily basis. Economic growth in Indian has been strong over the past decade. However, the caste disparities are increasing.

Who are the Dalits

Dalits are the poor and downtrodden. Generally, Dalit includes those termed in administrative parlance as Scheduled Castes (SCs), Scheduled Tribes (STs) and Other Back Ward Classes (OBCs). However, in day-to-day usage in political discourse, the term is so far mainly confined to SCs. They are the castes identified by the president of India under Article 341 and put under a Schedule. The term SC was first used by the British in the Government of India Act, 1935. Prior to this, some of these castes were included among the Depressed Classes – a category used for the first time at the beginning of the 20th century (Gupta 1985: 7-35). Traditionally, in the Hindu social order they are placed at the bottom of the hierarchy, considered Ali-shudras or Avarna, and are treated as untouchables. However, all ex-untouchables do not find a place in this Schedule, and all castes under the Schedule did not experience untouchability to an equal degree in the recent or distant past.

The caste system, in which SCs occupy the lowest position, per-petuates and maintains inequality. According to Dr. Babasaheb Ambedkar, the caste system has been legitimized through the Shastras. It has religious sanction. 'It is spiritual, moral and legal. There is no sphere of life which is not regulated by this principle of graded inequality' (Moon 1987a:107). Following Dr. Ambedkar's framework, Throat and Deshpande argue that as a scheme of distribution, the Hindu social order has failed miserably, and over time, produced appalling economic inequalities and poverty, particularly among the social groups located at the bottom of the social and economic hierarchy of the Indian society. Discrimination, which is an all-pervading character of the caste system, is just not confined to production relations alone but covers all possible economic spheres. This is evident from the land-ownership pattern. A vast majority of SCs (84%) live in rural areas. They are agricultural labourers, sharecroppers or self-cultivators. Nearly 13 per cent of the SC households, against 11 per cent of the others, are landless and among those who own land, a vast majority (nearly 86%) comprise small and marginal farmers.

Among bonded labourers, estimated at over 20 lakhs, Scheduled Caste labourers constitute a sizeable number, if not a majority. They are bonded against debts that they incurred dither for marriage and/or day-to-day expenses. Some of these bonded labourers work for the same master for several years or, in a few cases, even for life, they live a worst life.

While Bonded Labour System Act, 1976, and every labour 'shall stand freed and discharged from the obligation to render labour in lieu of loans', in practice the system still prevails. Though one can cite isolated cases of bonded labourers who were freed due to the efforts of some individual bureaucrats and activists, many such 'free' labourers reverted to bonded labour sooner or later. Throat and Deshpande have a reason to believe that there is systematic segmentation of Scheduled Caste workers into certain categories of low-paid economic activities, and this is possibly the result of the discrimination in terms of access to market, land, employment and capital formation.

Though segmentation and discrimination of Dalits in various spheres does continue, it is not total, thanks to capitalist development and competitive politics. The modern Indian state does not legitimize caste-based discrimination. Various land reforms related to ceiling and distribution of land have enhanced, to a small extent, access to land among a tiny section of SCs. Moreover, all SC households are not small section of SC cultivators – 4.5 per cent against 10.5 per cent of the others – are middle or rich peasants owning 4 hectares, or more. Though they are not as well off as Hindu in the same category, a few of them have certainly improved their condition in comparison with their brethren in that they have taken advantage of the so-called development programmes over the last five decades and produced marketable surplus.

A section of Dalits pursuit traditional caste occupations along with agriculture. They are leather workers, weavers, scavengers, basket makers, etc. The capitalist system has opened avenues for those whose skills and products are marketable. For instance, the Chamars in Agra have improved their condition by marketing their products, though their social position has not changed much (lynch 1969). In urban areas, SCs are employed in the organized and unorganized industrial sectors; they are petty shopkeepers, small entrepreneurs, scavengers and white-collar workers, mainly in the public sector. Scavengers in urban areas have become blue-collar workers, but their social status has not changed. Their occupation is still looked down upon as polluting.

Though the visible practice of untouchability has declined – certainly in public spheres (Desai 1976, Shah 2001) incidents of atrocities against Dalits have not shown a similar downturn and continue unabated in post-independence India in various forms of murder; grievous hurt, arson and rape. Caste prejudices often contribute, but are not solely responsible for the atrocities against Dalit. Conflicts over material interests and political power contribute a great deal to such incidents. Land-owning classes – upper as well as middle and OBCs do not tolerate land allotted to Dalit under various welfare programmes of the state. Disputes over public and common land and other resources such as forest and water, and wages, lead to clashes between Dalits and non-Dalits.

Thus, a very vast majority of SCs in spite of diversification of occupation, rise in literacy rate and urban migration, though at a slow pace-continue to experience discrimination and deprivation. Legislations relating to the removal of untouchability, control of atrocities and equality of opportunities have, by and large, remained on paper. But at the same time a small section of Dalits have improved their economic condition. They compete with the non-Dalit middle class and in the process, assert their dignity and share in political offices.

Dalit Identity

The term 'dalit' has its root in Sanskrit (Dal) which means broken, cracked, trodden down, scattered, crushed or destroyed. It is interesting to note that the Hebrew verb 'dal' also means the frail one or the weak one which denotes the poor and lowly of the society. (Gutierrez, 1973:291) The term was first used by Jyotiraj Phule (1827-1890), a backward class social reformer, to describe the untouchables and outcastes of India as the oppressed and broken victims of the Hindu society. The term is a constant reminder of their age-old oppression and deprivation. It does not actually mean poor or outcaste but, as Dr. Kuruvila points out, it is a state to which a certain section of the people have been reduced through systematic religious process and are forced to live continually in the predicament.

There are many names used to identify the untouchables of India but Dalit is the name they themselves prefer because it exactly describes their situation in the society. Mahatma Gandhi called them Harijans (people of God) but the untouchable considered it a misnomer because it did not signify their real status. They Indian social structure rooted as it is in the Hindu or Brahmanic caste system can indeed boast of creating children of a lesser god. A section of the people has been maliciously and deliberately made poor and outcaste because according to the sacred religious system they are outside the four-fold caste system.

Caste is what determines a person's status and dignity in the Hindu society. There is nothing that a person can do about the choice of the caste. He/she is born into a caste and his/her social status is therefore predestined and unchangeable. One has to perform the duties that one inherits by being born into a particular caste and that is the only way to salvation. Mahatma Gandhi, one of the staunchest supporters and advocates of caste system says that "Caste means the predetermination of a man's profession. Caste implies that a man must practice only the profession of his ancestors for his livelihood".

Gandhi asserts that a person who does not live up to the profession of the caste in which he/she is born does violence to oneself and becomes a degraded being. He expresses the common conviction of the Hindus when he says that caste has saved Hinduism from disintegration and that the Hindu society has been able to stand precisely because it is founded on the caste system. The four steps in the caste ladder are:

1. *Brahmins* (The priestly class) According to Hindu mythology they originate from the head of god. They do the learning and teaching of the scriptures besides performing sacrifice.
2. *Kshatrias* (The warrior class) They come from God's shoulder and their work is to protect people by fighting against enemies.
3. *Vysias* (The trading class), Originates from the thigh of God and their work is to feed the above two classes.
4. *Sudras* (The servant class), Originates from the feet of God. They are to be servants of the above three classes.
5. *Panchamas* (The fifth class), They are the impure, the unclean, and untouchables. These outcasts are the scum of the society-treated with contempt.

Indian history reveals that the Dalits were the original settlers of India. But the Aryans invaded India in around 1500 B. C., defeated the King and captured the people and made them slaves. Then they slowly created the caste system woven into their religion of Hinduism. Thus we see that this in human and barbaric practice of caste discrimination and untouchability has been given religious sanctions and blessings, and has been perpetuated on the Indian soil for nearly 3500 years. Since caste system is thought to be of divine origin any breaking of this system individually or collectively is considered to be a violation against God and his divine law. Very painstakingly every dimension of this divine ordinance was included in the Hindu scriptures. The Reg-Veda, the Upanishads and the Baghavadgita along with Manu Dharma are the principal channels through which the caste system is perpetuated.

Dalit – Always out Side

The dalits not only find themselves out of the four-fold caste system but are also forced to live in separate colonies (cherries) outside towns and villages. Manu Dharma, the Hindu religious code of conduct, which is believed to be divinely revealed spells out clearly the meticulous details of who the outcasts should conduct themselves, where they could live and what duties are ascribed to them. It is the practice of this code of conduct that still keeps the Dalits outside the village living in subhuman conditions. Most of the dalits are bonded labourers of the village landlords. They have no own land, property or houses. They still do the works that the society considers to be the corks of the slaves. They are the scavengers, street cleaners, cobblers, washer-folk, those who beat the drums for the dead, those who carry the dead and those who wait upon the upper caste lords. There are still many villages where a dalit can not sit on the same bench with a high caste person in a coffee shop. There are still villages where a dalit cannot ride a bicycle through the streets of high caste people or even walk with king of foot wear. The women can not go to the common village well to draw water. I do not want to paint an altogether dark and pessimistic picture of our society. Things have improved considerable in some villages. But there are hundreds of villages where the pathetic plight of the Dalits has hardly changed. Some Dalits who have come up in life due to education prefer to migrate to towns and cities where they can live in anonymity without the fear of the social stigma attached to their caste. It will not be a exaggeration to say that the dalits are still the poorest of the poor in Indian society. They are not even low people. They are 'no people'. The Hindu society has robbed their identity as human beings.

Mahatma Gandhi, an ardent champion for removing untouchability with in the Hindu Chaturvarna framework, called the untouchable, 'Harijan'-man of God. The denominator was used in 1931 amid conflicts between Gandhi and Ambedkar on the issue of political representation to Dalits on the basis of a separate community – distinct from Hindus. Gandhi borrowed the name from a Bhakti saint of the 17th century, Narsinh Mehta. He primarily appealed to caste Hindu to use the term Harijan instead of Antyaja. While giving currency to the word, he explained.

Gandhi hoped that…. 'probably, Antyaja brethren would lovingly accept that name and try to cultivate the virtues which it connotes. may the Antyaja become Harijan both in name and nature' (Gandhi 1971: 244-45). The congress party gave currency to the new nomenclature for untouchables during the freedom movement.

The term Harijan has been widely used by caste Hindus as a substitute for achchuta, *i.e..*, untouchable. Many SCs also began to call themselves so hoping that the caste Hindus would change their behaviour towards them. But the new category hardly enthused most SCs except a few who followed the path of Sanskritisation to cultivate the virtues of upper castes. It did not provide a new world-view, symbol or path to attain equal status, which they began to demand during this period. In fact, for Gandhi, the new category aimed at persuading caste Hindus to express repentance. By doing so, they were expected to change their heart and behaviour towards untouchables. Dr. Ambedkar and his followers did not find any difference whether they were called achchuta or Harijan, as the new nomenclature did not change their status in the social order.

Ambedkar believed 'Untouchables do not regard Gandhi as being earnest in eradicating untouchability' (Moon 1990: 254). According to him, saints (like Nardinh Mehata) never carried on a campaign against caste and untouchability. The saints of the Bhakti sect 'were not concerned with the struggle between man and man. They were concerned with the relation between man and God' (Kumber 1979). Later, a section of the SC leaders rejected the term Harijan, considering it an insult rather than an honour.

Dr. Ambedkar had a different approach and philosophy regarding the emancipation of SCs. He strived for an egalitarian social order. Such an order, he believed, was not possible within Hinduism whose very foundation was hierarchical with SCs at the bottom. The Chaturvarna system was part of Hinduism. 'The re-organisastion of the Hindu society on the basis of Chaturvarna is impossible because the Varnavastha is like a leaky pot or like a man running at the nose... religious sanctity behind Caste and Varnas must be destroyed... that the sanctity of Caste and Varnas can be destroyed only by discarding the divine authority of the 'Shastras' (Moon 1979:86-87). *Second,* Ambedkar did not have faith in the 'charitable spirit' of the caste Hindus towards the untouchables. He asserted that SCs should get organized and educated, and struggle for self-respect rather than depend on sympathy.

Though Dr. B. R. Ambedkar did not popularize the ward 'Dalit' for untouchables, his philosophy has remained a key source in its emergence and popularity. In a way, the word Dalit is of relatively recent origin – of the 1960s in public discourse. Marathi speaking literary writers, neo-Buddists by persuasion, began to use the word Dalit in their literary works instead of Harijan or achchuta. Dalit writers who have popularized the word have expressed their notion of Dalit identity in their essays, poems, dramas, autobiographies, novels and short stories. They have reconstructed their past and their view of the present. They have expressed their anger, protest and aspiration. Punalekar examines Dalit literary works and identity formation . The word gained currency in public spheres during the SC caste Hindu riots in Bombay in the early 1970s. Dalit panthers used the term to assert their identity for rights and self-respect. Later, the term has been used with a wider connotation. It includes all the oppressed and exploited section of society. It does not confine it self-merely to economic exploitation in terms of appropriation of surplus. It also relates to suppression of culture – way of life and value system – and, more importantly, the denial of dignity. It has essentially emerged as a political category. For some, it connotes an ideology for fundamental change in the social structure and relationships. According to Gangadhar Pantawane: 'Dalit is not a caste. Dalit is a symbol of change and revolution. The Dalit believes in humanism. He rejects existence of God, rebirth, soul, sacred books that teach discrimination, faith and heaven because these have made him a slave. He represents the exploited man in hinds country' (cited by Das and Massey 1995: iv). Gopal guru argues in the Dalit identity not merely expressed who Dalits are, but also conveys their aspirations and struggle for 'change and revolution'.

2 STATUS OF WOMEN IN INDIA

The Indian society like a number of classical societies was patriarchal. Patriarchal values regulating sexuality, reproduction and social production prevailed and were expressed through specific cultural metaphors. Overt rules prohibiting women from specific activities and denying certain rights did exist. But more subtle expression of patriarchy was through symbolism giving messages of inferiority of women through legends highlighting the self-sacrificing, self-sacrificing pure image of women and through the ritual practices which day in and day out emphasised the dominant role of a women as a faithful wife and devout mother.

The basic rules for women's behaviour as expressed in the Laws of Manu insist that a woman must constantly worship her husband as a god, even though his destitute of virtue or a womanizer. Women should be kept in dependence by her husband because by nature they are passionate and disloyal. The ideal women are those who do not strive to break these bonds of control. The salvation and happiness of women revolve around their virtue and chastity as daughters, wives and widows. This theme has been reiterated by the recurrent symbolism of seed and the earth. Man provides the seed, the essence for the creation of the offspring; the seed determines the kind: the child's identity is derived from the father for the group placement. The role of the mother is just to receive the seed and through her own blood provide warmth and nourishment and help it to grow. Renowned anthropologist Leela Dube while referring to this symbolism comments: "One of the most significant aspects of the symbolism is how the two partners are situated in the process or reproduction. In his body man has the seed; the woman, on the other hand is herself the field".. The two partners are not on par with one another in so far as the process of reproduction is concerned. The offspring belongs to the one to whom the seed belongs. In fact he also owns the field. Very sinister implication of this symbolism is that the man is the lord master owner, or provider. A daughter or a wife is a commodity or a possession.

Besides such symbolism relegating woman to a lower position there are rituals and practices for a woman which reinforce her role a devout wife is a doting mother. Women perform a large number of the yearly calendrical rites. These rites seek the protection and well-being of crucial kinsman (especially husband, brother and son) the general prosperity and health of family members. Men's rites are not concerned with having good wives or one who will have a long life.

Further, the ideal women of Indian mythology who have been extolled as paragons of virtue like: Sita, Savitri, Draupadi, Damyanti etc., are women who have been dutiful truthful chaste, self-sacrificing women of unswerving wifely devotion whatever the temptation. The legends associated with them consistently refer to their purity and self-less attachment to their consorts. At one place wives have been mentioned as restraining all their sense and keeping their hearts under complete control; they regard their husbands as veritable gods. For women neither sacrifice nor sraddh as (penances) are of any efficacy. By serving their husbands only, can they win heaven. This ideal gets re-enforced thoroughly numerous myths and legends. One important point in understanding the value structure in Indian society is the dual concept of the female in Hindu philosophy: On the on hand woman is fertile, benevolent bestowed of prosperity, on the other hand she is considered aggressive malevolent and destructive. This dual character manifests self in the goddesses also as there are dangerous aggressive malevolent goddesses like: Kali and Durga; there are equally important goddesses like: Laxmi, Saraswti, Mariamman who are benevolent. Veena Das while analysing the anthropological meaning of prevalence of the worship of goddesses, draws attention to the fact that in shakti form the goddess usually stands alone had is not encompassed with a higher male principle. She add: "The principle of power fins expression in the goddesses who represent shakti who come to the aid of man and gods in period of cosmic darkness, by killing the demon who threaten the entire cosmic order. The principle of renunciation on the other hand, finds expression in the ideals of sati.

This duality is confusing and attempts are made to explain it Susan Wadley for instance, considers that there is a cultural logic in this concepts. She says "The female is first of all shakti (energy/power) the energizing principle of the universe. The female is also prakriti (Nature) the undifferentiated Matter of the Universe". She further adds, "Uniting these two facets of femaleness, women are both energy/power and nature, and nature is uncultured… uncultured power is dangerous". Romila Thapar in this quality sees both contempt and fear. The latter doubtless derived from fear of pollution since women were regarded as impure of many occasions. Sushi Kakkar, while studying the inner world of an Indian child, harps upon the intimate relationship between the mother and the son. Wherein for the son, wherein for the son the mother's original perfection remains untarnished by reality a part of the iconography of Hindu inner world. He remarks, "in the case of a Hindu woman, at least in the imagery of the culture, maternal feelings of tenderness and nurturance occur in combination with a profound gratitude and the readiness for a poignantly high emotional investment in the child.

The value structure by presenting the dual character of woman, seems to have been successful in creating a myth that Indian woman possesses power, which is far from the position in readily. This whole concept is still unclear and needs more exploration. However, it is a very valuable concept in understanding the seemingly high and really inferior position of women in India.

In order to properly estimate the position of women in ancient society, a brief reference to the stratificatory system as expressed through varna and caste system is necessary. The varna principle of categorisation of society into four groups, *viz;* Brahmans, Kshatriyas, Vaishyas and Shudras existed in Vedic society. The four varnas are mentioned in order of hierarchy wherein the first three are called dwija, *i.e.,* twice-born while the Shudras occupy the lowest position in the society and they are expected to serve the other three varnas.

Brahmans occupy ritually and ideologically the top position of power and authority. The principle of stratification acquired normative significance, thus legitimizing the over-lordship of the Brahmans. The varna scheme were empirically expressed through various caste groups, indicating the adjustment of the system to the development needs of the society. A good deal of controversy about the caste system centres around its origin. Scholars are divided in their opinions with regard to the emergence of a stratificatory system which has such a powerful hold on both religious and secular activities of the Indian even today. The most popular and widely prevalent theory traces the origin to the Aryan invasion of India and links it to be process by which the invaders could sub-ordinate the indigenous inhabitants and integrate them as peasants and slaves in a stratified society. Thus the 'twice-born' castes are descendants from the non-Aryans.

Position of Women in India: An Overview

The status of women in India has been a chequered one as it has seen many ups and downs. In the Vedic age, they were worshipped as goddesses. In the Muslim age, their status suffered a sharp decline and in the British regime they were looked down upon as: 'Slaves of Slaves'. Since independence the tide seems to have gone in their favour. There is no denying the fact that women in India have made some progress, may be because of the social legislation, the progress made in the fields of education, health or economic or as a result of

Technological very small numbers, we find engineers, pilots, journalists, teachers, administrators, judges including a woman judge in he Supreme Court, State Governors, ambassadors, members of parliament and ministers. We have a women prime minister and a president of the U. N. Assembly. In spite of these achievements, the fact remains that the women's condition is a grim reality. Though concern is being expressed for her emancipation in every field, economic independence is of paramount importance. Efforts are on to ensure that she is economically not dependent of anyone. But these efforts have hardly been of any help. The woman is now burdened with two kinds of Jobs-her work within the house and the job outside. She does not find any free time to enjoy the fruits of her economic independence. Not only that in many cases she is the custodian of her salary till she arrives home. Her salary later becomes a part of the total development of the woman the awareness about her rights and responsibilities, the recognition of her role and the work that she does at home. If necessary the social system must change so that the woman does not have to ask for concessions.

The year 1990 was observed as the year of the girl child. Her well-being and her status in the family, the community and the nation may be the focal points of concern. Perhaps there may be an increasing awareness that the girl child is also human being with her thoughts, emotions, aspirations, will and individuality of her own. In fact, the post. Independence period, particularly in the case of women, has been a continuation of pre-independence era of social reforms, economic uplift and political recognition. The struggle for equality, Justice, Parity between women and men and for their identity continues.

The social reforms, which began in the 19th century, set in motion a number of legal measures with a view to improving the conditions of women. The laws thus enacted, among others, related to infanticide, child marriage, widow remarriage, sati etc. This even though was a step forward and an enabling factor in the development of women, the law could not achieve the desired results. For in the case of social legislation it is also imperative to have a change in the outlook, in the perception of women's role and support service. All these have been very slow to come by; consequently, even after more than a century of social reforms, the change, though discernible, is far from being indicative of a parity between men and women.

The overview of the situation generally is distressing. Rape, dowry deaths, misuses of the tests to determine the sex of the child in the womb and the termination of pregnancy in the event of a female fetus is given an indication of the horrible behaviour patterns. In recent years the Government has taken a number of steps to correct the wrong that is done to the girl child. We have the report of the committee on the status of women, the women's year followed by the women's decade, women's departments , national perspective plan for women, the inclusion of aspirate chapter on women's development in the 7th plan and now the national commission. All These measures show the concern for women.

The women have yet to travel a long way before they can be equated with men. Employment and income-generating production programme was stated in 1982-83 to train women belonging to weaker sections of society and provide them employment on sustained basis. It is implemented through public sector undertaking/corporations/autonomous bodies/ voluntary organizations. Assistance for the programme comes from Norwegian Agency for International Development (NORAD).

The concept and organization of self-help group (SHG) has been described as an illustration for understanding. Non-Governmental Organizations (NGOs) by organizing SHGs, facilitate a 'silent sustainable grass-root revolution' for ameliorating the lives of the rural poor, particularly women.

Women in Indian Society

There are a number of images of Indian women, some times complementary and sometimes contradictory. She is revered as a Goddess; but at the same time, her birth is not much preferred. She is considered as an embodiment of Sakti, but at the same time she is considered as one to be protected all through in her life-by father, husband and son respectively. She is worshipped as a Goddess but instances of treating her as slave are not unknown. She is honoured as a mother and loved as a child. But as a wife and of one's own age group, for example, a friend or a colleague, the attitude is not always positive or friendly. At times, general comments on entire women-folk irrespective of age and accomplishments, are not unknown. While the reverential feelings exist at ideological level, she is socially treated as inferior and is assigned discriminatory values.

Women, form about half of the population of the country, but their situation has been grim. For centuries, they have been deliberately denied opportunities of growth in the name of religion and socio-cultural practices. Before independence, women were prey to many abhorrent customs, traditional rigidities and vices due to which their status in the society touched its nadir and their situation was all-round bleak. At the personal social plan, women were victims of widespread illiteracy, segregation in the dark and dingy rooms in the name of purdah, forced child marriage, indeterminable widowhood, rigidity of fidelity and opposition to remarriage of widows turning many of them into prostitutes, polygamy, female infanticide, violence and force to follow SATI, and the complete denial of individuality. Besides, the economic dependence, early tutelage of husbands and in-laws, heavy domestic work-load which remained unpaid and unrecognized, absence of career and mobility, no-recognition of their economic contribution, poor work-conditions and wages, and monotonous jobs which men generally refused to do was also responsible for their pitiable conditions. At the socio-politically plan women suffered from the denial of freedom even in their homes, repression and unnatural indoctrination, unequal and inferior status, rigid caste hierarchy and untouchability. Consequently, most women were reduced to dumb cattle and had lead to inhuman beastly life. During pre-independent India nationalist movement led by Mahatma Gandhi strived to achieve equality for women. Women were Gandhi's 'last persons' whose tears he wanted to wipe and without their liberation, he thought the country's independence was superficial. The Fundamental Rights and Directive principles enshrined in the Constitution are the instruments to attain the national objectives of equality, liberty and justice. By these objectives, the Constitution abolished all discriminations flowing from sex, caste, creed, colour and place of birth. Women were placed at par with men in all respects. Women's sacrifices of pre-independence days were rewarded by the Fundamental Rights of equality between both the sexes. The Constitution of India had not only provided equal rights and privileges to both men and women, but has also gone a step further to make provisions for special measures to be undertaken by the Government to improve the conditions of women by enacting laws and establishing separate institutions. Thus, the Constitution has once for all settled the position of women in society. This recognition of political equality of women was a radical departure from socio-cultural norms prevailing in the country.

The status of women is intimately connected with their economic status which in turn, depends upon rights, roles and opportunities for the participation in economic activities. The economic status of women is now accepted as an indicator of a society's stage of development. However, all developments do not result in improving women's economic activities. Pattern of women's activities are affected by prevailing social ideology and are also linked with the stage of economic development. Undoubtedly, the scope of women's career has expanded during last forty years.

Women, throughout the country and more so in Uttar Pradesh are very inadequately participating in the development process. They are the recipients of an iniquitously small share of development opportunities. Their access to education, nutrition, health care, skill formation, jobs and decision-making is very limited. Many customs cause them harassment.

Wage discrimination and gender bias are both visible and widespread. Generally they are employed in low paid, low producing sectors, despite a lot of laws enacted for conceptualizing the equal status of women.

After Independence many steps have been taken to improve the lot of women. Many laws have also been passed. A National Commission on Women was setup to act as a watchdog on the matters concerning women in 1992. Many Programmes in the areas of education, health and employment have been initiated for development of women, rural as well as urban.

Women in India are subject to discrimination not just on the basis of gender but on the basis of numerous other factors such as caste, community, religious affiliation and class. India's caste system involves a social hierarchy and is a feature of Hinduism. People are born into a caste where they remain throughout their lives. Keer (1936), compared the Hindu society with a tower 'which have several stories without a ladder or an entrance' in which one 'was to die in the storey in which one was born'. On the basis of broad caste categories (Varnas), the caste groups can be separated according to occupation. Outside these categories are the 'untouchables' or dalits whose occupations like: sweepers, tanners - were viewed as 'polluting' and who are subject to segregation.

Ambedkar interpreted caste as a dysfunctional, disintegrative and undesirable institution. Ambedkar was of the view that in order to maintain the so-called purity and sacredness, the caste Hindus not only maintained physical and social distance with the untouchables and other backward classes, but they also developed different prescriptions and proscriptions which these caste were forced to follow. They were forced to lead a pitiable life and debarred from following the culture and tradition of higher castes. Those who dared to go through the process of what Srinivas called 'Sanskritisation' had to face rough weather Ambedkar (1936) criticized the socialists and their view points toward the caste system. According to him, we cannot understand social relations in

India on the basis of economic relations. There are about hundreds and thousands of Sadhus and Fakirs. We have so many religious places. We believe in the cycle of birth and death. Hence, if we have to understand India, we must take into account these undercurrents. He opined that without having social reformation, which includes withering away of the caste system and untouchability, we cannot think of economic reformation Keer (1981) said "caste is the cause of the downfall of the Hindus. Owning to the caste system the Hindu's life has been a life of continuous defeats. Caste has made the Hindus the sick men of India. Caste has ruined the Hindu race and has destroyed, demoralised and devitalized the Hindu society". The only way to improve and reform them is to reject the existence of the caste system. This is not possible because for the Caste Hindu, Caste and religion are more important than the people and the society.

Most of those belonging to dalit communities are expected to stay in the profession they are born into, and overall, members of dalit and adivasi communities are less well educated than their non-dalit counterparts. About 75 per cent of dalits live below poverty line. Economic backwardness of dalits is mostly due to injustice done to them by the high castes and also due to exploitation. From the time immemorial dalit women worked like slaves, sold as commodities resulting in their social discrimination, economic deprivation and educational backwardness. Literacy levels among dalit women are among the lowest levels of literacy of all groups in India (in rural areas, only ten % are literate). Till recently, many dalit women were ill-treated and educationally backward inspite of the facilities of free education. Their low level of literacy is due to three interrelated factors:

1. Continued monopolization of state, economic, cultural and other resources by middle and upper class groups.
2. The stronger influence of casteism in rural areas on dalit women.
3. The control of dalit men over dalit women and girls. As a result of which, dalit women's access to even basic literacy or education is limited.

Nearly ninety per cent of dalit women are in rural; most of them are landless or marginal farmers who live in abject poverty with grinding labour. Many work as coolies, or day-to-day manual workers without much re-turns. Their economic situation has worsened due to the overall deteriorating rural economic conditions as a result of the New Economic Policy. So too, the deterioration and privatization of common forest re-sources on which many Dalit women depend for survival. Water and fuel scarcity have a direct influence on Dalit girls' access to education.

Dalit women are the target of government population programmes and female literacy is viewed as part of this strategy, in other government programmes and schemes for rural and urban women, it is other back-ward castes (OBCs), middle and upper Hindu caste women who derive most of the benefits dalit women are left out with few exception. In all cases of caste conflict Dalit women are the first victims. Dalit women are invisible in school curricula and text books. Poverty, the root cause of many social problems compels most rural Dalit parents to send their children to work rather than to school. Many Dalit parents consider education for girls as a luxury, pointing out that it is expensive and later on there is lack of gainful employment opportunities. For example, Dalit women's participation in the organized sector is negligible. However, many parents also feel that education beyond the primary level of girls will affect their household management. Infant mortality due to neglect and malnutrition is very high. Among the several factors the gender division of labour, child marriage and restricted mobility also limit Dalit women's access to education. These factors directly contribute to a high dropout rate among dalit girls especially at the secondary school level and higher. Dropout and non-enrollment is also due to other factors including the lack of childcare facilities in rural areas, cooking, cleaning and other domestic chores; employment as child labourers to supplement the family income; education and marriage of siblings; and above all the attitudes of parents and the Dalit community. Fear of alienation of girls from their environment as a result of education is yet another factor for low literacy level among Dalit girls. Even if the education improves the marriage prospects of the girls, the minus point is the increase in dowry. Therefore, many parents wish to withdraw their girls from schools.

The present scenario seems to be better with reference to the rate of literacy among dalits. The literacy rate is 31.48 per cent for boys and 10.93 per cent for girls. In rural areas, Dalit girls need the assistance of government and other welfare organizations. In many Dalit association executive positions are occupied by male members whereas very poor representation is made by women. There is an urgent need to get a feedback about the welfare schemes where lot of money is allocated for the development of Dalits. The funds are not properly utilised for their development. Many of the schemes go unnoticed because they are not popularized properly.

The coaching programme conducted by the government for Dalit women are beneficial in training many women to compete in the competitive exams. These programmes do not reach the needy Dalit women, be-cause they are cornered by the very few creamy Dalit women. This needs to be monitored and schemes should be designed in such a way so that it is evenly distributed. The benefits should be directed towards the most deprived and constantly struggling Dalit women.

Because these Dalit women are neglected by socially advanced communities and also by the better off among the Dalits, which leads to an unhealthy socio-economic condition. There should be some scientific basis to pick up the poorest and they should be equipped with facilities. There are some pre-examination coaching centres offering training for Dalits which are doing good service. They are training them in vocational line for competitive exams, in medical and engineering field, railway recruitment boards, bank recruitment etc. These services also needs to be checked so that they reach the poorest deserving dalit women so as to make optimum use of the services.

3 DALITS AND DALIT WOMEN

Origin and Development of Dalit Community

They constitute nearly 15.75 per cent of India's population (Registrar General and Census Commissioner). Scheduled Castes named as Harijans by Gandhi are entangled in sub-human social existence, abject poverty, economic exploitation, sub-culture of submission and political powerlessness. "Centuries of continuous misfortunes have suppressed the heat of his anger and he patiently handles his miseries. He places his wife on work to supplement his income. She makes her baby lie and cry on the footpath and herself grooms the road-side near by. When the sons and daughters grow slightly up the age, they are at once put to the groomining task, denying them schooling, playing and loitering worthy of their age" (R. P. Dewan). It is India's untouchables, has withstood the psycho-economic pressures of social conformity for centuries.

The details of the origin of untouchability and the racial, ethnic composition of the Scheduled Caste population is shrouded in mystery. They have been the weakest constituent to the Indian social structure except the Adivasis. They are designated with a variety of nomenclatures such as: untouchables, harijans, depressed classes, dalits, servile classes, weaker sections, panchamas, atisudras, avarnas and antyajas and Scheduled Castes. The term *'depressed classed'* refers to those castes which belong to the lowest rung of the Hindu caste hierarchy and whose touch or proximity is considered polluting by the caste Hindus (G. N. Reddy). This is a British innovation from and article written by Dr. Annie Besant in the *Indian Review*, February 1909 with the caption '*The uplift of the depressed* classes'. The word '*Dalits*' denotes poverty and their oppressed conditions. The 'servile classes' phrase was used to denote the servile nature of their working relations with the higher castes and the degraded nature of work with which they were involved like Scavenging and sweeping etc.

(G. S. Ghurye). D. G. Tendulkar preferred the term 'Harijan' to Antyaja used by the Saint Narsimha Mehta. Later, it become a catch-word-cum-brain child of M. K. Gandhi who popularized the concept.

Limited exclusiveness and consequent practice of ceremonial purity show themselves as fundamental traits of culture and character of other and Western branches of Indo-European peoples. The Greeks even in the heydey of their philosophical thought, manifested this spirit. Their contempt of the slaves is almost proverbial and the bulk of the slave population differed from them in both race and culture. Plato, the maker of ideal laws, offers the finest testimony of the depth of this feeling and perhaps of the extent of the practice. His penalty of the heinous offence of striking one's parent is the perpetual exilement of the striker from the city. In order that this exile and ostracism may be completely successful, Plato further lays down a rule, which is redolent of the caste penalties of the Hindus on their erring members. It runs: And if any person eat or drink, or have any other sort of intercourse with him, or meeting him have voluntarily touched him, he shall not enter into any temple, nor into the agora, nor into the city, until he is purified for he should consider that he has become tainted by a curse (A. C. Pradhan). So in Greek, the slaves had a similar status of Dalits that we find in our Indian tradition the position of Harijans.

Ancient India

The origin of these dalits is a complicated theme. We trace it's origin from the Vedic period, *i.e.*, the coming of Aryans to

India during 2500 B. C. to 2000 B. C., and from the writings of Rig-Veda which was written during 1200 B. C. to 1000 B. C., so in the early Vedic time, it is said that, all men were equals and there was no trace of untouchability as we see it to-day. According to Rig-Veda, in those days, perfect brotherhood was prevalent. In course of time, when the Aryans, having grown in overwhelming numbers, scattered and colonised throughout the whole of *Aryavarta,* they divided themselves into four divisions according to their different qualities (*guna*) and actions (*karmas*) in order to organize their society and set it upon sound basis. This four fold division has been a pre-dominant feature of Hindu social fabric" (R. R. Prasad). Historically, untouchability was the social fruit of the Aryan Conquest of India.

In the process of social interaction, a portion of the indigenous conquered population was incorporated into the Aryan fold. The most backward and despised section of this incorporated population, it appears, constituted the hereditary caste of untouchables" (A. R. Desai) But many read a kind of caste structure with four varnas in the Rig-Veda, in its Purusha Sukta. Though doubts exist about the status of the Purusha Sukta as an integral part of the Rig-Veda, it is certain that functional division of society was known at the time of the Rig-Veda. The existence of the four fold divisions of society in Iran, *viz;* Athravans, Rathaestars, Vastria Fshouyants and Hiuti, corresponding to the four varnas in India, must have been known to the early Aryan colonizers, and a functional division of society on similar lines could have been practised. So untouchability as we now understand it seems to be not existent during the Vedic period. The reference about four varnas which we find in Purusha Sukta of Rig-Veda does not necessarily suggest the Brahminical supremacy over the three other varnas. It rather suggests that all the four groups are equally important for the preservation of total human race or Purusjati. Head, hand, thigh, leg, etc., are all vital aspects of human physiology and a balanced composition of all these is obviously necessary for the continuance of man.. Therefore, the so-called religio-philosophical outlook of Vedas seems to have been more directed towards human welfare in socio-ethical plane. Any reading of transcendental, mystical and supernatural theological concept of divinity regarding caste can be said as an unwarranted interpolation from without. The distinction concerning four Varnas is from the standpoint of certain qualitative standards (Guna, Karma, Veda) and it need not be interpreted in terms of birth. This point has been very much supported in the Upanishadic period when one finds not only non-brahmins like Kshatriya in the social plane on account of their qualitative mark and excellence.

So the lȧter Vedic literatures such as other three: *(i)* Vedas, *(ii)* brahmans, *(iii)* Aranyakas and Upanishadas and Vedangas or Upavedas, Smruties, Sutras and the epics give a glimpse of the concept of untouchability. If *Varna* (colour) *bheda* may be accepted as the basis of system there should have been only two castes; one of the Aryans and other non-Aryans. But this is not accepted, however, the origin of the caste system can be traced to their professions which they practiced and perfected hereditarily.

In the later Vedic Period this caste system was not absolutely rigid; rather, it was a mid-way between the laxity of the Rig-Vedic Age and the strong rigidity of the age of the Sutras. The term Varna was now used in the sense of caste not in the sense of colour in this age. In the Sutra period, caste system was rigid. Various restrictions were imposed.

Untouchability had begun to creep in the probability seems to be that in Vedic times the Varnas were classes rather then castes, and that post-Vedic scholars, looking for authority for the caste system in the earliest Vedas, have interpreted the nature of the Varna in terms of the caste system as they knew (J. H Hutton).

In Puranic period *i.e.* 3rd century A. D. to 1000 A. D., due to certain economic forces the people belonging to higher castes indulged in lower occupations and naturally they were declared as out castes and once they lost their position it was not possible for them to regain it.

The Dharmasutra writers declare the *chandals* to be progeny of the most hated of the reverse order of mixed unions, that of a Brahman female with a Sudra male. Kautilya agrees with the Dharmasutra writers and he has no objection if they treat them as Sudras. He regards the chandals so low that the advises all other mixed castes to avoid being with the Chandals. According to Manu they were to be the hangmen who were to be prohibited entry into villages and towns during day time, were to be stamped with some marks and were to serve as the undertakers for unclaimed corpses. The chandals were technically '*apapatras*' according to Manu. The earliest evidence of caste and untouchability is textual, and dates back to more than two thousand years. Varna if first mentioned in a late Vedic text (C. 1000 B. C), and by the time of the law book of Manu (C. 1000 B. C. to A. D. 200), Varna and jati (or caste) co-exist as isomorphically ranked social order (Michael Moffatt).

Untouchability is largely an outgrowth of the system of caste, and caste in its turn, is the illegitimate child of the concept of Varna. But, in the absence of any historical evidence, it is difficult to say with any precision or finality as to when the three or four Varnas or occupational divisions of society into Brahman, Kshatriya, Vaishya and Sudra came to be multiplied into numerous castes. The origin of untouchability also is lost in antiquity (V. S. Nargolkar).

Stuart Piggot, a British archaeologist and author of Prehistoric India has put forward a thesis that even before the Aryan arrival in India from the North-West, the Harappan civilization might have developed a caste system. He is, however, quite certain about fact. "The concept of caste', says he, "as known in the later literature is quite unknown in Rig-veda (V. S. Nargolkar).

So in the later Vedic period, specifically in the period of Smrities and Sutras we find little restrictions in interactions. There is the possibility that in this phase of development of human civilization, the healthy spirit of equality, gave place, in course of time of the tradition bound caste system and then again to the institution of untouchability which divided the Hindus, wrapped their thinking and eroded the structure of the community. The Hindu scripture interpolated the concept of Varna and legitimized the concept of Chaturvaran and gave it a divine origin. Those who did not recognise this system-mostly indigeneous people who had their own gods, religion and social system as well as those who opposed or violated this system were out caste and were put aside the Pale of Hinduism, they were forced to live outside the towns and villages and were treated as untouchable.

The idea that certain persons defile, while others sanctify the company if they sit down to a meal in one row is present in the sutras. In this idea may be discerned the origin of the later practice not to dine in the same row with people of other castes than one's own . The idea that an impure person imparts pollution by his touch and even by his near approach to a member of the first three castes finds definite expression in the law-texts of this period, generally with reference to the persons who are out caste and even specifically in relation to a class of people called chandalas.

In Post-Vedic times society was clearly divided into four Varnas. Each Varna was assigned well-defined functions, although it was emphasised that varna was based on birth and the two higher Varnas were given special privileges. The first three Varans were given or the twice-born, were entitled to wearing sacred thread and studying Vedas and the Sudras did not possess any such rights. The Sudras were treated as slaves and has the only right to serve the three other higher Varnas. Some of the Sudras were treated as untouchables. This Varna divided society with the concept of special privilege gave rise to tensions. The Kshatriyas, who acted as rulers, however, reacted strongly against the ritualistic domination of the Brahmins and seems to have led a kind of protest movement against the importance attached to birth in the varna system. The Kshatriya traction against the domination of the priestly class called Brahmanas, who claimed various privileges, was one of the causes of the origin of new religious sects of Hinduism such as: Jainism and Buddhism. Jainism did not condemn the Varna system. According to Mahavir, a person is born in a high or in a lower varna in consequence of the sins and virtues acquired by him in the previous birth. Buddhism made an important impact on society by keeping its doors open to women and Sudras. Since both were placed in the same category by Brahmanism, they were neither given sacred thread nor allowed to read the Vedas. Conversion to Buddhism freed the Sudras from marks of inferiority. But neither Jainism nor Buddhism could make any substantial change in the position of Sudras. Although Sudras could be admitted to the new religious orders, their general position continued to be low. It is said that Gautama Buddha visited the assemblies of the Brahmans, the Kshartiyas and the grihapatis or house-holders, but the assembly of Sudras is not mentioned in this connection.

Gradually, as the Hindu Varna system grew fashionable strong strict measures were adopted to enforce it. Social intercourse and inter-marriage were prohibited. Society became strictly endogamous and was divided into water-tight compartments. Those who violated the law of endogamy were ex-communicated and were forced to live outside the community. In, consequence they had no option other than the low and degrading occupations.

The Buddhist birth-stories called the Jatakas, written in Pali, may be taken to reflect mainly the conditions prevailing East of Allahabad about the second century B. C. We read in them of the chandalas as the lowest caste... The reference to chandalas are specific and almost invariably show them as a despised group, to see members of which is to see evil, to avert which one mist at least wash one's eyes. Chandalas are described as occupying sites outside village and towns whether in the West near Taxila or in centre near Ujjain. They could detected by their special dialect. Sweeping was their hereditary occupations (G. S. Ghurye).

By the close of the pre-Mauryan period rigidity had crept into the caste-system and inter-marriages were disfavoured but these were confined to higher classes alone the chandalas were looked down upon. They were doomed to miserable plight and lived outside the city. The untouchable, who were also known as the *Panchamas* (the fifth caste), or the antayajas (the last born), has been living outside the cities and towns for centuries. They were not allowed to enter the cities or to have contact of any kind with the nobility and the upper caste people. Mangesthnesis's account speaks volumes of forbidden inter-caste marriage and a rigid caste system.

Faihen, who came to India in the (399-414 A. D.) 5th century A. D., during the Gupta period in the of Vikramaditya (Chandra Gupta II), mentions about the untouchables who lived outside the cities and Vishnupurana mentions and incident in which Hindu Kings were condemned to be born as dogs, crows, pigs etc., for the sin of looking at or conversing with an untouchable (Bhagvan Das). Again, Faihen refers to this special class of people called chandalas, who lived outside the city gates and had to strike a bamboostick on the floor, while traveling on the road-side so that people might take precaution and were not touched by them. Their shadow was not to fall on the people. The chandalas reared pigs and birds and eate all kinds of foods.

In the Gupta times, the chandalas were a neglected section also, and have been described as living apart from village settlement. Harsha is called the last great Hindu emperor of North India (A. D. 606-647). The Chinese pilgrim Hsuan tsang who came to India (626 A. D. to 645 A. D.) gives an account of the condition of the untouchables. By fifth century A. D., the untouchables grew to only in numbers but by glaring disabilities. Whenever they entered the town the upper caste people kept themselves at a distance from them because the road was supposed to be polluted by them. The Chinese pilgrim takes notice of untouchables such as scavengers, executioners, etc., they lived outside the villages and took garlic and onion. The untouchables announced their entry into the town by shouting loudly so that people might keep away from them. Thus the untouchables were neglected and looked done upon.

"It can no be inferred that the Chandalas followed some degrading occupations and that they lived outside the villages. But it is very difficult to imaging that persons born out of forbidden sex contacts were numerous enough to form a separate caste group, since they are to be found practically in all villages of India. It is possible that because they were following occupations which were despised, they were characterised by the Dharmashastras as equivalent to the despicable progeny of forbidden sex relation. In other words, these statements should not be taken in literal sense as explaining the origin of these group (B. Kupuswamy). As observed in the Hindu Shastras in the eyes of laws these Antajas had no status.

Medieval India

Alberuni, writing in about A. D. 1020, grouped together Dom and Candelas, as two of the groups not reckoned among any caste of guild. They are occupied with dirty works. Like the cleansing of villages and other services and distinguished only by their occupations. So, the Hindus had developed a very complex social structure by the beginning of the 11th century. Inter-marriage and inter-dining were strictly prohibited. The untouchables lived outside the towns and villages. They suffered from may social and economic disabilities which made their lives miserable. The ruling elite and the orthodox Brahmins shout themselves into the ivory towers of caste-system and were cut-off from the main stream of the society or the masses. In central Hindustan, there was untouchability and Chandalas were required to make their presence known by striking a piece of wood while entering the market place or the quarters inhabited by upper class people. No wonder, more than half on the Hindu populace stood forth as mere spectators when the Rajput rulers had to fight a life and death struggle against the Turkish invaders. They did not consider themselves to be responsible for the defence of their own hearths and homes. During the Turkish rule, Hindus made the caste rules more rigorous.

So during the Muslim rule, amongst the Hindu caste system was so rigid that both inter-marriage and inter-dining were taboos. Because of much rigidity, the untouchable became a prey to the process of conversion started by the Muslims. Many of these untochables and low caste people embraced Islam and joined the invaders partly to avoid prosecution, partly in search of freedom.

Then the Mughals, like other Muslims had come to India not only to conquer the country, but also to convert its people to Islam. Islam is militant faith and its followers are zealous missionaries who look upon it to be their main duty to propagate the message of Mohammed. The Mughals, like early Turko-Afghan rulers, were foreign conquerors and despised the Hindus as inferior people. They were filled with conqueror's innate pride and were determined to retain their separated identity. So, Muslims refused to be absorbed in Indian Society. Hence Hinduism tried to defend itself by making the caste system more rigorous and the condition of the untouchables became more miserable. The worst effect of the cramping Mughal rule was that the Hindus could not speak or write the truth. They couldn't deal with the Muslims in equal terms, and developed low cunning, hypocrisy and even deceit to get on in the world. It is believed that caste-system was much more rigorous than the previous period and Mughals exploited this weakness by which some of the lower caste Hindus, notably in Bengal and in certain other parts, were converted into Islam and some high castes in Punjab and Kashmir had in the same manner, been compelled to abandon their ancestral religion.

Therefore the Bhakti movement from the 12th to the 17th century was nothing more than an attempt on the part of Hinduism to win the battle that was lost in the 10th century. It is a generic name for all the movements which are non-ritualistic and based on Bhakti. Under the patronage of Mughal administration Bhakti movement gained movement. But it is not historically true that Islam taught the Hindus monotheism. Islam did give an impetus to the movements against the supremacy of the Brahmans and religious rituals and indirectly promoted the cause of the Bhakti movement which offered a common meeting ground to the devout men of both creeds in which their differences of rituals, dogma and external marks of faith were ignored. This movement was geared by a set of saints in different parts of India: Ramananda, Kabir, Vallabhacharya, Nanak, Sur Das, Tulsi Das, Raidas, Mirabai in North, Chaitanya, Sankara Devin East; Namadev, Tukaram, Sant Gyaneswar, Eknath, Ram Das in the West, Ramanuja, Purander Das and Basava in South India. This movement was reformist in the sense that it attempted to correct some of the evils in Hinduism, Particularly the practice of untouchability without questioning the caste system. They were all initiated by caste Hindus and/or admitted clean caste Hindus also into the movements fold. Once castes with differing ritual ranks came to be associated with the movements, the participants developed a dual identity; a religious ideological identity with fellow movement participants and a socio-cultural identity with social collectivities (castes) to which they traced their origin. So the first initial protest movement had got its ignition in the traditional Indian society to uplift the Harijans' social status. It started with the Jainist and Buddhist revolt of 6th century B. C., against the central ideology of the concept of purity and pollution and Bramhminical supremacy. Again, it is for the second time that the Bhakti protest movement occurred against social discrimination. This movement confined its attention to the ideational realm without any proper socio-economic programme to uplift the Harijans, hence turned to the a mirage. Whatever might have been the efforts of the Bhakti movement to bring about social elevation of the untouchables, the Hindu social customs were powerful enough to nullify them. In spite of this reformist trend, the Harijans were debarred from worship at most Hindu Temples, from the services of the Brahman Priests and from the use of the village well.

Untouchability was expressed in the maintenance of physical distance between Scheduled Castes and high castes and in extreme restrictions of commensal relationships between untouchables and all others. Upper caste groups also enforced a code of conduct which symbolised this super-ordinate position vis-à-vis the untouchables and deferential behaviour in manner, dress and language was expected of the Scheduled Castes. Individual Hindu philosophers and saints often ignored the distinction between caste Hindus and untochables. They seldom concerned themselves with the reform of social institutions. Profound and universal ignorance was then natural consequence (J. R. Kamble).

After the Mughals, during the rule of Marathas and Peshwas, it is also recorded that, the Mahars and mangs were not allowed within the gates of Poona after 3 P.M., and before 9 A.M. It was because before 9 and after 3 their bodies cast too long a shadow which falling on a number of the higher castes-especially Brahmins-defiled them. Thus, untouchability was institutionalized.

Brahmins at the top-the most pure of human beings purifies himself in order to approach God. The (Dalit) untouchable a the bottom-the least pure of human beings makes personal purity possible by removing the strongest sources of organic impurity (removing of garbage, dead animals, etc.,). Thus the completion of the cycle by two unequally ranked units is equally necessary. In other words, the execution of impure tasks by some is necessary for the maintenance of purity for others. Thus the two elements are together the higher castes and the untouchables (G. N. Reddy).

Pollution and maintenance of social distance are specific forms of segregation and inequality bred within the Indian caste system. Hinduism sanctifies it through its theory of Karma and Dharma and the cycle of rebirth, those who are indispensable for the maintenance of caste hierarchy are excluded from it. The classification of certain sections of people as Periahs, obviously is not accidental. The overt bases of exclusion were menial occupations, constant contact with pollutant like leather, excreta, earth etc., yet with out the performance of such tasks by some, the other (*i.e.*, high caste people) couldn't maintain their purity. Thus some form of coercion had to be exercised over these village servants and dalits upon whom fell the exclusive responsibility of their performance (A. Ghosh).

However, the generally accepted notion is that, the untouchables were the aboriginal inhabitants who were conquered and enslaved by the Aryan invaders. Apart from they being known to perform all degrading service, they were alleged to have following characteristic: Drunkenness, shamelessness, brutality, truthlessness, nucleanness, disgusting food practices and an absolute back of personal honour. To be an untouchable is to be beyond the reach of the Hindu culture and society, to be almost cultureless. Among the savarnas the sudras are required to perform hard work (like: farming, cattle rearing and artisan work etc.,) but they are not expected to do degrading work like scavenging and sweeping public roads etc. The untouchables are described thus: persons of a discreet set of low castes, excluded for reasons of their extreme collectivity, impurity from particular relations with higher beings-both human and divine (Michal Moffatt).

The ideas of untouchability and unapproachability observes G. S. Ghurye arose out of the ideas of ceremonial purity, first applied to the aboriginal sudras in connection with the sacrificial ritual and expanded and extended to other groups because of the theoretical impurity of certain occupations (G. S. Ghurye).

The Varna system, in course of time broke into hundreds of castes and sub-castes as a result of the operation of a variety of factors, such as racial admixture, geographical expansion of the population, inter-regional isolation of the various parts of the country and growth of crafts which tended to become heredietary. The result was the emergence of the caste system, as found today in the Hindu society. While the untouchables stood outside the pale of the Varna system, they formed an essential part of the caste system (A. C. Pradhan).

So the concept of untouchability is peculiarly a Indian idea. There are several theories to support the doctrine of touch. Those who believe in the theory of sanctity, specify the idea, the more the sanctity the more the nearer to God. It is lost by touching objects of less or no sanctity and restored by a both or utmost by a paltry unmeaning ceremony of expiation. A common man who does not search for the reason of a practice which is sanctified by religion, believe it to be a sin to violate the custom and hence practices it firmly. The practice of untouchability thus was not the result of a deliberate conspiracy to suppress the Sudras or the untouchables. It was just the holding on to wrong beliefs about religious purity. From the modern point of view, the beliefs are not only completely wrong, but they amount to positive irreligion (V. S. Nargolkar).

Socially Scheduled Castes have been denied status in the traditional Hindu caste system, for they are ritually for below the pollution line. They fall beyond the varna system. But surprisingly they are accommodated in the local jati system in the villages. The Hindu caste system, despite severe inequalities, is marked by an organic unity among castes made possible through internalization of the inegalitarian values, embodied in the twin concept of 'Karma' and 'Dharma' observed both by upper and lower castes. This phenomenon was facilitated by a peculiar complex *'jajmani system'* (exchanges of goods and services among various castes), but the Scheduled Cates always stood on the wrong (exploited) side of exchange.

The Hindu Sanskritic have been closed to the Harijans since time immemorial. Their social and cultural marginality is well reflected in the villages settlement of Indian society-upper Hindu caste live in centrally located areas while Harijans live in the outskirts of the villages. The Hindu high caste feudals have enforced a culture of repression of Harijans. The status quo was maintained by sanctions and the Harijans were kept in a state of constant fear under a permanent threat of violence. This made, Harijans to avoid any danger and risk involved in contact with upper castes and now situations; hence they remained unexposed and inactive.

Renaissance and Reformation in British India

Along with the religious, cultural and linguistic diversity, Indian has also developed a unique form of social stratification known as the caste system. However, what is more significant than the caste system is the appearance in the Indian society of social groups which are identified as 'untouchables'. While those social groups who controlled the economic resources and wielded political power become the privileged upper castes, others were treated as social outcastes. Without access to the vital economic resources and bargaining power, they become the most exploited peripheral group in the Indian society (Jose Kanannikil). The social customs deprived the Harijans of their right to seek higher social status by taking to occupations other than the hereditary ones.

Economically they were the poorest of the poor toiling in most unremunerative and often degrading occupations. Traditionally predominantly rural, they have been mainly: landless, agricultural labourers and marginal sharecroppers and peasants-commonly indebted beyond redemption and held in varying degrees of 'bondage' in different parts of the country. Historical evidence shows that the Harijans have been completely by passed by the controlling elite group. They have been neglected by the elite formation and circulation process such as wars, Pre-British royal land grants, British India land settlements, industrial expansions and spread of English education (M. P. Singh). The British rule awakened Harijans to the enquiry of certain social customs and religious traditions. One such socio-religious tradition was the practice of untouchability among the Hindus. So before independence, the reform movements and political awakening during 19th century were urban and mostly remained as upper caste affairs.

The fight against social evils particularly untouchability based on ancient rules and customs become a nation wide debate. With the advent of British the upper caste Hindus and Muslims elite joined hands with British, representing a political triangle in which the British played a dominant role by completely neglecting the Scheduled Castes. However, the western education taught Indians the value of freedom and independence and dispelled from their minds the cringing, slavish mentality and freed them from the age-old superstitions and caste ritual. With the impact of western education, three groups emerged with different plans of actions to ameliorate the bondage of untouchables. One group was those who wanted to adhere to old society but wanted to reform by gradual process. The second group was revolutionary social reformers who wanted a complete transformation. The third group represented a revivalistic tendency. For a long time, education was the monopoly of the Brahmins. Christians were the first to open the doors of education to the untouchables. Those who embraced Christianity encouraged other members of their family to embrace Christianity. Those who did not embraced Christianity but got education become aware of their low condition. The British with a views to collect information regarding the subjects of its empire conducted the census in Punjab which was followed by a census of British India. These reports showed that the population of Muslims, Christians and Sikhs was increasing and that of the Hindus was falling. This was mainly due to large number of the low castes embraing Christianity or Islam.

Hence in 1814, Raja Ram Mohan Roy (1774-1833) founded the Atmiya Sabha. Fourteen years later in 1828 he founded the Brahmo Samaj which started preaching the gospel that unless religious evils were removed, the society could not advance. So, it successfully attacked social evils like casteism and untouchability, then came the Arya Samaj under the leadership of Swami Dayanannada Saraswati (1824-1883) in 1875. He decried casteism and untouchability on the ground that they were not sanctioned by the Vedas. Then Arya Samaj started opening schools and educated the masses. The chief significance of the Arya Samaj lies in the fact that it created a feeling of self-confidence and self-reliance among the Hindus and undermined the prevailing notions of superiority of western races and culture. But its greatest success lies in raising the social status of the untouchables among the Hindus and preventing them from leaving Hinduism and joining other religious denominations. It started a purification (Suddhi) movement or reconvert those who had accepted Islam and

Christianity. But the untouchables who were received into Hinduism continued to be treated as untouchables.

Ramakrishan Mission was set up by Swami Vivekananda (1863-1902) in the memory of his Guru Rama Krishna Paramhansa in 1896. Vivekananda tried to impart a social purpose to the Hindu religion and declared that he did not believe in a religion which did not wipe out the widow's tears or bring a piece of bread to the orphan's mouth. He asserted, "Him I call a Mahatma whose heart bleeds for the poor, otherwise he is a Duramta. So, long as millions live in hunger and ignorance, I hold every man a traitor who, while educated at their expense, pays not the least heed to them". So this is safely concluded to be a phase of Hindu renaissance. Anyhow, its gospel instilled in the hearts of millions of untouchables a sense of brotherhood. He was perhaps the first Indian to describe himself as a socialist and to declare that the Sudras (the Proletariat), who had all along been suppressed, must assert themselves and become the ruling force in society.

The depth of Vivekananda' understanding of the modern world and his farsightedness emerge perhaps most clearly from his attitude towards the oppressed and the downtrodden and in his remarkable prophecy: "A time will come when there will be the rising of the Sudra class with their Sudrahood.. A time will come when the Sudras of every country with their inborn nature and habits will gain supremacy in every society."

Jitirao Phule (1826-90)

Jotirao Phule was the first Indian to proclaim in modern India the dawn of a new age for the common man, the downtrodden, the underdog and for the Indian women. It was his aim to reconstruct the social order on the basis of social equality, justice and reason. As we have just seen, the 'Aryan theory of race' constituted the most influential common discourse for discussing caste and society in Phule's time. European 'Orientalists' like: William Jones, Charles Wilkins, James Prinsep and others (Marshall, 1970: 1-44) conveniently used it to assert an ethnic kinship between Europeans and the ancient Vedic peoples (see O'Hanlon, 1985: 57-59). The constant interest of European scholars like H. H. Wilson, C. lassen, H. T. Cplebrooke, Monier Williams, Max Mueller and others (Kejariwal, 1988) in ancient Aryan society and their appreciation and praise of this society provided an important moral boost to high-caste Indians. Thus, Indian civilization was seen as primarily derivative from Aryan civilization, and the caste system was lauded as a means by which people of diverse racial and cultural backgrounds were brought together and subjected to the civilisating influence of the Aryans (Omvedt, 1976:103).

At one level, Phule simply reversed this notion, arguing that the low castes, whom he sometimes called 'Shudras and Atishudras' and were simply listed as 'Kunbis, Malis, Dhangars... Bhils, kolis, Mahars and Mangs' were the original inhabitants of the country, enslaved and exploited by conquering Aryans who had formulated a caste-based Hinduism as a means of deceiving the teeming masses and legitimising their own power. It was the confirmed and sincere view of jotirao that the ancient history of India was nothing but the struggle between Brahmins and non-Brahmins (Keer, 1964:120). Hence, Phule consciously sought to bring together the major peasant castes (these were, besides the Kunbis or cultivators, the Malis or 'garden' cultivators and Dhangars or shepherds) along with the large Untouchable castes of Mahars and Mangs in a common 'front' against Brahmin domination (see O 'Hanlon, 1985; 131).

Jotirao's attack on Brahminism was uncompromising. He realised that the seeds of the Brahmins' power, supremacy and privileges lay in their scriptures and Puranas; and these works and the caste system were created to exploit the lower classes (see O'Hanlon, 1985-132). Phule also reinterpreted sacred religious literature. To give an example: by reading the nine avatars of Vishnu as stages of the Aryan conquest and using King Bali as a counter-symbol to the elite's use of Ram, Ganapati or Kali (see O'Hanlon, 1985:137; Keer, 1964:90-125). Thus, Jotirao attacked the Brahminical scriptures and Puranas, revolted against priestcraft and the caste system and set on foot a social movement for the liberation of the Shudras, Antishudras (Untouchables) and women.

Phule realised that the strongest hold of religious tradition in the people derived from the extensive integration of Hindu religious literature into the popular culture and oral traditions. Phule's answer to this to provide alternative accounts of the texts, myths and stories most common in popular Hinduism. He linked these with important symbols and structures from contemporary Mharashtrian society in order to convey the real community of culture and interest that united all lower castes against their historical and cultural adversaries: the Brahmins.

To fulfill his life's ambition to establish a casteless society, Phule founded the *Satya Shodhak Samaj* (truth-seeking society) on 24 September 1873. The Samaj set up the first school for girls and Untouchables. Phule also organized marriages without Brahmin priests, widow remarriages, etc. According to Phule, the performance of any religious ceremony by a Brahmin priest for a member of another caste expresses in a concrete form the relations of purity between them which make up the basis for Hindu religious hierarchy. It is the Brahmin priest alone who, in his ritual purity, has the power to mediate between the human world and that of the high gods, and so it is he who controls the entry of divine power into the world (Babb, 1975: 31-67). For this reason, Phule felt that the employment of Brahmin priests negated the very principle upon which he hoped a community of the lower castes would be based. The Satya Shodhak Samaj actively encouraged marriages without Brahmin priests. Thus, the Satya Shodhak Samaj assumed a vital role as the ideological conscience for all those who identified themselves with the lower castes, whether they belonged to the Samaj or to one of the numerous other groups working for lower caste uplift.

Gandhian Approach on Caste and Varna

Hindu reformers, including Gandhi, were of the opinion that the Untouchables could maintain a Hindu as well as a Vankar or Malliga identity without the stigma of being

Untouchable. The Hindu reformers delinked the problem of untouchability from the caste system. Untouchability, according to them was not an essential part of Hinduism or, for that matter, of the caste system. It resulted from a violation of the basic spirit of Hinduism. 'Varnashram,' Gandhi asserted, 'was for the preservation of harmony and growth of soul' (Shah, 1995:28). Gandhi repeatedly harped on the evils of untouchability. He himself adopted a Dalit girl as his daughter. He voluntarily decided to live with the Untouchables to become one with them. He symbolically called Untouchables Harijans, that is people of God. He started the Harijan Sevak Sangh to launch programmes to remove untouchability and improve the economic condition of the Untouchable (Shah, 1995: 28-29).

Periyar's (1879 – 1973) Vision for Justice

E. V. Ramaswamy Naicker, known a Periyar (Great Sage), was born in 1879 in Erode into a respectable middle-class family of artisans. He married at the of 13, but after six years he became a *sanyasi,* traveling as a religious mendicant over the whole of India. In his visits to pilgrim centres, he gained an intimate knowledge of the evils of popular Hinduism and also of the exploitation of the masses by Brahmin priests.

Periyar become convinced that casteism and Hinduism were one and the same. He wanted Hinduism, as he saw it to be removed altogether. His movement took a turn towards racial consciousness and became a 'Dravidian' movement, seeing to defend the rights of the Dravidians against Aryan domination. It blamed the Aryans for introducing an unjust and oppressive social system in the country (see Hardgrave, 1965: 17). Periyar realised that the important feature of all new ideologies of the elite was the 'Aryan view of race'. The 'Aryan view' was adopted enthusiastically by the Indian elite as a new model for understanding caste. That is, Brahmins, Kshartiyas and Vaishyas were held almost as a matter of definition to be the descendants of invading Aryans, while Shudras and Untouchables were those of the native conquered inhabitants. In thesis new language of caste and race, to claim

'Aryan' descent was equivalent to claiming 'twice-born' status, to say 'Dravidian' or 'non-Aryan' almost equivalent to saying 'Shudra'.

The high-caste elite of India began to take Aryan and Sanskritic culture as the basis of 'Indian nationality', but in so doing they were in fact taking a part- the culture of the upper castes and roughly more northern groups – for the whole. Periyar's movement sought to defend the rights of the Dravidians against Aryan domination. He saw in the Brahmins the representatives or Hindu arrogance and the stronghold of social injustice (Devanandan. 1960).

Naicker quit the Congress and attacked it as a tool of Brahmin domination. In 1925, he organized the Self-Respect Movement', designed as Dravidian Uplift, seeking to expose Brahmin tyranny and the deceptive methods by which they controlled all spheres of Hindu life. Naicker publicly ridiculed the Puranas as fairy tales, not only imaginary and irrational, but grossly immoral as well. Naicker attacked the Hindu religion as the tool of Brahmin domination.

Under the Congress ministry of C. Rajgopalachari in 1937, Hindi in the schools was introduce to the South as a compulsory subject. Taking this as an affront to Tamil culture and its rich literary tradition, Tamil patriots like: Annadurai, Karunanithi and others under the leadership of Naicker reacted with violent protest. Naicker saw the imposition of Hindi as a step towards subjugation of Tamil peoples by the North Indian Aryans.

The Hindu religion was denounced as an opiate by which the Brahmins had dulled and controlled the masses. A Hindu in the present concept may be a Dravidian, but a Dravidian in the real sense of the term cannot and shall not to be a Hindu' (A. S. Venu, cited and Harrison' 1960:127). Pains were taken to destroy images of Hindu deities such as: Rama and Genesha. According to Periyar, 'Rama and Sita are despicable characters, not worthy of imitation or admiration even by the lowest of fourth-rate humans'. Ravana, on the other hand, is despicable as a Dravidian of 'excellent character'. In his preface to *The Ramayana: A True Reading* he states that 'the veneration of the story any longer in Tamil Nadu is injurious and ignominious to the self-respect of the community and of the country' (Naicker, 1959: iii-iv).

On the eve of Independence, Naicker called upon the Dravidian people of South India 'to guard against the transfer of power from the British to the Aryans' (The Hindu, 11 February 1946). Fearing Brahmin dominance under Aryan 'imperialism', Naicker called for the formation of a separate South India state, Dravidasthan. Today, the several Dravidian political parties in Tamil Nadu trace back their inspiration to Periyar in their programme to build a Dravidian civilization in the Indian sub-continent.

Dalit Women Today

The situation of Dalit women in India needs special attention. They are one of the largest socially segregated groups any where in the world, and make up 2 per cent of world's total population. Dalit women are discriminated against three time over they are poor, they are women, and they are Dalits. Dalit women constitute half of the 200 million Dalit population, and 16.3 of the total Indian female population. The traditional taboos are the same for Dalit men and Dalit women. However, Dalit women have to deal with them more often. Dalit women are discriminated against not only by people of higher castes, but also within their own communities. Men are dominant in Dalit communities. Dalit women also have less power with in the Dalit movement it self. Women are active in large numbers in the movement but most leadership positions in the organizations, local bodies and associations have until now been held men.

Even as we are in the 21st millennium, caste discrimination, and age-old practice that dehumanizes and perpetuates a cruel form of discrimination continues to be practiced. India where the practice is rampant despite the existence of a legislation to stop this, 160 million Dalits of which 49.96 per cent are women continue to suffer discrimination. The discrimination that Dalit women are subjected to is similar to racial discrimination, where the former is discriminated and treated as untouchable due to descent, for being born into a particular community, while the latter face discrimination due to colour. The caste system declares Dalit women as 'impure' and therefore untouchable and hence socially excluded. This is a complete negation and violation of women's human rights. We urge this august body to pay special attention to this issue and come up with recommendations to eradicate the caste system.

Dalit women are thrice discriminated, treated as untouchables and as outcastes, due to their caste, face gender discrimination being women and finally economic impoverishment due to unequal wage disparity, with low or underpaid labour. According to the Hindu caste hierarchy, there are four castes namely: *(i)* the Brahmins (priestly caste), *(ii)* the Kshatriya (warriors), *(iii)* the Vaishyas (traders) and *(iv)* the Shudras (menial task workers). Below this four tier caste ladder is another rung, who are called the untouchables (Panchamas). Among the untouchables, the status of women is further eroded and closely linked to the concept of purity. This is what the rigid, fundamentalist Hindu promotes through continuation of caste system, imposing the Brahminical values to maintain the caste system. In order to trace the traditional status of *'Dalit'* women one has to turn over the pages of Indian history of the origin and features of the caste system.

The Caste System is probably the longest surviving hierarchical system in existence in the world today; its roots can be traced back to the *Manusmriti* a secred document of the Hindus. The Hindu social organization is traditionally divided into two substrata, known respectively as *Dwija* and *Ekaja*. The *Dwija* comprise three higher Varnas – *(i)* the *Brahmin* (the priestly caste) the *(ii) Kshatriya* (warrior caste) and *(iii)* the *Vaishya* (trading and artisans) with their future sub-divisions into castes but the *Ekaja* or *Shudra* consist of the lower castes, who are meant to serve the *Dwija* and are thus placed lower in the social order. The whole system is known as *Chaturvarna Vyavastha* or four-fold division of society in which a large chunk of people belonging to a number of the other castes do not find their place within this schematic structure. They are, therefore, called as *Panchama* (Fifth order) or *Chandala, Avama* (coloured), *Antyaj* (low born) etc., (Cf. Buhler, 1886: 14-24, Hocart, 1950: 127; Hutton, 1951: 64; Mayer, 1956: 136; Ghurye, 1960: 55-56; Srinivas, 1962: 63-69).

But a Dalit women, who fortunately had no fallen prey into the net cunningly women by Hinduism was more free and less dependent. She was physically strong and could work hard. Anti women feelings were not to be found in their social life. Child marriage, strict monogamy, widowhood, dowry practice and the heinous practice of '*Sati*' were all unknown to them. Dalit woman has more freedom than her counterpart in the higher castes. But this freedom does not really mean anything. This is the freedom given to her by men for their own conveniences.

In their vain attempt to be identified with and approved by the caste Hindus, tried to follow their practices, forced their women into subjugation; widowhood was thrust on them. They are forbidden to remarry. The freedom that the *Dalit* woman was enjoying was mercilessly taken away so in the present day society a Dalit woman is also considered to be unequal to her men. Today the Dalit women who constitute the major working force.

Being a Dalit is a reason enough to be ready to face a life full of miseries, suffering degradation and dehumanized way of life. Being a women means a life of exploitation in the name of sex, a weak variety of human subordinating to man, unwanted burden since birth and a domestic servant for life. Almost all Dalit spokesmen (and most, infact, are men) clearly recognise women to be the most oppressed of their groups, the "Dalit among the Dalit and the oppressed," as it is sometimes put. Dr. B. R. Ambedkar, the leader of Dalits, described the Hindu caste system as a pyramid of earthen pots set on one another. When Brahmins and Kshatriyas are at the top, Sudras and the Untouchables are at the bottom like crushed and wasted powder. And at the very bottom are the Dalits and below them are the suppressed Dalit women.

The Dalit/Bahujan women is a social force, a cultural symbol and has a historical background. She is the prominent feature of a farming culture. She is the true builder and heir of prominent face in the Industrial culture. She plays a big role in the construction of buildings and laying roads. *Dalit* women are estimated to contribute eighty per cent of total labour to strengthen the national economy. She looks after the family, she walks miles and miles to fetch water, fodder, fuel and so on. She gets up before the cock crows. Her day starts by sprinkling water mixed with cow dung in front of the house. As the sun-rises she goes out to work in the fields. She comes back in the evening and starts her routine household work. She eats very less and sleeps late in the night and she wears patched clothes. Such a hard working supporter and builder of the family, society and nation at large, today is suffering a lot in India. She is struggling for survival and existence. She is leading a life full of disadvantage of being Dalit and of being a women.

Dalit are not only a socio-cultural group but often represent an economic class as well. More than 50 per cent of the Dalit workforce were landless agricultural laborers. A number of social studies have revealed that Dalit women makes up a large number of professional sex workers 90 per cent of those who die of starvation and attendant diseases are Dalit. Their untouchability status accentuates their economic exploitation and their poverty, strengthen their polluting social status. Untouchability was made a legal offence by the Indian Parliament in 1955. However, untouchability as a social institution, was an still is kept alive by the use of brutal force. Untouchability is related to the oppression of upper caste women as well, as it become an effective means of patriarchal/Brahmanic control over high caste women's sexuality, which was essential for maintenance of caste privilege. At the same time, the potential threat to these system of domination that the rape of upper caste female by lower caste males represented, was negated by calling or branding them as 'untouchables'.

The same ideologies allowed upper caste men to violate low caste women's sexuality with impunity.

The status of the Dalit women and also presents a holistic picture of the position of the Dalit women at a micro level. What makes these women triple of the victims are factors like: class, gender and caste. There are large number of Dalit in the country. Only around 16 per cent of the Dalits live in urban areas and the remaining 84 per cent live in rural areas. Their contribution to society in terms of labour art and culture is enormous. Their share of the country's resources and culture is however, disproportionately lower. Dr. B. R. Ambedkar describes the Hindu Caste System 'as a pyramid of earthenware post, set on top of another'. Not only are Brahmins and Kshatriyas at the top and the 'Suhudras' and untouchables at the bottom, but within each earthenware pot, men are the top and women of that caste are at the bottom like 'crushed' and 'power'. At the very bottom are the Dalits and below them are the suppressed Dalit women. Dalit women have been kept powerless, their voices silenced, their dignity and personhood trampled on. In this chapter effort has been made to address their heart burning issues and related specific handicaps, difficulties and problems suffered by the Dalit women in the longer context of the social sphere in which they live. The Dalit problem has been universally acknowledged to be acute social malice that demands an immediate solution.

The Dalits today are receiving wide attention from both government and non-governmental organizations (NGO) by way of policies and welfare schemes to improve the position of these women. The Constitution of India provides for reservation in jobs, educational institution for the Dalits under Scheduled Caste (SC) category. There has been a rise in educational access to Dalits as a result of the post-independence educational programmes. Apart from reservations in educational institutions, other major programmer for upliftment of Dalit include, exemption from school fees, procisions of stipends or scholarships, precisions of facilities like: book grants and maintenance of hostels or assistance to hostels for SC students.

Dalit Women and Work

1. *Agricultural Labour*

The Scheduled castes, more particularly their women folk contribute significantly in agriculture sector, by their manual labour. In 1991, over 76 per cent of the SC male workers were engaged in agriculture and related pursuits and remaining 24 per cent in non-agriculture sector. By comparison, a smaller percentage, *i.e.* 62 per cent of male workers were engaged in agriculture and allied sectors among the non-SC/ST population; conversely the proportion of SC population on agriculture was more than that of non-SC/ST population. This dependence on agriculture was even higher among the SC women (*i.e.* 86%).

It is however, noteworthy to point out that disparity in dependence between women folk of Scheduled Castes and non-SC/ST population is relatively less when compared with that between men folk of the two social groups. In the non-SC/ST population, more males have taken to non-agriculture pursuits and that too possibly highly remunerative.

In the agriculture sector, the scheduled castes involved, are by and large, agriculture laborers and small and marginal farmers and tenant cultivators, the SC agricultural labour constitute nearly half (49.07%) of the total SC workers. In absolute number, the SC agricultural labourers are 24.47 million which constitute 32.80 per cent of the total agricultural labourers in the whole country. Men of the scheduled castes are sharecroppers of other forms of insecure tenants. In the rural economic structure, they are the weakest link. Then come to the marginal cultivators who constitute 25.45 per cent of the total SC workers. The marginal cultivators also somehow maintain very unstable economic condition which forces them to incur debts which results in alienation of land as also advance sale of their crops; the consequence is debt bondage. Whatever meager assets they have are depleted and in course of time they join the group of landless agricultural laboures. Economically, there is hardly any difference between a marginal farmer, a sharecropper and a landless labour.

There has been progressive swelling in the number of landless agricultural labourers as well, in the number of marginal operational holders since 1961. In 1961, 39.4 per cent of total workers were cultivators and about 30.0 per cent were agricultural labourers. In case of non-SC/ST population, however, the percentage of it was quite low as agricultural labourers. The incidence of agricultural laboures among the SCs was infact three times higher than of non-SC/ST population. This disparity in work force composition of SCs population. This expectation is not fully materialized. The population of workers engaged in agriculture, in fact has increased from 69.4 per cent in 1961 to 74.5 per cent in 1991, but in case of non-SC/ST group, it has declined from 62.0 per cent to 59.4 per cent during the same period. This implies that over a period of thirty years 1961-91 the gap between the two group has further widened. The difference which was 8.0 per cent points in 1961 went up to 15 per cent in 1991. The gap has enhanced by nearly 100 per cent . Fewer shifts in agricultural to non-agriculture occupations among the SCs faced lacking in comparable economic and social base in the agricultural sector itself.

2. *Work Participation Rate among Scheduled Caste Women*

Of 66.29 million SC females reported in 1991 census, 13.29 million, *i.e.* 20.05 per cent were reported economically active and classified as main workers. Besides, 3.93 million (*i.e.* 5.93%) of them were reported as marginal workers. In all 26 per cent of the SC females were reported as workers.

Among the SC females, *i.e.* 25.98 per cent was next to that of the ST females *i.e.* (44.76%) and higher than that of the non-SC/ST females which is 18.97 per cent, same trend is visible in both rural and urban context. Among the major states, the highest female workers among the SCs is found in Andhra Pradesh (46.71) and the lowest in Punjab (5.40) followed by Delhi (7.49) and Haryana (11.65). The SC population is largely rural-based which has a higher female WPR than the urban SC population, *Secondly*, the female-oriented; Thirdly, because of poor literacy level of SC women, the school going female population would be much less and there by increasing the participation of younger girls in economic activity.

The average female WPR among the rural SC population is 29.02. The states which have WPR higher than the average are: Andhra Pradesh (52.47), Karnataka (42.68), Madhya Pradesh (40.66), Himachal Pradesh (37.01, Gujarat (34.81) Kerala (33.57), Rajasthan (33.29) and Tamil Nadu (31.53). On the other hand, the WPR among rural SC women in Punjab is the lowest, *i.e.* 5.59 followed by Tripura (9.21), Haryana (12.8) West Bengal (14.12) and Uttar Pradesh (18.94) Regarding low WPR of Punjab and Haryana, the Census paper-1 of 1991 has observed that "it is commonly believed due to cultural factors and the reluctance among the higher caste women to report themselves as workers even though they may be participating in some economic activity, particularly in the agricultural sector". The practice is visible among the rural SC women as well, possibly because of the 'Sanskritisation' process commonly vogue in the Hindi speaking region.

The lives of Dalit women are largely circumscribed by their poverty and lack of access to productive resources like land, financial capital, or educational qualifications. In all states, the overwhelming majority of Dalit women work outside the home, most often as agricultural labourers. The only exception seemed to be Madhya Pradesh where, according to the 1991 census, 65 per cent of Dalit women were not employed. Certain agricultural tasks are typically assigned to women. In Punjab, for instance, women are employed to weed crops, pick cotton and sow potatoes, as well as clean the cattle sheds of big landowners. All over India, wherever women work for non-Dalit landowners, performing tasks that include: transplanting paddy, weeding, harvesting, threshing and winnowing, they are always paid less than men. Although there is no caste discrimination in the wage-rare since both Dalit and non-Dalit women are paid equally, Dalit women tend to be relegated to the most menial and arduous tasks.

In south Orissa, Dalit women who work as agricultural labourers are paid as little as Rs. 15 a day. Dalit women from Orissa report that they prefer to migrate to towns in search of work. Not only are the wages higher, they do not have to face caste-based discrimination. In rural Orissa, Dalits are made to wait for several hours before being paid, and non-Dalits place the money on the ground instead of directly handing it to the Dalit worker.

In 24 of the 52 sample villages in Bihar, women are paid Rs. 16-20 for 10 hours of work; in non villages, they are paid Rs. 10-15. Both women and men are paid much less than the legal minimum wage. While women do not generally migrate out of the state for work, some migrate within the state during the paddy season or to the brick kilns. Dalit women whose husbands are working outside the state reported being abused by the landlords. Since they are paid at 10 - or 12 - day intervals, they are forced to go to the moneylender, to whom they pay Rs. 10 in interest every month on a loan of Rs. 100.

In Perayam, Kerala, Dalit women reported distinctive caste discrimination in the division of labour in cashew processing factories. Dalit women are confined to the hardest task of breaking the roasted cashew nuts, a task which over time deforms and stains their palms and fingers. An educated young Dalit woman who asked to be assigned the easier job of peeling cashews was not allowed to shift. She protested against caste discrimination and fought the factory management.

Dalit women in Tamil Nadu say that they instinctively avoid touching non-Dalit women in the workplace. They eat separately. When working in the fields, if non-Dalit landlords provide the food, Dalit males and females have to either bring their own utensils or eat in leaf plant. When serving water, non-Dalits hold the pot at a height, pouring a trickle into Dalit hands to avoid pollution.

Yovelamma of Yadavalli village, Guntur district, Andhra Pradesh, works as an agricultural labourer. She points out that when landlords perform rituals for paddy transplantation and harvest, Dalits are not allowed to participate. Dalit women have to keep their food away from other workers and eat separately. On tobacco plantations, Dalits have to bring their own pots to water the saplings, where as non-Dalit workers can use the landlord's pots.

3. *Other Employment Outside the Home*

Many Dalit women are also employed to do domestic and other chores in non-Dalit agrarian households. These tasks include cleaning the cattle shed, sweeping the courtyard or outer areas, washing clothes, and sometimes cleaning cooking utensils. These activities are spatially defined so the Dalit women do not enter particular parts of the non-Dalit house, especially the kitchen. In all states, Dalit women pointed out that non-Dalit women are more rigid about maintaining practices of untouchability than non-Dalit men. In more than 50 per cent of the villages surveyed, Dalit women reported that they were discriminated against by upper - caste women. This may be because non-Dalit women internalize the caste ideology that stresses the role of women as upholders of caste purity for the entire household. Non-Dalit women may also practice untouchability as one of the few ways in which they are able to yield power over others, given their limited opportunity to do so.

In Jayntira village in central Orissa, they have to enter through the back door, work in the backyard and leave from there. In Sarriya, Narsada, Dashrathpur and Ramput Gohania villages in Uttar Pradesh, non-Dalit women do not touch Dalit workers when they have to give them something. Women in Hullahalli, Karnataka, say that if they accidentally touch their non-Dalit women employer, she takes a bath and changes her clothes. Dalit women are not employed to wash the cooking utensils in Brahmin or other upper-caste households. Untouchability seems to have wakened to some extent in rural Punjab where Dalit women are employed in well-to-do upper-caste households to clean the house, wash clothes and even kitchen utensils. In some households, although they are still not allowed to enter the kitchen, they are served food in separate vessels set aside for them.

Even if Dalits violate pollution norms accidentally, that are punished severely. Rangamma, a Dalit woman of Appannapeta village in Karimangar district, Andhra Pradesh, recalls that one day she was called by her master's wife saw this and became furious, scolding and slapping her. Later she washed going to her house to collect leftovers.

Dalit washer women from Betarsing village in south Orissa report that upper-caste women will not touch them while taking clean clothes, but do not mind physical contact while giving dirty clothes. Dalit women from Ghumar village in south Orissa who have formed a weavers' cooperative note the contradiction that non-Dalit women avoid their touch while purchasing saris, but don't mind wearing Dalit-made fabric even when performing religious rituals.

It was reported from Agali, Kerala, where Dalit women are hired to do kitchen chores, that they are not allowed to enter the puja room. When they are given food, it is served in separate wells. In Elamkunnapuzha, kerala, Dalit women vendors say that they get fewer customers that non-Dalit vendors in the market.

Working in the fields and homes of non-Dalits exposes Dalit women to sexual abuse and violence, which they are often powerless to resist. The dependence on non-Dalits prevents Dalit women from devising work routines that avoid non-Dalit spaces and the experience of being humiliated every day. Women in Perayam, Kerala, says that when they work in upper-caste households, they are sometimes forced to give in to men's sexual advances. Fearful of losing their jobs, they silently submit to sexual harassment. If the case somehow becomes public, the Dalit woman is blamed, without any stigma being attached to the non-Dalit man. In Punjab, Dalit women not only go to work in the fields of the big farmers but also collect fodder from there. While in most cases they get shouted at for centering the fields and cutting plants, some of them are also sexually abused. As a well-off Dalit from a village in the prosperous Doaba region of Punjab asserted:. 'As long as we remain dependent on the jats for collecting fodder for out cattle, and out women keep going to their fields, there is no way that we can uphold out dignity'. When Dalit men are able to afford it, they stop their wives and other female kin from working outside the home. Dalit women seem to appreciate this restriction on their mobility because their burden of work is reduced and they do not have to face sexual and other harassment.

Many Dalit women also perform tasks of scavenging, midwifery and prostitution. Each of these activities becomes the site for specific forms of discrimination. The devadasi form of prostitution was found in Karnataka in Maraldini, Hebbali, Pettlur and Navalgi villages. Navalgi has 400 devadasis; all Dalit households in this village seem to have women engaged in prostitution and they are discriminated against in several ways. The women serve upper-caste men who refuse to recognise the paternity of children born to Dalit women. In Bihar, Dalit women are allowed into non-Dalit houses to act as midwives, but cannot enter the kitchens or the puja room. Older Dalit women who work as scavengers in Hullahalli village in Karnataka are generally given leftover, even spoiled, food. Women from the Award region of Uttar Pradesh are compelled to wash clothes because there is no other job available. They complain that upper-caste women tell them to wash even the clothes soiled during childbirth and menstruation, which they cannot refuse.

4. *Domestic Work*

In addition to working outside their homes, Dalit women also shoulder the responsibility of running their own households. Their domestic tasks include collecting fuel and fodder, fetching water, cooking, cleaning, bringing up children, as well as tending livestock or land, if they have any. These activities in turn expose them to particular practices of discrimination, untouchability and violence.

In Orissa, discrimination and abuse are highest at the water sources. When Dalit water sources dry up, they are not allowed to use tube wells in the non-Dalit areas and if permitted have to wait until all the non-Dalit women collect the water. Dalit women from Badabasul, Bikramguda and Karlakote villages in south Orissa and from Similpur in central Orissa said that whenever they collect water from the tube well in the upper-caste hamlet, non-Dalit women abuse them and wash the tube well. Women say that they would rather get water from muddy ponds or walk long distances to other Dalit hamlets than face upper-caste harassment. The notable exception is Muktapur village in central Orissa where Dalits and non-Dalit use the same tube well for drinking water, without any discrimination. In Mouda village in central Orissa, discrimination seems to have instituted recently. Women report that earlier, there was only one well in the village and there were no caste-based restrictions around it. However, when two tube wells were installed in the village, access to their water was immediately divided by caste. When bathing and washing clothes in streams or rivers, Dalit women in Orissa experience untouchability. Even though Dalits have separate bathing ghats downstream, of soapy water from their ghat accidentally reached non-Dalit ghats, they are subjected to a string of caste and character abuses.

Dalit women in Lanke, Karnataka, also report that when that are compelled to fetch water from the non-Dalit colony, they are made to wait until the upper-caste women have had their turn. After wards, the non-Dalit women clean the taps with tamarind. In Salgunda village in the same state, where there is a common well, upper-caste women do not let Dalits touch the pulley and bucket. Instead, they draw water themselves and pour it from a distance into Dalit pots.

Since most Dalits do not own land, women are compelled to collect fuel and fodder and graze their livestock on either non-Dalit private lands or on village common land. This exposes them to constant harassment and abuse for trespassing. Even a basic human need like defecation becomes a constant ordeal for Dalit women because they have nowhere to go besides the non-Dalit lands.

A Dalit girl was raped by a non-Dalit in Bhooni village, Nagour district, Rajasthan, while she was grazing her animals.

A case was lodged and the police arrested the culprit who has since been released on bail. Without access to indoor toilets, Dalit women in Kesharay Patan tehsil of Bundi district, Rajasthan, live in constant stress. They are forced to go to relieve themselves in a group, and that too only early in the morning or late at night, surreptitiously, when non-Dalits cannot harass them in their fields. As a result, many women suffer from chronic gastrointestinal problems.

In Punjab, almost all available land has been brought under cultivation through the Green Revolution. Rich and powerful landowners have appropriated most of the village common lands and grazing grounds for cultivation. Some land has also been converted into housing plots. Even village ponds have been taken over. As in other parts of India, poor villagers use fallow land on the outskirts of the village for defecating. The grabbing of the commons has left poor Dalit women with nowhere to go. They are forced to defecate before sunrise or at night. It they go to the fields, they get abused and shouted at by farmers. It becomes particularly difficult for the old and the sick. While many of the landowning upper-caste families have constructed regular flush toilets in their houses, most.

Dalits lack the resources to build these. Even though the state government gives grants to promote rural toilet construction, most Dalits who lack even a *pucca* house to live in, cannot afford to spend a few thousand rupees on a toilet. Even Karnataka Dalit women have complained about the problems they faced because of the lack of toilets.

In Madhar village, Chhattarpur district, Madhya Pradesh, when a Dalit girl was going for her evening ablutions through their fields, she was raped by two Thakur boys. They coerced her not to reveal the incident but the matter came to light when the girl became pregnant. A police case was registered against the boys, but no action has been taken.

Status of Dalit Women in India

In India, according to the Census report of 1991, dalit women constitute 49.96 per cent of the 200 million of Dalit population, 16.3 of the total India female population. The Dalit women literacy rate in India was only 23.76 per cent, 7.7 per cent in Bihar, 8.31 per cent in Rajasthan and 10.69 in Uttar Pradesh showing distinct biases that state structures and contingent biases have that directly exclude the dalit women. One of the major reasons for the high dropout rate among dalit women in primary school if the discriminatory and insulting treatment that they receive first from their non-dalit teacher and form their fellow students.

The dalit women labour force constitute the backbone of Indian agricultural economy. Although the Indian state consistently defaulted over the fast 55 years is not recognising this truth by its abject neglect of their right to livelihood and education. 32-40 per cent of the household sector and large number of them employed as unorganized labour in the urban areas. Feminisation of labour and poverty amply illustrate in the light of dalit.

According to Kumud Pawada a Marathi writers means "a person Completely broken, destroyed and downtrodden. Because of public persecution, Complete and in human neglect, the group of human beings that are down trodden are completely neglected ignored" (P. G. Jogolanad). For ages together, they are living away from the society and civilization. The social structure is so stubborn that it does not allow anyone to make reforms in its. In India the caste system is so strong that even today people believes in the old and worn out classifications of society as the basis of the four varnas. Though there are laws and atrocity acts, people are still dominated and discriminated against because, laws cannot change the minds and hears of the people. Dr. Ambedkar burnt the Manu Smriti, which gives second class treatment to the Dalits Shudras and women.

In India basically women are oppressed and are not treated on par with men. Moreover the Dalit women are oppressed among oppressed and slaves. People living outside the boundaries of village, away from civilization, education religion and culture and dalits. One even with a little human sensitivity gets stunned with the realistic and authentic accounts of the life conditions of the Dalit women, her suppression, humiliation sufferings dilemmas and exploitation. Her suffering are two fold: she has her own share of universal suffering as a women and additionally, she is victim of a variety of exploitations social, religious economic and cultural as a Dalit women. Her experience of patarichal domination is qualitative, more sever than that of non-Dalit women and opportunities and avenue available to her voicing her grievances and agonies are vary few (P. G. Jogolanad). Indian society is a male dominated society. All men dominate women. Therefore it is very obvious for a Dalit man to dominate a Dalit women. After fifty years of independence, she has to work hard for earning livelihood for family. She has to undergo atrocities committed on her by her family drunkard husband. She has to protect herself from the people where she works and she has to fight against all the exploitation. Poverty is a great course for the Dalits. Because of weak economy, the Dalits cannot progress. The women working as constructions working in houses as maid – servant, is municipal corporations road broomo, breaking stones on roads, putting coal tar as road – buildings are mostly done by dalits. Dalit women have to make as two – way struggle, one in the house and the other, out of the house women due caste system which has strong hierarchic and patriarchal bias discriminate against dalit women denying them just and equal wages, fare share in economic distribution, maternity benefits, the security and protection of property rights etc.

Social Status of Dalit Women in India

In India, the traditional fourfold caste system, called varna, consists of Brahmins (the priestly caste), kshatriyas (the warrior caste) and Vaishyas (the trading caste) – all of whom are considered twice-born and are allowed to read the holy texts. The fourth group, shudras (the servile caste) are not allowed to read the holy books. Dalits were an even lower caste, the so called 'outcaste' or 'Untouchable' groups, whose very shadow was considered polluting to caste Hindus. For example, the peshwas introduced especially limiting strictures on mahars dalits, such as carrying post for their own spittle and brooms to erase their own footsteps from the road. Many untouchable groups could not draw water from the wells and tanks used by the caste Hindus. They were denied the use of public roads and transport. Dalit women could not dress in the manner of other hindu women are could they wear jewelry, and as domestic labor by women of the upper caste.

Dalits may or may not be hindus; *e.g.*, holiya and madiga are hindus; but so are former 'untouchable' converts to Buddhism, Christianity, Islam, Sikhism and other religions. However, only 'Hindu' and Sikh Scheduled Caste can claim the benefits of reservation. The marthi word dalit, was chosen by the group itself and it means literally 'ground', or 'broken or reduced to pieces'.

Compared to the women of other social groups, Dalit women are more awakened and aware of the existence in the society now a days. They have – a revolutionary mind. In India, caste system can only be comprehended when it is realised it is essentially permeated by religious conception the Caste system has established "direct link between the religious beliefs and the social differentiation (Max weber). "Each group of caste, each Caste and sometime even sub-Caste was allowed to cultivate its distinctive styles of life in the matter of diet, dress. Worship, marriage etc., (Ander Beteill). Very often these observation have made to think about the relationship between caste hierarchy and the various customs and religion beliefs and practices existing in the Indian social scene.

The term Dalit is an imposed category, for many 'untouchable' and former 'untouchable' groups do not identify themselves with the term, and furthermore, none of the women and girls in the study sample referred to here, identified themselves hamlets at the edge of a village. They are a small and vulnerable minority in any given region, main resistance to exploitation and violence is very difficult. Dalit constitute over 16 per cent of the total Indian population. The 1991 Census estimates the total Dalit population in India at 138 million, and in Karnataka state as seven and a half million (7.5), or 16 per cent of the total state population.

Dalit are not only a socio-cultural group but often represent an economic class as well. The 1971 census figures show that over half of the Dalit workforce were landless agricultural labours, compared to 26 per cent of the non-dalit workforce. A number of social studies have revealed that Dalit women make up a large number of the professional sex workers. Studies reveal that 90 per cent of those who die of starvation and attendant diseases are Dalit. Their untouchability and poverty support each other – their untouchable status accentuates their economic exploitation and their poverty strengthen their polluting social status.

Untouchability was made a legal offence by the Indian parliament in 1955. However, untouchability as a social institution was and is kept alive by the use of brutal force. The caste Hindus insisted of enforcing the inferiority of the dalits in many ways, and if they tried to improve their standards of living they were cruelly.

There are various barriers for Dalit women not to take participation in the active politics, such as Social, Economic and Political inequality in the India society the social barriers such as practice of untouchability, casteism, illiteracy, socio-cultural variation, religious exploitation and superstitions and class variation in the society.

Devdasi System

Married to God before puberty, the devadasis (servants of God) may of whom live in the temples become sexual servants to the villages upper-caste men after their first menstrual period. In some villages devadasis are kept as conubines but the men she bought them. In others they are public shuttle, who can be used by men free of charge.

Indian can't seem to shake off one of the sruelest traditions of its hidebound caste system. Dedications of devadasi girls have been supervised by village priests in southern India for thousands of years. The British tried to outlaw the tradition, and the Indian government has banned it too. But according to human-rights activists, as many as 15,000 girls in rural areas are still dedicated to God each year. "The parents simply don't see any other possibility," says Pailey "Somebody has to be dedicated, or the goddess will be angry." Religious duty often ends up as prostitutions; many dalit women leave the villages to earn money in the filthy brothels of Bombay. Activism and education are starting to change attitudes.

Educational Status of Dalit Women

"I pray to you with folded hands that you give me blessings I am going to do divine work. I want your blessings and good wishes" (Champa Lernaya). The person who was making this request was Smt. Savitribai Phule, Mahatma Phule's wife and she was praying before the Brahmins of Pune who were pelting stones at her, curising her and throwing cowdung on her. Her clothes used to get stained with blood. The heinous crime that savitribai and committed was to teach girl. This incident occurred in the first half of the 19th century. In the state of Maharashtra, the city of Pune was the strong hold of orthodoxy. In those days to get educated was supposed to be the greatest sin for women. The orthodox people thought that if women would begin to read and write and become literate, they would take to apth of sin women were threatened that if they become literate they would become widows. In those days women were tied down by shalkles of customs and traditions and were confined within the four walls of their homes in change of the kitchen and child care persecuted. Perhaps the most effective weapon which helped in the perpetuation of the untouchability was the institutionalized bias and denial of access to educational resources.

Untouchability is related to the oppression of upper caste women as well as it became an effective means of patriarchal/ brahmanic control over high caste comen's sexuality which was essential for maintaince of caste privilege. At the same time, the potential threat to these systems of domination that the rape of upper caste females by lower caste males represented, was negated by defining offspring of such unions as untouchable. These some of the ideologies allowed upper caste men to violate low caste women's sexuality with impurity and without consideration of issues around caste purity and female honor.

Even the process of Sanskritization or approximation to upper castes' code of conduct' did not help Dalits to cross the barriers of untouchability. Dalit all over India have tried to change their lifestyles, marriage practices and caste names but to no effect.

Alarmingly for the past several years, official Indian figures on violent attacks against Dalits have routinely exceeded 10,000 cases per year. Indian human rights workers report a far larger number go unrecorded, buried by collusion between police and local privilege. Justice is rare, even when charges are filed.

Suganabai Kshirasagar looked after him. The orthodox people tried to put a lot of obstacles in the path of Jyotibe's education Sagunabai left no stone unturned to teach Jyotiba English language as she knew his caliber. One 1st January, 1884 Jyotiba started the first school for girls in Pune and he stated another school for untouchable children in 1891. The orthodox (so-called religious) people created a lot of hurdles in Jyotiba's work.

Before Jyotiba, the Missionaries had tried to start girl schools but their efforts proved to be futile. However, taking inspiration from jyotiba's attempts, some of his Brahmins and non-brahmin friends helped him in his work. The first school started in the house of Shri. Bhide who instead of taking rent, promised to donate Rs. 5 per month as help to the school and for the initial expenditure of the school donated Rs. 101. Savtribai become the first teacher and the Principal of this school. They registered the names of their friends' daughters. The students were of the age of 4,5, 6 years. The couple started convicing the people and though at first people were frightened, gradually the number of girl students started increasing. Any good work is at first looked down upon, but later on people feel curious about it and ultimately accept it, as it happened in Jyotiba's case. The public preferred the schools started twenty schools in Pune and its Vicinity. Afterwards male teachers like Shri. Vishnupant Atre and Shri Vamanrao Kharadkar began working in the schools. Usman

Shiekh's sister Fadtima Sheikh started teaching after she had taken training. He was the first Muslim teacher.

Savitribai was very beautiful. When she was teaching in her youth once a good a tried to molest her on the way. But Savitribai was not only beautiful but also physically strong and mentally firm. She could understand the intention of the goonda and attacked him like a tigres and gave him three-four slap. The goonda was flabbergasted and ran away from there. This news spread ever where and people realised savitribai courage. So nobody dared cause her any trouble there after. Otherwise people of orthodox attitude used to throw stones at her every day but she faced the assault peacefully and courageously.

At time when even the shadow of a person from scheduled caste used to be shunned, when people were averse to giving water to thirsty untouchables and had no compassion for them, jyotibe savitribai spend the well in their house for the use of the untouchables. It was a great miracle. It was a challenge thrown at the orthodox, reactionary people. The Brahmins cried out, "the entire city of Pune is drowned in sin. The Kaliyug evil age has arrived. Now the day of deluge is soon coming". It is a sorry state of affairs that even today after a hundred years, things have not changed much. In villages and small townships the untouchables have to pine for water.

Economic Status of Dalit Women

Economic disability is the main thing which concerns the scheduled castes in the state. Large numbers of them have been landless agricultural labourers working for others as daily Wages. With the mechanization and improvement in agricultural economy most of them have lost their traditional occupation. One of the Constitutional provisions with regard to the reservation of job for scheduled caste in governmental and public undertaking. But due to ignorance, illiteracy, poverty and official apathy these advantages are not fully made use of by them. The economic oppression of Dalit women has made them live below the poverty line. The Dalit women often decend below the subsist. Once the line with the disappearance of their means of earning and livelihood, women work both in organized and in unorganized sector. The Dalit women employed mainly is unorganized sector, and work as labourers in agriculture, construction work, landless labourers, factory work and other house hold and marginal works, as daily wages workers (P. C. Jain and Shashi Jain, Shudha Bhatnagar).

The basic problem that affects the Dalit women is role and opportunities for employment in this sector spring from this helpless dependence supposed by lack of adequate employment autonomous limited skills illiteracy, restricted mobility and lack of autonomous status. The lack of control ones predictive resources and a persistent gap between consumption and expenditure leading to perpetual indebtedness, deprive them of all bargaining power and occupational mobility. The proportion of Dalit women below the poverty line is comparatively higher than upper caste women. The structural adjustment in the new economic policy lists women, which leads to decline in employment and income by the introduction of imported technology.

Political Status of Dalit Women

Women constitute about 50 per cent of the population of India and 80 per cent population of women resides in the rural areas. Most of the rural women are engaged in the domestic and household activities. Some of them are also engaged in the economic activities to earn livelihood for their families. Even after fifty years of independence, they have not been able to participate effectively in various occupations. The role differentials created by the culture in a specifies society can be changed through educational development, change in social values and political will of the state. Thus the concept of gender in political participation is abstract and it can be used successfully for women's participation in political life of the nation (Hoshior Singh and Ajmer singh Malik). Some researcher evaluated the status and position of women in the society, especially is terms of political participation. Change finds the that discrimination against women is deeply rooted is the structure of society is the role women play and in a sexual division of labour, which relegated females primarily to the domestic spheres of life (W. H. Clage). Jahan points out that women generally participate in large number in voting but their participation is very low in the political activities (R. Jahan). Kaushik (Sushila Kaushik) state that the right to vote is the starting point in the struggle for women's political equality and their participation by way of voting has been growing but not steadily ones the years. Mohanti reveals that it is necessary to create proper socio-economic and political conditions to enable women to participate effectively in the Panchayati Raj Institution without endangering the positive values of the prevailing family system (Bidyut Mohanti). Sudha pai's in her brief study of three villages from Meerut district of Uttar Pradesh warns that unless reservations are accompanied by female literacy, independent voting rights and change in status of family and society, women will continue to act a more name sake representatives of the male members of their family (Sudha Pai).

Weaker section mean the weak groups of society need special care and protection. It refers to both economic and social weaknesses and both of these weaknesses to together, each kind re-inforcing the other. Weaker sections are the alientated sections of society comprising SC, ST, OBC, marginal and small farmers, rural artisan and landless labourers etc. Social and economic backwardness is considered as a criterion to be eligible as a weaker section (U. Gurmurthy). Dalits are the people who are socially and economically backward and most of them are landless labourers depending on the land owing classes for their livelihood. The Scheduled Tribes are victims of isolation, primitive economy and all sorts of exploitation. All the political parties in India speak much about equality of women, and have totally ignored the Dalit women, where their political status and participation is insignificant. It is regretable that the Dalit women have not been given the representation in all the political parties which reflects the social difference. By recognising the seriousness of women's participation in politics, in the year 1987 the Janata Government in Karnataka announced 25 per cent reservation for women in Zilla Parishad and Mandal Panchayat as per Zilla Parishad Act 1932, with a special provision of 5.1 ratio reservation to Dalit women in 25 per cent women reservation, which is a very important and significant aspect. This reservation a number of Dalit women had an opportunity to take part in active politics, 19 dalit women against 211 upper caste women in Zilla Parishad and 2469 Dalit women's against 14025 upper caste women in Mandal Panchayats were elected. The Participation of these representatives in active politics vares. A few women have really showed good performance in the participation. The representation of Dalit women in Zilla Parishad and Mandal Panchayat does not widen the reality of women's political visibility. There fore efforts should be made to increase the scope and percentage of reservation in legislatures and in parliament. All the Political parties should strictly implement the reservation specifically for Dalit women. And it is the responsibilities of voluntary social organizations, Dalit organizations and the implementation of reservation also to create the political awareness and its importance among women.

Government Economic Policy for Dalit Women

Scholarship schemes for the scheduled castes were one of the important constitutional provisions. But for this incentive it would not have been possible for many scheduled caste students to Continue their higher studies at different levels. The parents of their respondents, being financially in a difficult position and educationally backward, would perhaps not have allowed their children to go to schools and colleges. Very often the parents consider children as economic assets when they are young, since children are employed in many areas in the village, which supplements family income.

Reservation of jobs of the Scheduled Castes in government and public undertakings are being extended from time to time but as it is time-bound, it will come to an end at one stage.

Dalit Women and the Public Sphere

There are fewer reports of Dalit women experiencing discrimination and untouchability in the public sphere as compared to men. Yet this absence does not indicate the women are treated fairly, but that women do not even enter many public places. Prescribed norms about women's 'proper place' mean that they rarely go to post offices, banks or even the panchayat office. As women from Ganiari Khurd, Garhwa, Bihar, said, 'What work do women have in the panchayat'. Only men go there ' In Tamil Nadu, Dalit women cannot enter village temples, hotels and eating places. In Andhra Pradesh, women cannot enter village temples. Subordination keeps most Dalit women out of the public sphere. A major departure from this is the reservation of one-third of the posts in gram panchayats for women.

(i) Panchayats

Dalits in India, officially termed scheduled castes, form the largest discriminated community. Their discrimination is based, *first*, on their descent or birth into specific 'untouchable' castes, and *secondly*, on their traditional 'polluting' work. As a result, although almost one in five Indians is a Dalit, half of whom are women, their political participation as a large minority community in India remains disproportionately low. Looking specifically at Dalit women, the current Indian Lower House of Parliament has only 12 Dalit women MPs, a mere 2.2 per cent of Parliamentarians. In its consideration of the Government of India's report in 2007, the Committee on the Elimination of Racial Discrimination noted its concern over the under representation of Dalits in all levels of government. The Committee went further to state that: "Dalit candidates, especially women, are frequently forcibly prevented from standing for election or, if elected, forced to resign from village councils or other elected bodies or not to exercise their mandate, [and] that many Dalits are not included in electoral rolls or otherwise denied the right to vote"...

To just take the example of Dalit women's political participation in local governance institutions in India called the panchayats. The simple reason is that this is the largest political space open for Dalit women today to participate in public affairs. Moreover, at this level, there are separate quotas for Dalit women, aside from quotas for Dalits and women in general, meant to facilitate their inclusion in local governance.

It is true that the quota system has resulted in over 100,000 Dalit women elected representatives across the country today. Unfortunately, however, political representation through quotas has not led to effective political participation for the majority of Dalit women. The main obstacle is the multiple discrimination these women face arising from the entrenched caste hierarchy, chronic poverty and patriarchy.

Dalit women are excluded from caste councils (jati panchayats). Many of them are unable to participate meaningfully even in the gram panchayats. Lacking political-economic authority and formal education, and unfamiliar with administrative procedures, Dalit women who are elected to panchayat posts find themselves unable to function effectively. Many Dalit women in south Orissa complain that non-Dalit women do not inform them about panchayat meetings and so they never get to participate.

(ii) Health Services

Dalit women deal with government officials most frequently when they seek health services for themselves and their children. The village anganvadi worker and ANM (auxiliary nurse-midwife) discriminates against them. Dalit women from Sanjhiki, Bahabal and Randa villages in north Orissa say that upper-caste anganvadi workers do not allow them to enter the anganvadi centre. Their children are also discriminated against. Dalit women in Maouda village, central Orissa, note that their anganvadi worker is an adivasi; she does not visit their hamlet and refused to let them enter the centre. In Similpur village in central Orissa, women report that the health worker takes Rs. 150 from them for every visit to the Dalit hamlet. Dalit women across Uttar Pradesh report that the ANMs practice untouchability; hardly any pregnant Dalit women approach health workers for their services.

In pandalam Thekkekara, Kerala, Dalit women report that the doctors at the local hospital spend for more time in examining and treating upper-caste women. In Attipra, Kerala, the non-Dalit anganvadi worker discriminates against her Dalit colleague.

Dalit women from Tamil Nadu say that upper-caste families don't send their children to the anganvadi because it is run by Dalit women. In two villages, non-Dalit women avoided using the health centre because the health worker was Dalit . Premlatha, a Dalit women from Andhra Pradesh, is a graduate who is working as an anganvadi teacher. Despite being educated and employed in a government job, she still encounters caste-based discrimination. As she puts it : 'Chinta chacchina pulupu chavadu' (A tamarind may die but it does not lose its sourness).

The practice of untouchability in Lon Khurd, Parbhani district, Maharashtra, become apparent when researchers for this study held a group discussion with three upper-caste and four Dalit women. The meeting was held in anganvadi centre where the worker is a Dalit women. The researcher opened the meeting by asking the anganvadi worker to apply haldi-kumkum (turmeric – vermilion) to each woman's forehead, a common way of welcoming women in Maharashtra. The three upper-caste women refused to let the Dalit woman touch them to apply haldi-kumkum to their foreheads. Instead, they took the powder and applied it themselves.

In the rare cases when a Dalit women manages to become a government employee, she encounters discrimination from her colleagues and clients. Forty-year-old Pralaya Senapati is the ANM of Telipalsh village in district Kalahandi, Orissa-a great achievement for a Dalit. But whenever she goes to the upper-caste women and children, they change their saris and bathe to purify themselves after she leaves. That is why non-Dalit ask Senapati to come early in the morning so that they can deal with her before they have had their morning bath . If non-Dalits need her help later; in the day they ask her to place medicines so that they can avoid touching her hand. Senapati says' 'I do my work sincerely. I feel so insulted by this behaviour'.

(iii) Self-Help Group

Villages in several states now have women's Self-Help Groups (SHGs) where women regularly deposit small savings and use the funds to provide loans. In 30 to 40 per cent of the villages surveyed, Dalits reported that they were discriminated in SHGs. In Tamil Nadu and Karnataka, in instances, where the SHG includes both Dalit and non-Dalit women, Dalit women are made to sit separately. Dalits and non-Dalit women do not eat together. Dalit women from a now-defunct SHG in Lon Khurd, Parbhani district, Maharahtra, report that Maratha women members used to sit apart from women of other castes. When Sheela Athavle, a Dalit, was made the head of the group because she was literate, Maratha women members refused to accept her and stopped paying their monthly contributions to her. The group stopped working two years ago.

(iv) Schools

In some schools in Kerala, boys have started making friends across the Dalit/non-Dalit divide. They visit each other's homes and occasionally eat food together as well. Compared to boys, socializing between girls of different caste is still very limited. Premlatha, a Dalit from Andhra Pradesh who succeeded in becoming a graduate, recounts her ordeal in school where non-Dalit teachers and students would humiliate her by calling her by her caste name. When she was in the fourth standard, she accompanied her upper-caste friend to her house, only to be ordered out immediately. Premlatha dreams of a society free of discrimination, but to her disappointment, even the next generation has had to confront untouchability. Recently, Premlatha's daughter visited her upper-caste classmate's house to pick up a textbook. As she was thirsty, the friend offered her water in a tumbler. Just then, her friend's mother walked in and, finding a Dalit girl drinking from the tumbler, grabbed the vessel and threw it down, shouting caste abuses at her. In another case, the upper-caste head – master of a village school in Tamil Nadu refused to accept a boiled egg because a Dalit cook had removed its shell.

(v) Other Public Spheres

On local buses in Bihar, upper-caste women are allowed to sit in the seats reserved for women, while Dalit women are asked to sit at the back, along with the men. In Tamil Nadu, Dalit women say that they are made to give up their seat in the bus when an upper-caste women boards. Kanakarathnam, the leader of a Dalit SHG in Andhra Pradesh, encounter the same discrimination when she boarded a bus along with women from the upper-caste SHG in her village to go for a meeting at the mandal headquarters. The upper-caste refused to let Kanakarathnam sit on the seat reserved for women; they shouted at her saying: 'Have you forgotten your caste?' However, the conductor intervened and insisted that they share the seat with Kanakarathnam.

Resistance and change in Many Dalit women so not submit to discrimination; they act against it. In Kuanrput village in central Orissa, Kamala, a Dalit woman entered the village temple and confronted the priest: 'Has God debarred us from the temple and allowed only upper castes to enter, or is it your rules that you are imposing on us?' This led to a big fight between Dalits and non-Dalits. Today Dalits dare not venture near the temple.

A few Dalit women in Kerala have breached the caste divide by marrying upper-caste men. In Attipra, a Dalit girl said, she is happy with her husband and his family. Her only sorrow is that her in-laws do not allow her to meet her parents or others in her natal family. In order to marry the person of her choice, a non-Dalit, she has been forced to sacrifice her ties to her kin. In Kerala, it seems that the rules of kinship and marriage are being intensely renegotiated. When the Dalit girl's upper-caste mother-in-law was interviewed, she revealed the domestic politics behind her decisions. This women has four sons. She says that her second son had an affair with a Dalit girl slightly older than him. The mother created scenes and vigorously opposed the affair. To her relief, the boy abandoned the Dalit girl and has now married someone from their own caste. Later, her youngest son also got dragged into a similar 'foolish affair' with a Dalit girl. However, in this case, the boy was determined. The mother loves him marry the girl. But she makes sure that her youngest daughter-in-law's relations are not allowed to visit her house. She admits that she likes her daughter-in-law, but confesses that she cannot give up her 'other' feelings about Dalits.

New projects in Kerala that use decentralized planning to focus on women's particular needs are beginning to change women's access to the public sphere. Many Dalit women are benefiting from schemes and projects that, for inscance, train women to drive auto-rickshaws and buses, provide bicycles (for school girls), skills training, and instruction in karate. In a cultural milieu where women are not supposed to stand on the street other than for unavoidable reasons like shopping or waiting for a bus, these projects given women a new visibility and confidence. Women-driven auto-rickshaws enable the embodied presence of Dalit women in spaces where they are usually excluded. In the process, they challenge the age-old patriarchal prejudice that the public sphere is a male domain.

The specific forms of discrimination that Dalit women struggle against are produced by the combined weight of caste, class and patriarchy. Social beliefs about pollution, the economic compulsions of being dependent on upper-castes for work and livelihood, and the vulnerability imposed by gender sub-ordination, fuse to make the lives of Dalit women especially hard.

Social Change among the Dalit Women

Compared to the women of other social groups, Dalit women are more awakened and aware of their existence in the society now a days. They have revolutionary mind. They are participating in all kinds of social gatherings organized on various social issues. Dalit women are always ahead in the huge procession on the Dhamma Chakra Parivartana day. They are seen in large numbers on the Diksha Bhoomi at Nagpur. Dalit women today are living like burning flames in the society. To name some of them, Mayawati and Phoolan

Devi are championing the cause of Dalits through their political activities. The political awakening is definitely more among Dalit women as compared to the women of the higher castes. They are very conscious in the matter of their right to vote and keeping in mind the qualification and work of the candidate rather than the symbol.

Social

Even the killing of a Dalit women is explicitly justified as a minor offence of the Brahmins: equal to the killing of an animal (Manusmitri). If the killing of an untouchable was justified as a minor offence, you can imagine the treatment they received throughout their lives.

In a male dominated society, Dalit women suffered unimaginable oppression, not only through caste, but gender too, from which there was no escape. The laws in the Manusmriti and other Vedic scriptures close all economic, political social, educational, and personal channels through which Dalit women could be uplifted (Thind n.pag). the horrendous laws in the Manusmriti were incorporated into Hinduism because they were favourable only to the Upper caste, which form the majority of Indian. Even today, in modern times, we see the severe oppression and exploitation of Dalit women. The Laws of the Manusmriti have a devastating effect on the level of education reached by dalit women.

The caste discrimination inherited by birth results in Dalit women facing multiple oppression that violates their economic, political, social and cultural rights. The most deprived section of the society comprises of Dalit women who are the poorest, illiterate and easy targets for sexual harassment. The women face not just caste violence inflicted on them by the dominant castes, but also state violence.

Achievements in Education

A large majority of the illiterate population comprise of Dalit women with 76.24 per cent of Dalit women being illiterate. The girl drop out rate among Dalit families is increasing with girl-children are forced to work as child laborers, More and more girl children from Dalit communities are school drop outs and working as child labourers. Dalit illiterate because they have less access to education which is an inherent part of the caste system. There are not enough facilities for education, taking care of small children and they join the adults to add top the income of the family. Dalit girl children are involve mostly in hazardous work like: Beedi making, working in match factories and in the fire-works industry.

Traditionally dowry, which is not a practice of the Dalits has now became a bane. Due to Sanskritisation by the caste Hindus, the Dalits have begun to emulate the customs and rituals of the Hindus. Dowry is one such custom. The Dalit families have succumbed to the societal pressures, added to this the fear of sending the girls to schools which are usually located in distant places deprive them of education.

Girl children are deprived of access to education as belonging to economically weak families, they are unable to pursue their education. They do not get uniforms, school books, special fees, and have to walk long distances to reach their school. This is a limiting factor for Dalit children.

The major achievement in absolute term has been noticed in the filed of education. The level of literacy among the Dalits has grown up considerably during the past two decades. But there is a considerable gap between upper caste women and the Dalit women. Education is the means of realising one's life-desire which help to develop one's personality and it accentuates in improving one's status in all respect. Education has direct association to the socio-economic and political status of women. It is due to the lack of education the Dalit women are not able to come out of their poverty and marginalized situation. Being illiterate they are not aware of their own rights and their own life-situation. It is because of their innocence and ignorance that upper caste people can easily exploit them and oppress them. Due to lack of education there is no knowledge of health among them and they do not care about their health, and easily becomes the victim of pandemic diseases.

Following are the reasons why Dalit women bother least about education of their children are:

Their main aim is to earn their livelihood, for education is not needed. By seeing other people as domestic workers, sweepers, weavers, etc., they can earn their living. When the mother goes out for work, the girl children, stays back at home, in order to assist in cooking, looking after the young ones and grand parents. They don't show any interest in educating their girls. Girl children help them at domestic chores and even these women discriminate between male children and female children.

Dalit women are ahead in the educational field, but still they have to enter many more areas such as business, professional education, medical etc., But still economic progress is needed. Until recently, the contribution of women to the Indian economy through self-employment and home based work has not received much attention. Employment of women in organized and unorganized sectors has drawn large number of women out of the family and the house hold who make their contribution to the economy visible.

It is important to note that under Dr. B. R. Ambedkar's leadership the Dalit women took active part in Dalit protest movements on a number of occasions. Until and unless there is an improvement in the status of Dalit women and their equal participation in the society all talk of nation's progress and development is meaningless.

Economic

Of the total population, Dalit women constitute 16.3 per cent of which 18 per cent women live in rural areas. The women perform hard domestic labour which is unpaid and as agricultural labourers or casual labourers they continue to toil under the burning sun, with no protection or benefits that labour laws should provide, since majority of these women are in the unorganized sector. They do not even get the minimum wages that the state/country has specified, since they are unable to organize and demand for decent wage. Dalit women undertake manual, low paying, tedious, time consuming work. They earn less than one U.S. Dollar.

The women have to walk miles to fetch drinking water and often the water is not safe and potable. Dalit hamlets are usually at the end of the main village or in the village outskirts. They live in small huts and even the few who may have slightly better housing are devoid of basic amenities such as sanitation, light and safe and clean drinking water. The women work on construction sites, carrying heavy loads of construction material. They also work in brick kilns for long hours, as casual labourers to lay roads with hot tar in the burning sun, without sandals and any other protective gear. The women have to walk miles not just for collecting water but also fuel and fodder for their domestic chores. Dalit women are victims of bonded labour, they are abused, sexually exploited by other caste, humiliated and are easy targets of insult.

A study conducted come up with some shocking facts about the work of Dalit women. What is horrifying is that Dalit women work more than bullocks and men. Bullocks and men work in a hectare in a year for 1064 hours and 1202, respectively, while women work for more than 3485 hours. The caste and patriarchal norms legitimize the poor economic conditions of Dalit women. She has to work to survive. She is powerless and has neither access nor control over resources.

Manual scavenging continues as an occupation in India and most of the manual scavengers are Dalit women. The women are subjected to do this humiliating and degrading work, which further results in discrimination and social exclusion.

Health

The health condition of Dalit women is alarming with high incidence of maternal mortality and infant mortality. This is due to the fact that Dalit women are unable to access health care services. Due to denial and sub standard healthcare services the life expectancy of Dalit women is as low as 50 years. The infant mortality rate is 90/1.000. The sex ratio of Dalit women is 922/1000 compared to 927/1000 for rest of the population in India. Due to poverty, Dalit women are malnourished and anemic. Early marriage and multiple child births causes the women to suffer from prolapsed uterus. Continuous bending, working while sowing and harvesting in agricultural causes acute back pain. They also develop skin irritation and allergy due to excessive use of pesticides. As they work barefoot and the soil is damp and wet, the women develop soars between their toes. Due to lack of awareness and medical care, many of them suffer from reproductive health complications, including STDs and cervical cancer with white discharges.

Dalit women are easy target for the Government Birth Control Schemes. Women face forced sterilization, are tested for the use of new invasive hormonal contraception like guinea pigs. They are force to use long-acting, hormonally dangerous contraceptives. They do not get basic medical facilities . Pregnant Dalit women receive discriminatory treatment in hospitals and there are instances where doctors have refused to conduct the delivery of Dalit women.

Political Power

Dalit women are excluded from decision-making. They are not in a position to exercise their power. Wherever Dalit women have contested, they have faced stiff opposition and even been brutally attacked. The 73rd amendment provides for mandatory reservation for Dalit women to be elected to the local governing bodies. They are elected but not able to exercise their power. Menaka (a Dalit women and a village Panchayat President was killed in broad day light).

Ranganayaki was deposed for solemnizing an inter-caste marriage. Banwari was gang raped when she objected and reported to the authorities against child marriage in her village. Gowri was made to parade naked for hoisting a flag on Independence Day. Dalit women are militant and powerful. They are now fighting for political power within this caste system.

There are instances where Dalit women have been elected into local governance and through the reservation policy nominated as the President of the local governing unit called

Panchayat. But when these women have endeavoured to exercise their role, it has met with resistance even to the extend of physical violence. A Dalit woman President is not allowed to sit on a chair, if the other caste members do no allow this. She is forced to be a mere figure head, while the functioning of the Panchayat is taken over by other upper caste members.

There are several traditional practices and customs that violate human rights. The practice of dedicating girl-children to become Devadasis, Basavis and Mathammas. This practice is a violation of Dalit women's rights. Dalit women are discriminated and treated as untouchables. The shoemakers. Arunthathiar, practice Mathamma, dedicating Dalit girl children to their goddess Mathamma.

Superstition coupled with poverty and illiteracy is responsible for such practices. It is also using religion to sanction prostitution through the interpretation of mythology by the upper caste so that they can both economically and sexually exploit Dalit women. It also is a form of upper caste manipulation to control the lives of Dalits. Further the lack of medical services, allows for such practices to flourish. There is a strong belief that the goddess has dealing powers. So when a Dalit girl is sick. She is taken to the temple and left there till she is cured of her sickness. As already mentioned the economic situation is another reason that Dalits are unable to spend money to buy good health service. Once the child is cured, the child is named after Mathamma and married to the goddess with the 'Pottu Thali' (wedlock). After she becomes a dancer she belongs to the temple. During temple festivals she dances and earns her livelihood. She is not treated with respect and publicly humiliated by men who harass her sexually.

The team which plays music with her exploits her by having a share in what she earns. Once the girl is dedicated to Mathamma, she cannot marry and lead a family life, as she is wedded to the Goddess. Therefore, she is sexually exploited by her partner who leaves her, to fend for herself and her child. Other men also tend to sexually exploit these Dalit women. Mathammas have no family, no security and left all alone with a child, so she has to struggle life long to maintain herself and the child. Dalit women who are dedicated to Mathammas end up in the sex trade and become vulnerable to sexually transmitted diseases including HIV/AIDS.

Dalits facing Human Rights violations is a legion. A random sampling of deadlines in mainstream Indian newspapers tells their story: 'Dalit boy beaten to death for plucking flowers'; 'Dalit tortured by cops for three days'; Dalit 'which' paraded naked in Bihar'; 'Dalit killed in lock-up at Kurnool'; "Seven Dalit burnt alive in caste clash'; "Five Dalits lynched in Haryana'; "Dalit women gang-raped, paraded naked'; 'Police egged on mob to lynch Dalits'.

Dalits in India, officially termed scheduled castes, form the largest discriminated community. Their discrimination is based, first, on their descent or birth into specific 'untouchable' castes, and secondly, on their traditional 'polluting' work. As a result, although almost one in five Indians is a Dalit, half of whom are women, their political participation as a large minority community in India remains disproportionately low. Looking specifically at Dalit women, the current Indian Lower House of Parliament has only 12 Dalit women MPs, a mere 2.2 per cent of Parliamentarians. In its consideration of the Government of India's report in 2007, the Committee on the Elimination of Racial Discrimination noted its concern over the under representation of Dalits in all levels of government. The Committee went further to state that: "Dalit candidates, especially women, are frequently forcibly prevented from standing for election or, if elected, forced to resign from village councils or other elected bodies or not to exercise their mandate, and that many Dalits are not included in electoral rolls or otherwise denied the right to vote"...

I want to just take the example of Dalit women's political participation in local governance institutions in India called the panchayats. The simple reason is that this is the largest political space open for Dalit women today to participate in public affairs. Moreover, at this level, there are separate quotas for Dalit women, beside from quotas for Dalits and women in general, meant to facilitate their inclusion in local governance.

It is true that the quota system has resulted in over 100,000 Dalit women elected representatives across the country today. Unfortunately, however, political representation through quotas has not led to effective political participation for the majority of Dalit women. The main obstacle is the multiple discrimination these women face arising from the entrenched caste hierarchy, chronic poverty and patriarchy.

Globalisation

The process of Globalisation has affected Dalit women considerably. With the introduction of new farming techniques such as, mechanization for harvesting and transplanting, women have lost their traditional work in the agricultural sector. Food crops have been replaced by Cash crops. Horticulture has been introduced by big agrobusiness corporations for export purposes. This has deprived Dalit women of their land and the common resources in the village. Formerly women used to collect greens, fish, and shells from fields free for their food requirements. This is no longer available to them. The abject poverty condition has driven large numbers of Dalit women into sex trade to earn for their families. The Globalisation process has increased the feminisation of poverty and this has affected Dalit women in every sphere of their lives. There is also large scale migration from rural areas to the urban centres in search of better livelihood options. Women are left behind to bear the responsibility of the family. This further adds to the existing burden that Dalit women are trying to cope with. More and more female headed households emerge and most of them are Dalit women. Such situations push the women into further situations of impoverishment, making them more and more vulnerable to all forms of discriminations and violations.

4 REVIEW OF LITERATURE

In this chapter a brief review of various research studies conducted in the areas related different issues of status of Dalit women are presented.

Sudha Umashanker (The Hindu 26th July 2011). Is it easy being a Dalit in India? And a women at that? Have things changed for the better for the Dalits who constitute roughly 16.23 per cent of our population, since the Constitution of India "caste a special responsibility on the State to promote with special care for the education, economic interest of the Scheduled Castes and promised to protect them from all forms of exploitation and social injustice (Article 46)".

Ask Ruth Manorama, relentless crusader and rallying point for Dalit women, and she tells it like it is, without mincing words, in a no-holds barred conversation.

"Dalit women in India are the Dalits among Dalits and suffer from three-fold oppression – on account of gender as a result of patriarchy, caste 'the untouchable', and class – as they hail from the poorest and most marginalized communities. Eighty per cent of Scheduled Castes live in rural areas, are dependent on wage employment and have to contend with high rates of under employment which results in greater incidence of poverty," argues Manorama forcefully.

A grassroots person with her ear to the ground, Manorama is well aware that discrimination is indeed a regular and daily experience for Dalit women. "Less than equal wages at the workplace, beings force into dehumanizing jobs like manual scavenging and garbage picking, pushed back by the grueling cycle of generational poverty, landlessness and hunger, facing threats to their personal security and a lifelong cycle of indebtedness including religious prostitution and the Devadsi system, are the major hurdles. It is this linkage that makes Dalit women a vital and special concern for the UN Committee on the Elimination of Discrimination against women (CEDAW) and the UN Committee on Racial Discrimination (CERD) and the Human Rights Council".

Silent Abuse

Yet another issue that deeply angers her is incidents of violence against Dalit women and the silence that surrounds this. "Studies have shown that rape against Dalits and tribales are among the highest. Structural violence like caste and communal violence are deep-rooted in our psyche. It is often used to suppress women in countering Maoist attacks, organized rape and sexual violence (she refers to the Uttarakhand State rape) wherein police suspected women to be informers, are all such inhuman acts".

Bhupendra Yadav (The Hindu, 19th July 2011). Caste is inlaid in a pre-determined hierarchy. It is something one cannot choose, but inherits. Caste matters a lot in everyday life, and marriages are negotiated on that basis. It plays a decisive role in elections and, as the saying goes, 'Indians do not cast their vote but vote their caste'.

Dalits, as is known, are a bloc of castes in the lowest rungs of the social hierarchy that stand condemned as 'untouchables'. If every sixth person in the world is an Indian is a Dalit. In spite of the constitutional guarantee of civil rights and the special law enacted (in 1989) to prevent atrocities against them, the Dalits continue to be the victims of social discrimination and oppression across the country.

While the 'outcaste' is abhorred, there is, ironically, a craze for acquiring the 'Scheduled Castes' tag. In fact, the demand is so high that producing fake SC certificates has become a small-scale industry of sorts. In the current era of liberalization, governments are gradually relinquishing their role as service providers and taking on the role of facilitators or policy initiators. As a result, governments have been tightening their fists in some crucial segments of social sector. But they extend small tokens of help to the SCs, and the reasons are obvious. In a sense, the 'lust' for SC certificates is a pernicious fallout of the spasmodic pleasantness shown by governments for their self-preservation.

Irony

In this book, Anupama Rao examines the irony of the Dalits having no security of life or dignity, despite all the legal protection they enjoy. She has based her work on a study of Madras, a socially oppressed group of western India. Members of this community rebel against the discriminatory practices, individually as well as collectively – both as a caste group and as a constituent of the SC bloc. The strategy they adopt included the demand for recognition and separate political representation as a 'minority', apart from embracing Buddhism.

Dalit history is the 'history of India's political modernity', Rao reminds us and adds, thoughtfully, that 'Dalit democratization' – a term that refers to a democratic process which recognises and works for the collective rights and group emancipation of Dalits – happened not because of the expansion of liberal individualism or of any violent subaltern revolution. For the 'liberals' – those who believe in individual autonomy and least regulation by state – separation from community will mean emancipation. For Dalits, however, individual freedom can be achieved only by removing the 'caste stigma' that attaches to the community. Hence, unlike any liberal assertion, the movement for 'Dalit democracy' lunged forward seeking group recognition and minority rights. Similarly, unlike subaltern militants, Dalit leaders (including B. R. Ambedkar) invoked constitutional and political rights to seek social and religious emancipation.

Vulnerable

A question of worth investigating is whether Dalits are more vulnerable to violence after Independence than they were earlier? And if 'yes' – as indeed it seems – is it because they have become more assertive now? Previously, religion and tradition could be blamed for Dalits' vulnerability and discriminatory treatment. But now, for all the help they are getting from government, Dalits seem to have become more vulnerable and much less self-reliant than earlier. Instead of enhancing the level of self-confidence in them affirmative action by the state would appear to have rendered them unwilling to resist domination by the upper castes. The terms of Dalit enfranchisement and forms of governmental help have increased 'conjunctural violence' against Dalits, says Rao. If the literature of Dalit Panthers is replete with 'warnings' and 'threats', it is because Dalits as a class meet with so much of violence in their lives these days.

V. Sridhar 2011. A series of papers presented at the national seminar on Dalit households in village economics painted a grim picture of deprivation among Dalits in rural India. These papers, based on a series of village studies since 2004, pointed to Dalit relatively poor access to official sources of credit, their lack of command over assets and amenities, and lower levels of employment and income.

Commenting on the papers, Abhijit Sen, member, planning Commission, pointed out that the value of these village studies conducted by the Foundation of Agrarian Studies (FAS) and other researchers was enhanced by the fact that they were not aimed at finding out how Dalits were faring exclusively in socio-economic terms. Instead, the extent and nature of deprivation among Dalits was being demonstrated as a part of a study of agrarian relations in the country, in which caste played an important role.

Drawing on data from all the villages surveys conducted by the FAS, Vikas Rawal, Associate Professor, Jawaharallal Nehru University, New Delhi, pointed out that ownership of land accounted for an over-whelming proportion of the value of assets among Dalits as well as non-Dalits. There is 'a huge disparity' in the levels of landholdings between the two social groups, he observed.

Madhura Swaminathan, Professor-in-charge, Social Sciences Division, Indian Statistical Institute (ISI), Kolkata and Shameshr Singh, a research scholar at the ISI, demonstrated the inequality, in terms of access to basic amenities such as housing, water, sanitation and electricity, faced by Dalits. Based on 'pooled data' from surveys of 12 villages in five states, they pointed out that about one-fourth of Dalit households lived in kutcha houses and 30 per cent lived in 'single-room structures'.

'There appears to be a strong statistical association between caste and access to the basic amenities,' Prof. Swaninathan Observed. Pointing out that public intervention '(did) make an impact' she said the provision of homestead plots for Dalits was 'central' to any programme aimed at improving their quality of life.

Venkatesh Athreya, advisor, M. S. Swaminathan research Foundation, pointed out that the village surveys filled a serious gap in the data required for studying agrarian relations in India. V. K. Ramachandran, Professor at the Sociological Research Unit ISI, Kolkata, said, "Caste not only matters, but is right up there as a major explanation for inequality".

Another paper, drawing on official data sources, provided on account of how Dalits' access to official credit sources has declined since liberalization. The seminar, which concluded on Saturday, was organized by the Sociological research Unit at the ISI. It was supported by the ISI, the Indian Council of Social Science Research and the Foundation of Agrarian Studies.

The Navsarjan Trust and The Robert F. Kennedy Centre for Justice and Human Rights, 2010". It was carried out over three years in randomly selected 1,589 villages in the State. They compiled report of the findings was released here on Wednesday by University Grants Commission Chairman S. K. Thorat.

The report said that not only was untouchability practiced against Dalits by caste Hindus, it was practiced by the relatively 'upper' sub-caste Dalits against the 'lower' sub-caste Dalits. It said that while 98 forms of untouchability was practiced by caste Hindus against the Dalits, 99 forms of caste discrimination was found with in the Dalit sub-castes.

Giving example, the report said a Dalit woman was 'assaulted' for trying to take part in a village 'garba' dance organized by caste Hindus. Even the sarpanch, if he happened to be a Dalit, was expected to sit on the ground while caste Hindu panchayat members sat on a pedestal. The Dalit passengers were required to vacate the seats in government-owned state transport buses for non-Dalit passengers.

- *Reprimand;* It said inter-caste marriage was strictly prohibited in 98.4 per cent of the colleges and such marriages within the Dalit sub-castes was found banned in 99.1 per cent of the colleges. Any violation of the 'rule' would invariably attract a violent reprimand against the defying couple, who were often forced to leave the village.
- *Separate Cup;* Even in tea kiosks, cups and saucers were kept separately for the Dalits and such customers were required to clean their own utensils before putting the same back in the rack meant for the Dalits. In schools, separate sitting arrangements were made for caste Hindus and Dalits for mid-day meal schemes. Dalit students were not served water in schools. They were expected to go home or carry their own water with them. "The report shows that the existing legal system has failed to address the problem of untouchability and it is time for human rights activists to act strongly" Navsarjan Trust executive director Manjula pradeep said.

Meera Velayndhan 2010. Action Aid, 2000 A study of 555 villages in 11 States, including Karnataka, Andhra Pradesh, Orissa and Gujarat, held that in 36 per cent of the villages, Dalits were denied casual work in agriculture. Denial of use of water sources (well, pond and tubewell) and restrictions on access to common property resources (grazing land, fish ponds and other resources) in 21 per cent of the villages affected Dalit women's entitlement to medicinal and food plants and increased their burden of household tasks. Also, Dalits were denied the right of sale of vegetables and milk in the village co-operatives or to private sellers.

S. Viswanthan 1st November 2010. The Hindu News Paper. "The Plight of Dalits and the news media" (October 25th, 2010), has generated a lively and interesting response from several readers. The column was about the prioritisation of the tasks before the National Commission for the Scheduled Caste (NCSC) by its new Chairman, P. L. Punia (not P. J. Punia as erroneously mentioned in the column.) The concern of most who wrote was over the failure of successive governments to achieve the empowerment of Scheduled Caste and Scheduled Tribes, the most vulnerable of the country's poor, 63 years after Independence. This reveals not only their awareness of the pain of these victims of anti-human oppression, but also of official and bureaucratic indifference to their predicament. Readers are also aware of the lack of political will among those in power to help find a way out of this shameful situation. This is a far cry from the situation prevailing, say, 15-20 years ago, when reports that untouchability was still being practised in many parts of the country as harshly as ever carried little credibility among readers.

As recently as in 1990 Political leaders tended to deny that discrimination was prectised against Dalits in tea shops, where the beverage was served to Dalits and non-Dalits in two different sets of tumblers. These leaders asserted that it might have happened in one or two remote villages. It was as thought they believed, and wanted others to believe, that the constitutional ban on untouchability had abolished it on the ground. The atrocities against Dalits were depicted by most political parties and much of the media as 'inter-caste clashes' and the outcome of some needless provocation, usually from the Dalit side. Further, there was a marked tendency to equate the perpetrators of oppression and violence with the victims. Policemen, the overwhelming majority of whom were 'caste-Hindus,' almost always threw their weight behind their kin.

Dalits thus became the victims of both caste oppression and hatred and the custodians of law.

I was only during the first decade of the present century that large numbers of newspaper readers apparently began to see the Dalit question in fact-based perspective. In turn, there was a perceptible improvement in the media's approach to, and overage of, what may broadly be termed the Dalit Question, a critical challenge facing rising India. Unlike the previous decade, when reader ratings of Dalit-related reports were generally poor, the past decade has seen a spurt of lively responses to reports and editorial articles on poverty, caste-based oppression, and social injustice. Young men and women entering the field of journalism after being sensitized to the issue by good teachers in serious journalism schools or departments began writing on Dalit issues boldly and with élan. At least a few of the mainstream newspapers turned their focus on the plight of the poor and the oppressed. This is a heartening trend in agenda building, which in turn has sensitized and influenced readers.

The responses to last week's column on Mr. Punis's appeal to the central government to provide job reservation came from readers with different backgrounds. Almost all the them showed great concern for the victims. The NCSC has prioritized the tasks ensuring reservation for Dalit in the private sector and maximizing the benefits of such plans to Dalits.

Speedy and Effective Action Called For: A former Governor of Mizoram, Dr. A Padmanaban, who now lives in Chennai, pointed out in his comment on the column that reservation for Scheduled Castes in the private sector had been discussed and debated over along period: "The Bill introduced in Parliament some years ago was deferred and not dropped on the assurances and promises given by leading industrialists led by Mr. Ratan Tata in the form of a statement for affirmative of Mr. Ratan Tata, to the Prime Minister of Social Justice and others on 25/5/2005. This proposal includes training, scholarship, reservation in private sector companies etc." He added that it was on the basis of these assurances and in good faith that the Government of India deferred the Reservation Bill. Dr. Padmanaban's assessment is that "the measures taken by private sector to implement their affirmative action plan have been tardy and unsatisfactory". He has been in correspondence with the Prime Minister, the Minister for Social Justice, Mr. Ratan Tata, and organizations such as CII-Assocham and FICCI on this matter. "Speedy and effective action is called for. The Indian industrialists have to be more liberal and discharge their social responsibility effectively", Dr. Padmanaban concluded.

The Bill on Reservation, pending before Parliament, seeks to provide job reservation for the weaker sections of society in view of privatization of several public units in the country. The assurance was part of the electoral commitments made by UPA (2004-09) in its National Common Minimum Programme. According to some newspaper reports, the representatives of the industry chambers recently conveyed their 'inability to implement' the suggestion made to these organistaions by the Union Commerce and Industry Ministry to reserve five per cent of jobs for Scheduled Castes and Scheduled Tribes. In turn, Mr. Punia has recently at a meeting with the press at Hyderabad served notice on the private sector that it "will…have to do something for the disadvantaged sectioned," failing which he would press for legislation to bring this about.

Another reader, Mr. Punitha Pandiyan, who edits a popular Tamil magazine, Dalit Murasu, referred in his letter to the diversion of funds meant for Dalit welfare projects under the Scheduled Castes Sub-Plan to the commonwealth Games. He regarded this as a notable omission in this column. A report in The Indian Express of August 26th 2010 cited by Mr. Pandiyan said that the government admitted in the Rajya Sabha that over Rs. 670 crore meant for Scheduled Castes welfare projects was diverted to CWG work by the Delhi Government. Explaining the diversion of funds, Home Minister P. Chidambaram told the House that from 2006-07 to the current fiscal, out of Rs. 7,062 crores (under indivisible funds) Rs. 678.91 crores were given for CWG projects such as building stadiums, bridges and flyovers. In Mr. Padiyan, S view, this diversion of funds amounted to a breach of trust.

This reader also cited a report dated October 15th, which said that Mr. Punia took serious note of the Delhi Government's alleged diversion of funds meant for the welfare of the Dalits to the commonwealth Games and 'demand refund in case it had happened'. He was quoted as saying: "As a Chairman of the Commission, I would not allow any government whether of the Congress-ruled States or the Opposition-ruled State, to divert the funds meant for the Dalits to other purposes." Mr. Pandiyan wanted Mr. Punia to take action to get the money refunded, in the light of the August 26 statement of the Union Home Minister.

Another reader, M. N. Sanil from New Delhi, contended in his e-mail the "reservation in the private sector is liked to the cultural capital (in the Bourdieuan sense) of Dalits, which they acquire from education and families. The oppression they face in the education system and outside the system discriminates and excludes them in a conscious-brutal fashion". He expressed optimism in his belief that "contemporary Dalit struggles that are non-ngoised in nature can challenge the diverse and existing ideological forms of caste."

Feudal Foundation

S. V. Venugopalan of Chennai was clear about the root of the problem: "The feudal foundation of this vast nation is too deeply entrenched and the roots of social discrimination lie embedded in our genes... When people of various social strata play an equally important role in building a nation and nourishing it (the) casteist perspective has no place in any modern society". Another reader, S. Raghavan of Chennai, commented: "If only our governments had organized a massive education programme for Dalit solved by now". This progressive observation has some truth in it but the challenge is clearly not as single-track or as simple as this assertion suggests.

Thorat and Lee, 2010. A survey conducted in 531 villages in Rajasthan, Uttar Pradesh, Bihar, Andhra Pradesh and Tamil

Nadu exposed patterns of caste-based exclusion and discrimination in the government's MMS and PDS. In Rajasthan and Tamil Nadu, the MMS is predominantly located in dominant-caste localities.

In Uttar Pradesh, the distribution of dry grain to children of government schools takes place in dominant-caste localities in 90 per cent of the respondent villages, while in only 10 per cent of the villages the distribution is conducted in Dalit localities. Access can also be conditional and depend on the state of inter-caste power relations. Often, Dalit children's access to the MMS is cut off by dominant castes to assert their domination. The opposition to Dalit cooks, mainly women, also represents a power struggle over livelihood rights, that is, Dalit entry into new livelihood domains such as government employment as MMS cooks at the village level.

Dr. A. G. S. Rao and G. S. Rao 2010. The Development and empowerment of women is one of the most crucial issues of today. It is universally accepted that there have not considerable governmental efforts, on one of the sections of women namely Scheduled Caste and Scheduled Tribe women lag woefully behind others in development and they continue to be among the weakest and the exploited. Moreover, women in transition economics are finding that their specific skills are becoming absolute. In weaker sections women play a major role, especially in economic field. Inspite of the development taking place all around, it has to be conceded that the bulk of the Scheduled Caste Women will continue to live and earn livelihood in their own environment.

The Hindu 20th Oct 2010. Dalit women attending a State-level conference of the Centre for Dalit Rights at Dholpur in Rajasthan over the weekend demanded utilisation of resources of the Scheduled Caste Sub-Plan for ensuring their welfare and economic development, besides rendering social justice to them.

About 600 Dalit and nomadic women, mostly from eastern Rajasthan districts of Bharatpur and Dholpur, attended the day-long conference, which was inaugurated by

National Federation of Indian Women general secretary Annie Raja. While Ms. Raja called upon the Dalit women to organize themselves and wage a battle against 'patriarchal practices' prevalent in villages, National Federation of Dalit Women president Ruth Manorama exhorted the women to fight for dignity and equal status in the society.

Shri Mukul Wasnik 2009. He was addressing the Conference, Minister of Social Justice and Empowerment, Shri Mukul Wasnik stressed on education and better health facilities for Dalit women. He said NGOs should work among the Dalit women to promote education and awareness against social evils like female feticide and dowry. The Minister announced that by March 2010, all scavengers will be rehabilitated. Shri Wasnik said that his ministry has successfully started capacity building programmed for scavengers for self-employment.

The Ministry of Women and Child Development 2009. The one-day Dalit women's Congress organized by the Ministry of Women and Child Development was attended by a large number of groups of Dalit women, NGOs and civil societies. The Congress had breakout sessions on different issues related with Dalit women including economic upliftment of Dalit women, crèche, short-stay homes and help line services for Dalit women. It also had discussions on research, innovation and opportunities for Dalit women.

Major Recommendations of the Dalit women's Congress with regard to programmes run by Central Social Welfare Board.

Short Stay Home: More Stay Home to be opened in J. J Colonies where the population of Scheduled Castes is more. The percentage of SC beneficiaries to be decided in each Short Stay Home.

Women Help Line: More Women Help Line to be opened in areas where SC population is more and also in local police stations. Special training to be given to staff of Help Lines.

Creches: More crèches to be opened in SC dominated areas and special budget allocation to be made for these areas. Free books, writing material and uniform to be provided to

SC children. Special nutrition as per ICDS Scheme to be given to children of SCs.

Irudayam, Mangubhai, Sydenham, 2009. Another study on women's role in panchayats in Tamil Nadu and Gujarat shows that only one-third of the 200 women researched were able to, with support, act with freedom to win panchayat elections. Eighty-five per cent were pushed into panchayat politics by dominant castes or husbands (as proxy), and only one-third of the 119 panchayat presidents were able to work with freedom, with only 35.3 per cent of them calling panchayat meetings, 31.9 per cent chairing the meetings, and 27 per cent voluntarily signing resolutions. Only 21 per cent voluntarily authorised panchayat payments and only 23.5 per cent approved contracts for panchayats. Among the representatives who served as proxies, about 59 per cent served as proxies to husband/male relatives, and others to people of the dominant castes and political parties. Over 52.4 per cent of the 166 panchayat presidents and members attended many or all meetings, while only half of them raised development-related issues. In the case of over half of the 90 women who raised issues, the issues were not discussed or approved. Dominant-caste members used abusive language or refused to share information with Dalit women representatives and prevented them from speaking.

Separate seating arrangements and pressure to stand up before dominant-caste members and use separate utensils for tea or food during meetings were the other discriminatory practices. The status of being a proxy, fear, lack of confidence, lack of knowledge, poor level of education, and traditional caste and gender roles were cited as related issues that led to low political participation, according to 120 Dalit women (72.3%) members.

Venkitesh Ramakrishna and Ajoy Ashirwad Mahaprashasta 2009. Dalit women face the worst atrocities as both women and Dalits. A seminal study conducted by the NCDHR ('Dalit Women Speak Out', 2006) enumerating the experiences of 500 Dalit women from Andhra Pradesh, Bihar, Tamil Nadu and

Uttar Pradesh presents a shocking picture of the conditions they live in. The study records the violence – physical, sexual and mental – inflicted on Dalit women. The study reinforces calls for comprehensive preventive measures to be put in place to eradicate caste discrimination and violence against Dalit women, in conjunction with measures to help Dalit women achieve their rights.

Valjibhai Patel says that though the Act mentions punitive measures against negligence, to date not a single official in India has been punished despite serious violations of the Act all over the country. He says the judiciary should also be made accountable, not just the police and the district administration. "There are many cases of atrocities where the accused has been punished under the IPC but has been acquitted under the S.C./S.T. Act. In Gujarat, one of the professors who raped his Dalit student got life imprisonment but was acquitted under the S.C./S.T. Act. The Khairlanji case is a big example where the people now serving the death penalty were acquitted under the S.C./S.T. Act. How is this possible? This means there is some problem in investigation and pursuance of the Act," he says. The CSJ has filed a petition in the Supreme Court regarding the violation of the Act, the first hearing of which will be on December 3.

The International Labour Organisation Report 2007. According to the International Labour Organisation Report 'Equality at Work – Tackling the Challenges', with limited access to education, training, and resources including land and credit, Dalits are generally not considered for any work involving with food and water meant for non-Dalits. They also face discrimination in a wide range of work opportunities in both the public and private sectors.

Hindustan Times 18th Feb 2006. (Dalit women tortured in jail - Punjab) There Dalit women from Muktsar district in Punjab have accused the police of torturing them, including administering electric shock to their 'private parts' and confining them illegally. Talking to reporters at the BJP headquarters in Chandigarh on Friday, Amarjit Karur, Virpal Kaur and Rarni alleged they were picked up by the police after they rejected the overtures of two drug traffickers to join the flesh trade. Amarjit alleged she and Virpal were detained for five days at the police station. "We were tortured in the presence of the SHO. We were stripped and electric shock administered to our private parts," she said, adding that she suffered a miscarriage due to this. Virpal said their families were silenced with threats. Both claimed they were let off without registration of any complaint or FIR after five days. They alleged the SHO was acting at the behest of the drug traffickers. Rani's claims were similar. The district BJP unit are not buying the DSP's claim that the women were picked up for trafficking poppy husk and plan to approach the Punjab Human Rights Commission, National Women's commission and SC/ST Commission.

Kumar, N and Raj, M 2006. Traditionally, leadership in the village was confined to 'rural elites', who were aged and belonging to higher castes. In the year 1993, 73rd amendment in the constitution granted reservation to dalits, tribals and women in local government. This amendment made it compulsory that one third of the seats are reserved for dalits be filled by dalit women. In some states, there has been little or no acceptance for reservation for the lower castes and dalit women by upper castes. This has resulted in atrocities against Panchayat members including women. Dalit who stood for election were beaten, and dalit women were raped and ill-treated. The members of the higher castes, who are not prepared to relinquish power to the lower castes, grabbed their land. An easier method to retain power is to put-up proxy candidates but keep the control in the hands of the dominant castes, always men.

The Hindu 5th June 2006. The National Campaign for Dalit Human Rights has demanded a CBI enquiry into the death of a Dalit women in Chomu police station of Jaipur district on Thursday. The women, kamla, who was brought to the police station to meet her son who was in police custody on a charge of murder, had died of mental shock and agony due to police misbehaviour, and enquiry report by NCDHR and Centre for

Dalit Rights said. The main opposition in the State, the Congress party had made a similar demand. Pradesh Congress Committee president B. D. Kalla in a statement on Friday demanded a judicial enquiry into the case. The party has alleged that the death had taken place at the police station following the ill treatment of the victim. The Chomu police last week and arrested Kammla's son Sumit on a charge of murdering a history sheeter Sikandar Khan. Kamla, a schoolteacher was taken to the police station on Thursday last by five constables, including two women constables to meet her son in the lock up. The police version is that the woman, apparently depressed over the act of her son had consumed poison at home before leaving for the police station. She gave a dying declaration to this effect but her family members had challenge this. The NCDHR team, which visited the spot, found the role of the police and administration 'doubtful'.

Hindustan Times 28th Feb 2006. (Dalit women denied passport) Girija Devi, a Dalit woman who was scheduled to attend a UN seminar in US, failed to get her passport. Opposition parties in the state have threatened to take up the issue in the assembly, Girija Dev, a 59 year old mother of four from the Musahar community, was scheduled to address a seminar on 'Women Environment and Development Organization' in Bhojpuri. "It was the state government's fault. This was done to stop her from attending the UN convention to present her views" said RJD leader Shauam Rajak. Musahar Vikas Manch leader Amar Kumar Majhi said red-tapism was to blame. "The old Dalit women was forced to run from one office to another. She would had Bihar proud by speaking at an international convention" he said Chief Minister Nitish Kumar said, 'I will take action. Let me collect the facts'.

Soni, Jayashree, 2006. A study of water accessibility in eight villages in Gujarat Soni, Jayashree, 2006 indicates the hardship and humiliation Dalit women face in the collection of water. Dalit women wanted separate water spots or sumps to avoid quarrels at the time of collection and over the location of collection. Considering food security as an entitlement, the public distribution system (PDS) and the midday meal scheme (MMS) assume significance for Dalit women in ensuring the survival of their households and education for children, in particular to daughters.

Irudayam, Mangubhai, Lee, 2006. Intrinsic to these denials and exclusions is violence, in particular against Dalit women and girls. A study of 500 women from 32 panchayat unions/ blocks/mandals in 17 districts of Andhra Pradesh, Bihar, Tamil Nadu and Pondicherry, and Uttar Pradesh showed that the most frequent forms of violence included verbal abuse (62.4%), physical assault (54.8%), sexual harassment and assault (46.8%), domestic violence (43%) and rape (23.2%). Other forms of violence included forced sex work, kidnapping, medical negligence, sexual exploitation and child sexual abuse.

The multiple sites of abuse included public spaces, home, workplace, the perpetrator's home and government offices. Those who inflict violence included dominant-caste landlords, police and forest officials, business persons, goondas and thugs, professionals, those involved in politics, other dominant caste members and other Dalit persons. The issues included Dalit women's perceived sexual availability, rejection of sexual advances and attempt to leave forced sex work; women breaking caste norms, accessing resources, speaking up, and participation in religious and cultural life; arrest of family members; and women's assertion of their rights to land/wages/forests/common property resources, indebtedness, upward social mobility, exercise of political rights, failure to be dutiful wives, failure to bear sons, control over earned income, inheriting marital property, or showing the spirit of independence.

In 40.2 per cent of the cases, women were unable to secure justice from the law and the community. Women were also prevented from seeking justice by the perpetrators, the police and sometimes even by family members. Only in 1.6 per cent of the cases were women able to secure informal form of justice. The study highlighted the need for government policy that understood the intersection of caste and gender.

Asian Age 21st, June 06. (Doctor robs Dalit women of Kidney) In a bizarre incident a Dalit women has been robbed of her kidney by an Uttaranchal-based. The woman has been waging a line battle to get a case registered against the doctor but the police has, so far, refused to lodge her complaint. The victim has now written to the President of India and the National Human Rights Commission for justice and is also preparing opt to go to the court. According to Phool Singh, a resident of Akbarpur patti village in Jyotibe Phule Nagar, his wife Maya, 45, had been diagnosed as having stones in the uterus in December 2003.

Kumar, 2006. Traditionally, leadership in the village was confined to 'rural elites', who were aged and belonging to higher castes. In the year 1993, 73rd amendment in the constitution granted reservation to dalits, tribals and women in local government. This amendment made it compulsory that one third of the seats reserved for dalits be filled by dalit women. In some states, there has been little or no acceptance of reservation for the lower castes and dalit women by the upper castes. This has resulted in atrocities against panchayat members including women. Dalits who stood for election were beaten, and dalit women were raped and ill-treated. The members of the higher castes, who are not prepared to relinquish power to the lower castes, grabbed their land. An easier method to retain power is to put-up proxy candidates but keep the control in the hands of the dominant castes, always men.

Asian Age 24th Sept 06. (Dalit women in UP protection force) In a move that will lead to empowerment of Dalit women in Uttar Pradesh, the Mulayam Singh government has decided to enroll dalit women in the Prantia Rakshak Dal. The Prantiya Rakshak Dal (PRD) is a state level protection force that is usually deployed to maintain law and other in villages, in large congregations like the Kumbh Mela in during elections. The strength of the PRD force un UP is 24,000 and PRD jawans are sent for refresher training every three years. This will be the first time that women will get a chance to be a part of the PRD which, till now, is an all male force. The state government has now cleared the way for enrolment of more than 500 Dalit women in the PRD and recruitment will begin shortly from the district to the block level. Talking to this newspaper on Saturday, a senior official of the PRD department said," This is being done for the first time to empower Dalit women in the age group of 20 to 30. Under the gender budgeting programme, nearly 30 per cent of the PRD force will comprise of women. In the coming assembly elections, people will see Dalit women dressed in khaki PRD uniforms deployed at Dalit women but will also take them away from traditional menial jobs. Once the PRD enrolment begin, we see Dalit women moving away from menial jobs and becoming increasingly aware of the need for education", the official said. According to sources, the state government has decided to encourage women to seek enrolment through a massive publicity campaign next month. "We will convince the women in the SC/ST categorise to step out of their homes and join the PRD which will give them financial independence, dignity and status in society,".

The Pioneer, 28th April 2005. Finally, in only 13.8 per cent of instances of violence in this study is *appropriate, police or judicial action underway*. The majority of these cases are all pending: investigations are being carried out, charge sheets are yet to be prepared, cases are currently before the courts, etc. Hence, leeway still exists for the cases to be scuttled by the police and/or perpetrators and their community. Notably, only 3.6 per cent of all instances of violence have actually reached the court, and of those, only three cases (that is, less than 1% of total instances of violence) have ended in convictions. Eight other cases have been dismissed by the courts or ended in acquittals of the accused, due to either a forced 'compromise' dictated by the accused while the case was under trial, or the perpetrator pressurising the woman victim-survivor or witnesses into turning hostile, or the victim-survivor being unable to obtain the requisite evidence for her case, or the perpetrator dying before the end of the trial. Hence, the long process to obtain justice for Dalit women victim-survivors of violence is too often effectively stymied by different actors – the perpetrators, their caste community, police, the traditional village panchayats or formal elected panchayats. The brahminical patriarchal discourse of 'honour' and fear of further dominant caste reprisals, moreover, influences Dalit women, their families and their communities, not to seek justice where violence takes place. Impunity for violence, therefore, is an intrinsic factor in the maintenance of the caste system and caste-and-gender based norms circumscribing Dalit women's fundamental rights and freedoms. The overall performance of the Indian State, therefore, comes into serious question when measured against the standard of due diligence to prevent violence against Dalit women. This is true for violence at the hands of both non-state actors, as well as state actors themselves. Giving effect to Dalit women's rights requires not only building structures of protection – including investigation, prosecution, fair punishment and compensation for violence – but also rigorously implementing laws and policies designed to facilitate the enjoyment of equal citizenship rights for the 80 million Dalit women in the country today. Taking into account the situation of rising rates of crimes against Dalits, combined with failure of the state machinery to check this rise with stringent action, the Parliamentary Committee on the Welfare of Scheduled Castes and Scheduled Tribes has stated that atrocities on Scheduled Castes and Scheduled Tribes constitute an internal disturbance under Article 355 of the *Indian Constitution*, and has called for Central Government intervention under various provisions to take strict action against offending states. The Committee has also castigated the Home Ministry for using 'police and public order' being 'state subjects' as an excuse for absolving themselves of the responsibility implied under Article 355. Finally, the Committee recommended taking 'extreme steps' wherever warranted to protect the Dalit community and punish perpetrators of violence against them.

Nanivadekar, Medga 2005. In India, women are given equal civil and political rights, including universal adult franchise under the Indian constitution. Right from it's inception, the principle of affirmative action has been instituted in the Constitution of India in articles 15(1), (3) and (4), which prohibit discrimination on the grounds of religion, sex, caste and place of birth and also provides for the state making special provisions for women, children and the advancement of any socially and educationally backward classes of citizens. The 73rd and 74th amendments to the Constitution of India that were made in 1993 provided for 33 per cent of the seats to be reserved for women in local self-government institutions in rural and urban areas respectively. This created a landmark situation which enabled more than a million women to enter the political field for the first time.

One of the standard assumptions behind the landmark amendment was that if women entered politics in large numbers, they would change the whole texture of present-day politics since they were expected to bring different values, preferences and perspectives into the political arena. It was expected that they would ensure women's issues were given a high priority on the agenda of political parties and that their presence in decision-making positions would lead to the elimination of discrimination against women.

Chitnis 2005. With the realisation that violence is one of the potent threats to the peaceful existence of human beings, whole hearted and all round efforts are made at international, national and local level. The preamble to the Universal Declaration of Human Rights (UDHR) serves as a foundation and philosophy of Human rights. There are a host of international conventions including those for prevention and punishment of genocide and elimination of all forms of racial and gender based discrimination.

Thorat, 2005. Social acceptance and the multilayered nature of the caste system inform not only the social but also the economic and occupational aspects of the lives of Dalit women. Their occupational pattern is impacted by resource rights such as land and credit, access to education and modern skills, and restrictions on labour mobility. Several village studies (Thorat, 2005) have pointed to exclusion in the hiring of labour and low wage rates, the discrimination being greater in the case of Dalit women than men.

Chattopadhyay and Duflo 2004. In a study on Panchayats in the Indian states of West Bengal and Rajasthan. They found that women pradhans in reserved GPs were less likely to be literate they were less educated and less politically knowledgeable, and they were younger and poorer than women pradhans in unreserved GPs. Women pradhans coming into the system through quotas are more likely to be socially and economically disadvantaged and the researchers hypothesized that they were likely to be controlled by dominant local elements.

Thorat and Umakant, 2004. The World Conference Against Racism (WCAR) related to racial discrimination, xenophobia and intolerance held in Durban, South Africa in 2001, brought the issue of caste and untouchability based discrimination on the agenda of UN Conference in Durban. Among the several organisations, the National Campaign on Dalit Human Rights (NCDHR) – a collective of dalit NGOs, other NGOs, academicians', activists and large number of supporters spearheaded the national campaign in India for inclusion of the issue of caste and untouchability based discrimination in the Durban Conference.

Tirmare, 2004. A prominent researcher and sociologist while sharing her experience from a research on gender and land issue, informed that, when she enquired with dalit women about land owned by them in their names, they wondered about permissibility of owning land in their name. This indicates that neither do they own any land nor are they aware of their rights on land. When enquiries were made with Stri-mukti sanghatana and Prerana, Mumbai based organizations working on the issue of rag picking and prostitution respectively, to ascertain the proportion of dalit women in these occupation, it was learnt that NGOs usually do not keep record of caste.

National Human Rights Commission Report 2004. The National Human Rights Commission has summed up recommendations from the National Commission for Scheduled Castes and Scheduled Tribes, national conferences and various non-state organisations such as the National Campaign on Dalit Human Rights vis-à-vis protection of Dalits' rights to life and security of life: sincere and effective implementation of the law to protect Dalits against 'untouchability' practices and atrocities; capacity building within government to protect and promote Dalit human rights; capacity building of statutory watchdog bodies; strict enforcement of Supreme Court guidelines on treatment of persons in custody; convergence of regulatory and development programmes; information for social change in civil society; code of conduct for state agencies; overcoming procedural handicaps to Special Courts taking cognisance of atrocity cases without prior committal by Magistrates; right of separate settlement for Dalits; enhanced central share in schemes for Dalits; and the setting up of independent, non-official monitoring agencies to review cases of atrocities against Dalits.

Report of the Special Reporter on Violence against Women 27th February 2003. Any case of violence against a Dalit woman has to pass through the hands of the local police and the judiciary in order for the woman to receive justice under the law. Safeguarding the impartiality of this process, the Indian Constitution stipulates in Article 14 that all Indian citizens have the right to equality before the law. However, deeply ingrained normative values of appropriate gender and caste roles and behaviour patterns influence government officials, police and even judges who have the power to interpret and actualise rights. These socio-culturally-religiously rooted biases enforce the discriminatory status quo to the detriment of Dalit women's right to justice where violence takes place. As the United Nations Special Report on Violence against Women has noted with regard to the situation in India, "constitutional and legislative provisions that have been enacted to protect women from discrimination have not proved to be an effective deterrent."

Bandhu P. 2003. Dalit women's daily diet is the leftover of family meals, inadequate in quantity and quality. Health services are either not available in case of illness or unaffordable even if available. In addition to that, due to early marriage and too many pregnancies their health is always at risk. If birth control is practiced at all, 5 91 per cent cases of tubetomy are performed on the women who have to carry the burden of family planning. In an overall situation where dalits are prone to ailments in general, women suffer from more serious and more varied kind of sickness. More than 80 per cent of women in reproductive age group (15 to 45) are anemic. Poor health status of dalit women pushes her then into more vulnerable situation.

Dietrich in Rao 2003. Under conditions of grinding poverty and severe exploitation at work place, Dalit women also suffer caste specific ban on water access from upper castes and may be beaten up in their own houses as well. A poem by a dalit poetess Teressama, a teacher from Guntur puts the situation in the following words: *"We go to work for we are poor But the same silken beds mock us, While we are ravished in broad daylight Ill-starred our horoscopes are Even our tottering husbands Lying on the cots in the corner Hiss and shout for revenge If we cannot stand their touch".*

Sainath Rao. P. 2003. The incapacity of women, particularly Dalit women, to assert their rights is at the root of the problem. The reservation for dalits, particularly for women, is accepted in form but seldom in substance. Any change in the status quo is resisted. Dalit women's sitting on chairs is seen as threat to social hierarchy. So, the upper castes in the village vetoed chairs in the panchayat office.

Chakrvarti Rao 2003. The focus on education of low caste women is one of the important factors responsible for the emerging identity of Dalit women. Reformist intervention by Savitribai and Mahatma Phule of opening school for untouchable girls way back in 1848 was a turning point for changing status of dalit women.

Rege Rao 2003. After independence in 1960's and 70's, the dalit movement and women's movement emerged to demand their rights against caste and gender respectively. However, specific problems of dalit women were not acknowledged by these movements. Hence in 1990's there were several special, independent and autonomous assertions of dalit women's identity; a case in point is the formation of National Federation for Dalit Women (NFDW) and All India Dalit Women's Forum (AIDWF) at the state level. The Maharashtra Dalit Mahila Sanghatana (MDMS) was formed in 1995. A year earlier, the women's wing of Bhartiya Republican Party (BRP) and the Bahujan Mahila Sangha (BMS) was set up the Bahujan Mahila Parishad. In December 1996, at Chandrapur, a Vikas Vanchit Dalit Mahila Parishad (VVDMP) was organised and a proposal to commemorate 25th December (the day on which Ambedkar had set Manu smriti on fire) as Bhartiya Smriti Divas was advanced. The Christi Mahila Sanghatana, an organisation of Dalit Christian Women was established in 1997. These organisations have come together on several issues such as celebration of Bhartiya Stree Mukti Divas and on the issue of reservation for OBC women in parliament bodies. Indian Association of Women Studies (IAWS) network with dalit feminist across different regions had brought special issues on problems and identity of dalit women.

Zelliot Rao 2003. Dr. Ambedkar's thought and action made important differences in the lives of dalit women. His movement and especially his organisations encouraged many dalit women to become educated to be active in public life and to gain leadership, self respect in the contemporary period encouraged women to participate in organisastion for dalit women at regional, state and national level.

Chandra Ramesh and Mitra Sangh 2003. The situation of Dalit women in India is just unexplainable. They are one among the worst sufferers of socio-cultural, political and economic exploitation, injustice, oppression and violence. Their woes and miseries are boundless. They are the ones who form 'real' teeming millions in India, and are affected by all kinds of social and economic oppressions. They are mainly employed in unorganized sector of the Indian economy as daily wagers and marginal workers. The lack of adequate employment opportunities, limited skills and illiteracy have made their mobility extremely limited and prevent them from achieving independent status. The persistent gap between consumption and expenditure leads them to perpetual indebtness. The proportion of Dalit women living below the poverty line is just enormous. They do not enjoy any social security, maternity benefits, pension schemes or any other kind of economic protection. With the adoption of policies of globalization in India, their employment opportunities are likely to be further reduced as they will have to suffer from competition from foreign technology and modern methods of agriculture.

They are oppressed by the broader Hindu society, their own community's men and also their own husbands. Thus, they are triply disadvantageous. The issues of Dalit women are different from that of other Indian women. They have been deprived from all kinds of human rights, education, income, dignity, social status, religious rights, etc. They have to face outside world necessiated by economic deprivation, and an urgent need to earn for livelihood. Thus, their subjugation is more acute- being Dalit they are treated with great contempt by upper caste men and women alike, and their own menfolk. Despite that they have hugely contributed to the development of India by their seer hardwork and labour. But, their contributions have never been recognised. Their voices and protests are almost invisible. In fact, when we talk of marginalization of women in the development process, or feminization of poverty or woman's contribution to the unorganized sector in India, we are referring to them without even being conscious about their specificity.

Dhital 2003 For a large majority of Dalits livings in rural India has only been a disabling structure, affecting entitlements, capabilities vis-à-vis their functionings. Decentralized governance initiatives due to strong hold of caste culture and the agrarian structure have proved to be exclusionary for

Dalits. They have benefited neither socially nor economically from emerging participatory initiatives. The participation of Dalits in current development initiatives is rightly termed as inferior participation.

Bilgrami 2003. Observes, 'the social psychology of the Hindu caste system consists of an exclusionary attitude. For each caste, there is a lower caste which constituted the other and which was to be excluded from one's way of life, again by the most brutal physical and psychological violence. Caste in India-without a doubt the most resilient from of exclusionary social inegalitarianism, in the history of the world-its hard to avoid the conclusion that even the most alarming aspects of religious intolerance is preferable to it. To say, 'You must be my brother', however wrong, is better than saying, 'You will never be brother'.

Meenai, 2003. It is seen that gender inequality retards economic growth. There is growing evidence to suggest that several aspects of gender relations, the gender based division of lab our disparities between males and females in power and resources and gender biases in rights and entitlements act to undermine economic growth and reduce the well being of men, women and children (E of SC Women by S. K Singh and S. P. Pandy).

The Hindu, 29 June, 2003. The concepts of Social Capital and Common Property Resources dominate most of the discourse in development; however the former is neither social nor the latter common in a caste society. For instance, Dalits of Kanganaickenpatti in Namakkal district were forced to live as refugees in their village because they made a claim for a share in common village resources. The demand from Arunthathuyars for a share in the proceeds of sale of sand, which was being mind, provoked a strong reaction from caste Hindu, who imposed a series of restriction on the 50-odd families all farm labourers. Piqued by the persistent demand, the panchayat comprising 10 caste Hindu, issued a 'diktat' banning the Dalit from participating in any village function. The local shopkeeper was instructed not to supply groceries to the Dalit and various basic amenities including water and important source of livelihood like farm work were checked.

National Federation of Dalit Women 2002: It is the institutionalised inequality of the caste system that underpins and reinforces gender inequality in India, rendering marginalised Dalit women particularly vulnerable to violence with impunity. Therefore, an understanding of the intersection of gender and caste discrimination incorporated into government policies is vital to ensuring that Dalit women's rights to life and security of life are respected and protected. This also throws open the challenge to Dalit and women's movements, as far other social movements across the country, to incorporate a gender-and caste perspective in their work, in recognition of the specific identity and corresponding unique intensity of Dalit women's sub-ordination by gender and caste. By fulfilling its national and international obligations to protect Dalit women from violence, complemented by adequate focus on improving the socio-economic conditions of Dalit women, the Indian State could contribute to enlarging the choices and agency of Dalit women. Increased Dalit women's agency, in turn, would contribute to social change not only for their families and their communities, but also for the wider Indian society. As the National Federation of Dalit Women has stated in it's Declaration of Dalit Women's Rights 2002, Dalit women have the right to life and to freedom from oppression and violence, the right to expression, conscience and autonomy.

Paswan and Jaidev, 2002. In 1991, literacy among the dalit women was indeed quite low. In rural areas only 19.46 percentage women were literate. A report published by Ministry of Welfare, Government of India in 1998 showed that there is much difference in the literacy rate of dalits and non-dalits in general, and gender specific. Literacy rate of non-dalits is 64.13 per cent and literacy rate of women is 39.29 per cent, where as dalit women's literacy rate is only 23.76 per cent. There is a large disparity in the literacy rate due to wide spread prejudice based on casteism and patriarchy against dalits and women in general and dalit women in particular.

Jodhka, 2002. Indian races have been familiar with representative institution from the time immemorial….. The word panchayats is household word throughout the length and breadth of Indian and it means a council of five elected by the class of the people whom the five belong, for the purpose of managing and controlling the social affairs of the particular caste.

Narayanamoorthy and Kamble 2002. Education is one of the factors in human development. It can play a vital role in enhancing capabilities of individuals especially in oppressive social structure. A study by Narayanamoorthy and Kamble (2002) reveals that literacy rate of the Dalit rural population though has been increasing; it is much less compares to non-Dalit population. Literacy amongst the rural Dalits is 33 per cent compared to 45 per cent amongst the non-Dalits. The condition of Dalit women is said to be worse. International human rights group Amnesty International condemned the Uttar Pradesh and Rajasthan governments for the poor literacy rate among Dalit women in their domain, saying it directly violated their rights. The poor educational status of Dalits is attributed to the intense socio-economic deprivation of Dalits.

The Indian Express, 26th March, 2002. A good example of caste culture as culture of fear could be evidenced from Maduri. As part of empowerment of Dalits, positions of power in panchayats are reserved for them. Like upper-caste in various parts of India, the Thevars in Madurai district opposed this move. They ensured that the scared Dalits do not come forward to file nominations, and that they won't serve under a Dalit. The demand of the Thevars was to de-reserve the councillorship for 4 panchayats. Saraswati Dalit woman, filed nomination at Nattarmangalam, one of these four panchayats and had her house stoned.

Times of India, 26th March 2002. Subban, a daily wage earner at Pappatti in Madurai traveled 500 Km to Chennai to file his nominations for panchayat elections. He grieved 'How do you expect me to file nomination there. The Villagers would have killed me'.

V. M Rao 2002. Maintain that a review of the genesis and development of SHG's in India reveals that the existing formal financial institutions have failed to provide finances to landless, marginalized and disadvantaged groups. The origin of SHG's could be treated tom mutual aid in; India village community. SHG's encourage saving and promote income-generating activities through small loans. The experience available in the country and elsewhere suggests that SHG's are sustainable to have replicability, stimulate savings, and in the process help borrower to come out of vicious circle of poverty.

Jodhka's 2002. Study on Caste in Punjab has interesting findings. In some cases it was found, despite Dalits becoming Sarpanch, the real power remained with the landowning Jat, whose faction had supported his/ her candidature. In a village of Amritsar for example, a Dalit called Surat Singh could get elected because the local Jats did not let any other Dalit contest elections. Similarly Dalits were not treated equally in the Panchayats building. Nearly 40 per cent Dalit felt that they were not treated equally in the Panchayat and that discrimination is also practiced in sitting arrangements. The Panchayat and buildings are seen as upper caste community canters and Dalits have therefore built their own community canters. Even when the seats were reserve for Dalits, dominant castes often had a say in deciding who amongst Dalits should contest elections.

Waghmore 2002. Has brought to light how unparticipatory, participatory initiatives could be. They could well degenerate the existing inequalities; Dalits as people's representatives are mere pawns readily available at the hands of the dominant castes. Even when the seats were reserve for Dalits, dominant castes often had a say in deciding who amongst Dalits should contest elections.

Jodhka 2002. Maintains Ambedkar's thoughts on villages are caste to the anthropologists who have studied caste from below. Due to the rigid structure standing upon the strong foundations provided by the caste culture, the village and the village community infer different things for the dominants and the subalterns. A question that arises then is how exactly do the initiatives of decentralized governance promote development of Dalits.

National Policy for the Empowerment of Women 2001: The Indian Government has identified in its 10th Five-Year Plan 2002-07 the empowerment of socially disadvantaged groups such as Dalits and women as priority strategies for development of the nation. Complementing this development priority is the elimination of discrimination and all forms of violence against women and the girl child, which is a central objective of the National Policy for the Empowerment of Women 2001 in attempting to bridge the gap between *de jure* equal status and *de facto* pervasive gender inequality as the National Policy of states.

All forms of violence against women, physical and mental, whether at domestic or societal levels, including those arising from customs, traditions or accepted practices, shall be dealt with effectively with a view to eliminate its incidence. Institutions and mechanisms/schemes for assistance will be created and strengthened for prevention of such violence, including sexual harassment at workplace and customs like dowry; for the rehabilitation of the victims of violence and for taking effective action against the perpetrators of such violence. A special emphasis will also be laid on programmes and measures to deal with trafficking on women and girls.

Crook and Manor 2001. Dalits due to their unequal position are not equal participant. In their study of panchayats in the state of Karnataka observe that despite high level of electoral participation by the historically disadvantaged groups, their influence on Mandal and District council remains minimal.

Satish 2001. In his paper raised certain issues related to the functioning of SHG's Adequate care should be taken to ensure homogeneity of socio-economic status of the members, while forming SHG's. The process of SHG formation has to be systematic whether a Bank or an N.G.O forms it. He emphasised that SHG's experiment has to be spread throughout rural India rather than being concentrated in a few pockets of the country.

NGO's are more suited for forming and nurturing of the SHG's and therefore, it is essential to strengthen them and their resources so that they should increasingly undertake this work.

Barbara and Mahanta 2001. In their paper maintained that the SHG's have helped to set up a number of micro-enterprises for income-generation. Rastriya Gramin Vikas Nidhi's credit and saving Programme in Assam has been found successful as its focus is exclusively on the rural poor. It adopted a credit delivery system designed specially for tem with the report of a specially trained staff and a supportive policy with no political intervention at any stage in the implementation of the Programme.

Puhazendhi, and Satyasai 2001. In their paper attempted to evaluate the performance of SHG's with special reference to social and economic empowerment. Primary data collected with the help of structured questionnaire from 560 sample households in 223 SHG's functioning in 11 states representing four different regions across the country formed the basis of the study The findings of the study revealed that the SHG's as institutional arrangement could positively contribute to the economic and social empowerment of rural poor and the impact on the later was more pronounce than on the former. Through there was no specific pattern in the performance of SHG's among different regions, the southern region could edge out other . The SHG's Programme has been found more popular in the southern region and its progress in other regions is quite low, thus signifying an uneven achievement among the regions. Older groups had relatively more positive features like better performance than younger groups.

Manimekalai and Rajeshwari 2001. In their paper highlighted that the provision of micro-finance by the NGO's to women SHG's has helped the groups to achieve a measure of economic and social empowerment. It has developed a sense of leadership, organizational skill, management of various activities of a business, right from acquiring finance, identifying raw material, market and suitable diversification and modernization.

K. C. Sharma 2001. Maintained that through SHG's women empowerment is taking place. Their participation in the economic activities and decision-making at the household and society level is increasing and making the process of rural development participatory, democratic, sustainable and independent of subsidy, thus macro-financing through SHG's is contributing to the development of rural people in a meaningful manner.

Johnson 2001. In a detailed discussion on decentralized governance and poverty reduction observes. 'Central states have an important role to play in ensuring the development and implementation of substantive pro-poor policies.... A certain amount of re-centralisation may be needed to ensure that the needs of poor not neglected'. Most of the pro-poor policies implemented at decentralized level run a high risk of being appropriated by the elites or rampant corruption.

Sengupta and Singh, 2001. In India, the plight of women is no better than their counterparts in other developing countries. Despite the honour a ad reverence accorded to them as deities in mythology and personified tribute paid to them in historical monuments, the ground realities remain opposite. In a patriarchal society like Indian, there exists the unfounded belief that man is the bread winner of the family and hence the male child gets the best of limited facilities and resources within the family. The girl child is under constant risk of being aborted through the misuse of modern technology. She is mostly deprived of schooling for sake of taking care of siblings at home. Since she is to be married off soon, investing in her education is a liability. Despite the fact that women are massively involved in almost all sectors of economy, their work and earnings do not count. Their activities as producers of the household are not reflected in National Income Statistics, thus, making their contribution unaccounted for. In an effort to uphold cultural heritage, the past is glamorized and with it, the equality of women and enhancement of their role in development gets inhibited.

Meennakshi et al. 2000. A Study on estimating the poverty for SC, ST and Women headed household observes, 'irrespective of the deprivation measurement, the SC and ST communities have uniformly higher poverty rates' The importance of the landholding as a main source of livelihood in rural areas can hardly be over emphasised. The land distribution pattern ensures that patron-client relationship exists between Dalits and the upper castes sustains. The Dalits account for a sixth of India's population, but of Land. At best, they hold a tiny fraction of a sixth of land owned by Indians. Secondly, irrigation of the India has clear caste geography. Upper caste cultivate at the headwater; intermediate caste at the middle and Dalits cultivate near the tail waters.

Mungekar, 2000. The percentage of marginal farmers amongst Dalits is as high as 71, nearly 50 per cent of them are agricultural labourers; out of every 100 bonded labourers 66 belong to the Dalits; their share in industrial employment was as an abysmally low 4 per cent as a consequence of all this the extent of poverty among the Dalits is high as 50 per cent compared to 30 for the population as a whole.

The Opioneer, 30th Jun, 2000. In this study he mentioned briefly, during the period, which India calls Independence, 3 million Dalit women have been raped and one million Dalits have massacred. This is 25 times more than number of Indian soldiers killed during the wars it fought after Independence.

Nagayya 2000. Maintains that an informal arrangement for credit supply to the poor through SHG's is fast emerging as a promising tool for promoting income-generating enterprises. He has reviewed the initiatives arrangements to support this Programme for alleviation of poverty among the poor, with focus on women. He maintained that NABARD and SIDBI are playing a prominent role at various stages of implementation of this Programme. There are other national level bodies also supporting NGO's/VA/s, *viz.* Rastriya Mahila Kosh (RMK), Rashtriya Gramin Vikas Nidhi (RGVN) etc. He called for an imperative need to enlarge the coverage of SHG's in advance portfolio of banks as part of their corporate strategy, to recognise perceived benefits of SHG's financing in terms of reduced default risk and transaction costs.

Gurumoorthy 2000. Maintained that SHG is a viable alternative to achieve the objectives of rural development programmes. SHG's are viable organizational setup to disburse micro credit to the rural women for the purpose of making them entrepreneur and encouraging them to enter into entrepreneurial activities. Credit needs of the rural women can be fulfilled wholesomely through the SHG's. The women led SHG's have successfully demonstrated how to mobilize and manage thrift, appraise credit needs, maintain linkages with the banks and enforce financial self-discipline. SHG's enhance the equality of status of women as participants, decision-makers and beneficiaries in the democratic, economic and social and cultural spheres of life. They encourage women to take active part in the socio-economic progress of the society.

Bhatia and Bhatia 2000. Through few case studies highlighted that recovery of SHG's is higher than other credit extended to borrowers. Moreover, involvement of SHG's had helped the bank branches in recovery of old dues. They observed that there has been perceptible changes in the living standards of the SHG's members, in terms of ownership of assets, increase in savings and borrowing capacity, income-generating activities and income levels as well.

Rakesh Malhotra 2000. In this study of 174 women beneficiaries, in Rae Bareilly of the state of Uttar Pradesh, drawn and covered randomly from four formal agencies of credit *i.e.* CB's, PACS, and ARDB's revealed that less than half a per cent of female population against 3.5 per cent of male population in the study area were clients of the banks. Further more, only 7.64 per cent of the total quantum of credit extended by RFI 's have gone to women. It was observed that 83 per cent of loan cases availed for the end use of credit.

Dasgupta 2000. Informal journey through Self Help Group observed that micro-financing through informal group approach has effected quite a few benefits *viz; (i)* savings mobilized by the poor; *(ii)* access to the required amount of appropriate credit by the poor; *(iii)* matching the demand and supply of credit structure and opening new market for FI's;

(iv) reduction in transaction cost for both lenders and borrowers; *(v)* tremendous improvement in recovery; *(vi)* heralding new realisation of subsidy less and corruptionless credit; and *(vii)* remarkable empowerment of poor women. He stressed that SHG's should be considered as one of the best means to counter social and financial citizenship not as an end in itself.

Datta and Raman 2000. Highlighted that SHG's are characterised by heterogeneity in terms of social and economic indicators. The success of SHG's in terms of high repayment is mostly related to the exploitation of prevailing social ties and cohesion found among women members. Social cohesiveness among members spring not only from their diverse background of knowledge base, skills occupations and income levels, but also die to the dynamic incentive system of progressive lending to the groups on the successful completion of loan repayment. However, SHG's are heavily dependent on external financial agencies for their lending operations.

Government of India Report 1999. Hence, violence, which serves as a crucial social mechanism to maintain Dalit women's subordinate position in society, is the core outcome of gender-based inequalities shaped and intensified by the caste system. This situation exists in India today despite constitutional guarantees of non-discrimination on the basis of caste and gender *(Article 15(1)),* the right to life and security of life *(Article 21)* and the constitutional directive to specifically protect Dalits from social injustice and all forms of exploitation *(Article 46).* Moreover, the Indian State has enacted a series of laws protecting the rights of Dalits and women, acknowledging the prevalence of discrimination and violence against these sections of society. A key law in this regard is the *Scheduled Castes/Scheduled Tribes (Prevention of Atrocities) Act 1989.* The presence of laws, however, without concomitant implementation to ensure personal security to Dalit women, and without concerted efforts to emancipate the Dalit community and eradieate entrenched gender-and-caste biased notions of inequality and (in) justice, is not enough. The Indian government has itself acknowledged that the institutional forces – caste, class, community and family – arraised against women's equal rights are powerful and shape people's mindsets to accept pervasive gender inequality.

Jogdand, 1999. Women constitute half of the total population, but are unable to get equal share in active politics. Their socio-economic status directly depends on their participation in politics. Political parties in India speak much about equality of women but have totally ignored the dalit women.

Pal and Bhargav 1999. A careful look at the economic situation of dalit women reveals that their work force structure is such that they rarely own any land. A large majority of them are agricultural labourers. The rate of unemployment among them is also quite high. About 90 per cent of women working in unorganized sector are mainly from lower castes *Jogdand 1999*. In 1991, about 71 per cent of dalit women workers in rural area were agricultural labourers. Only 19 per cent of them owned land.

Pillai, cited in Michael 1999. The main complaints of the poor dalit women are that they have no good houses. In urban areas most of them stay in unhygienic slums and in rural areas their houses are away from main stream of society.

The Annual Report of University Grant Commission for 1999-2000, shows that Dalits in general have very low participation rates in higher education (*Annual Reports of University*). The main reasons for the very low literacy rate among Dalit women could be some or all of the following:

1. The Lack of educational resources especially in rural areas.
2. Privatization of schools and colleges.
3. Extreme poverty, because of which they cannot afford the expensive fees for the private schools.
4. The demand for an increase in the Dowry for educated girls.
5. Humiliation and bullying by the high caste students and teachers.

Rege, S. 1998. If human rights are the legitimation of human needs, then the needs of Dalit women for personal security, socio-economic development and social justice are priority areas for intervention. In order to understand, the reality of Indian society in general, and the Dalit community and Dalit women in particular, an analysis of caste-class-gender dynamics is imperative. It is only by adopting this three-fold lens focusing on the cultural and material dimensions of the intersection of gender and caste discrimination that a true comprehension of key social relations and social inequalities in India emerges.

Human Watch Report, 1998. It is easy for the historically dominating caste and gender to violate human rights of dalit women who are at the lowest rung of the hierarchical ladder. The type of violence inflicted on dalits is in the form of severest violation of human rights. Dalit and tribal women are raped as part of an effort by upper caste leaders, land lords and police to suppress movements to demand payment of minimum wages, to settle share cropping disputes or to reclaim lost lands.

Manipal, 1998. Dalit women also faced many problems in performing their duties due to illiteracy, lack of information and dependency on the male members of their families. An important obstacle is the no-confidence motion against dalit women as pradhan by the dominant sections. Rural elites are unable to accept the power, which has been given into the hands of the poorer and disadvantaged women.

National Commission for Women 1996. Vulnerably positioned at the bottom of India's caste, class and gender hierarchies, Dalit women experience endemic gender-and-caste discrimination and violence as the outcome of everely imbalanced social, economic and political power equations. Their socio-economic vulnerability and lack of political voice, when combined with the dominant risk factors of being Dalit and female, increase their exposure to potentially violent situations while simultaneously reducing their ability to escape. Violence against Dalit women presents clear evidence of widespread exploitation and discrimination against these women subordinated in terms of power relations to men in a patriarchal society, as also against their communities based on caste. As the National Commission for Women has commented, "in the commission of offences against... scheduled caste (Dalit) women the offenders try to establish their authority and humiliate the community by subjecting their women to indecent and inhuman treatment, including sexual assault, parading naked, using filthy language, etc".

Pandit 1995. Article 17 of the constitution provides for removal of untouchability. Based on this article Protection of Civil Rights Act' (PCR), was passed in 1955. However, there was no conviction/under this Act, hence Thirty-four years after the introduction of PCR Act, the Scheduled Caste and Schedule Tribes (Prevention of Atrocities) Act 1989 was enacted to bring various forms of atrocities to an end. In this Act the complainant is given more weightage. There are stringent provisions against the police for negligence.

5 PROFILE OF THE STUDY AREA

The economy of any nation depends entirely upon the socio-economic characteristic features of its people, which are the consequent outcome of the geographical and demographical factors of that nation. Geographical features of an area generate various aspects in relation to the life style and living conditions of the people. Besides, demographical features do demonstrate the socio-economic conditions of the people which ultimately reflect their impact on the national economy. Hence, in this chapter, the agro-economic features like: cropping pattern, land use pattern, farm size, production, productivity of crops are presented besides, geographic, demographic and physical characteristics. This chapter is divided into three sections. *First*, *Second* and *Third* sections presents the profile of the Andhra Pradesh, Guntur District and Tenali Mandal respectively. These sections deals with agro-economic profile of the state of Andhra Pradesh and Guntur District, which has been discussed in terms of physical features, demographic features, climate, rainfall, water resources, pattern of land utilisation, and pattern of crops as well as distribution of land possessions.

Profile of Andhra Pradesh

Physical Features

The State of Andhra Pradesh is situated in a tropical region between the latitudes 13° to 20° North and the longitudes 77° to 85° East and is bounded by the Bay of Bengal in the East with a coastal line of 960 km. The other boundaries to the State are the States of Orissa, Madhya Pradesh and Maharashtra in the North, Karnataka in the West and Tamil Nadu in the South. The state has an area of 2.75 lakh hectares constituting 8.4 per cent of the total geographical area of the country. As per 2001 census, the population of the state is 762.10 lakhs and 73 per cent of the population lives in the rural areas. Agriculture is the main occupation of the people and 70 per cent of the people depend on agriculture and allied activities for their livelihood. The state consists of 23 districts and has been divided into three regions, *viz*; Coastal Andhra, which comprises 9 districts, Rayalaseema, which consists of 4 districts and Telangana, which covers 10 districts.

Andhra Pradesh is endowed with a variety of soils ranging from poor coastal sands to highly fertile deltaic alluviums. Red soils occupy over 66 per cent of the cultivated area and are mostly situated in Rayalaseema and Telangana districts. These soils have a low nutrient status. Red soils can be sub-classified as: *(a) Dubba* soils (loamy sands to sandy loams) *(b) Chalkas* (sandy loam soils) *(c)* sandy clay loams *(d)* loams including *silty* soils *(e)* deep loamy sands and *(f)* sandy loams with clay sub soil. *Chalkas* occur mostly in the Telangana districts, while red loams combined with sands are found in the upland regions of coastal districts.

Black soils cover nearly 25 per cent of the cultivated area and are generally associated with poor drainage. They are also called *Regurs* or *Vertisols* and are of two types. The first category is *in-situ* soils while the other one is transported soils. While the first category can be noticed in the coastal districts and parts of Telangana and Rayalaseema, the second category occurs in the valley regions of the slopes with calcareous concentrations. The *in-situ* soils are generally heavy in texture with high salt concentration.

The alluvial loamy clay soils are found in Krishna and Godavari deltas which cover 5 per cent of the cultivated area. The coastal sands occupy only 3 per cent while the remaining

2 per cent is covered by laterite soils in certain corners of the State. Forest areas, which cover about 23 per cent of geographical area in Andhra Pradesh, yield timber products such as: teak, eucalyptus, cashew, casuarina, softwoods and bamboo.

Demographic Features

Demographic aspects influence economic development of any region. The demographic features of the study area are presented in Table 5.1 With a population of 762.10 lakhs (2001 census) constituting about 7.43 per cent of India's population, Andhra Pradesh is the fifth most populous state in India.

Table 5.1: Population of andhra pradesh state

Sl. No.	Category	2001 Census	
		Number of Persons	Percentage to Total Population
1.	Male	385.27	50.55
2.	Female	376.83	49.44
3.	Rural	208.09	72.69
4.	Urban	762.10	27.30
5.	Schedule caste	123.39	16.19
6.	Schedule tribe	50.24	6.59
7.	Literates	399.34	52.39
8.	Total workers	348.94	45.78
9.	Cultivators	78.61	10.35
10.	Agricultural Labourers	138.31	15.25
	Total Population	762.10	100.00

Source: Directorate of Economics and Statistics, Government of Andhra Pradesh, Hyderabad

The density of the population is 277 per sq. km., as against India's density of 312 per sq. km. Out of the total population, the male population is 385.27 lakhs and the female population is 376.83 lakhs representing 50.55 and 49.45 per cent respectively. The Percentage of literacy of the State is 60.47 while the literacy of the country is 65.37 per cent. Most of the population in the state lives in rural areas (73%) while the percentage of population living in urban areas is 27 only. The working population of the state is 348.94 lakhs, of which 78.61 lakhs are cultivators and 138.31 lakhs are agriculture workers representing 10.31 and 15.25 per cent respectively of the total population.

Climate and Rainfall

Diversified climatic conditions prevail as per the changing seasons. Piercing sun heat in summer followed by opening of sluice gates of sky, for which agriculturists anxiously await, paving a path for pleasant winter, prevail in perpetual periods in Andhra Pradesh. The state has generally a hot summer and a pleasant winter. The maximum and minimum temperatures in the state are 41.5°C. and 11.1°C. respectively. The state welcomes rain from the south-west and north-east monsoons. Region-wise rainfall in Andhra Pradesh state is presented in Table 5.2. The average rainfall varies from about 74 c.m., in South to about 200 c.m., in North with considerable fluctuations. It has a mean annual rainfall of 92.5 c.m., of which, 68.5 per cent is received during south-west monsoon period (June to September) and 22.3 per cent is received during north-east monsoon period (October-December) and the remaining 9.2 per cent of mean rainfall is received during winter and summer.

Table 5.2: Monsoon-wise rainfall distribution (2008-09)

(Rainfall in m.m.)

Monsoon	Actual	Normal	% to Total Normal Rainfall
South West Monsoon (June to September)	747	624	69.20
North-East Monsoon (October to December)	163	224	15.10
Winter Period (January and February)	41	14	3.79
Hot Weather Period (March to May)	128	78	11.85
Total (June to May)	1080	940	100.00

Source: Directorate of Economics and Statistics, Hyderabad, Andhra Pradesh

The rainfall varies among the three regions of the state as per the varying seasons and monsoons. The influence of south-west monsoon is predominant in coastal region followed by Telangana and Rayalaseema, whereas the north-east monsoon provides high amount of rainfall in Coastal Andhra area followed by Rayalaseema and Telangana. There are no significant differences in distribution of rainfall during winter and hot weather periods among the three regions.

Water Resources

Andhra Pradesh is endowed with rich water resources and it is appropriately called a river state. Three major rivers, namely: *(i)* the Godavari; *(ii)* the Krishna; and *(iii)* the *Pennar,* drain 70 per cent of the land area of the State. The water potential of Andhra Pradesh is estimated to be 2746 TMCs which cover 7.78 m. ha. The major rivers are seasonal and more than 90 per cent of the total flow which occurs between June and December depend on the rainfall which varies from year to year. The ultimate irrigation potential from all the sources is estimated to be 9.50 m.ha. This includes 7.30 m.ha., from surface water and 2.20 m.ha., from ground water.

Land Utilisation

Table 5.3 presents division-wise pattern of land as per its utilisation. The total geographical area of the state is 275.04 lakh hectares, out of which, nearly 50.68 per cent of the area (135.66 lakh hectares in 2008-09) is the net sown area. Forests spread over a reporting area of 62.10 lakh hectares forming 22.60 per cent of the total geographical area in the state and it is much less than as aimed at in the National Forest Policy resolution. An area of 6.50 lakh hectares of cultivable waste land forms 2.40 per cent of the total geographical area and offers scope for extending area under cultivation. The other fallow lands and current fallow lands consist of an area of 14.88 and 26.24 lakh ha., and account for 5.40 and 9.60 per cent respectively in the total geographical area.

Table 5.3: Land utilisation in andhra pradesh (2008-09)

Sl. No.	Category	Area in Lakh Hectares	Percentage to Total Geographical Area
1.	Total Geographical Area	275.04	100.00
2.	Forest	62.10	22.60
3.	Barren and Uncultivable land	20.55	7.50
4.	Land put to Non-Agricultural uses	26.52	9.60
5.	Cultivable waste	6.50	2.40
6.	Permanent pastures and other grazing lands	5.69	2.10
7.	Land under Misc. Tree crops, Groves not included in Net Area Sown	2.98	1.00
8.	Other fallow lands	14.88	5.40
9.	Current fallow lands	26.24	9.60
10.	Net Area Sown	109.58	39.80
11.	Area sown more than once	26.24	10.22
12.	Total Cropped Area	135.66	50.68

Source: Directorate of Economics and Statistics, Government of Andhra Pradesh, Hyderabad

Cropping Pattern

The area under the cultivation of principal crops in Andhra Pradesh is shown in Table 5.4. It is evident from the data that food crops occupy predominantly higher place in the cropping pattern constituting 66.92 per cent of the total cropping land. Among the food crops, paddy being an important crop occupies about 30.83 per cent of gross cropped area. Among the non-food crops the share of groundnut is the highest representing 12.42 per cent followed by cotton accounting for 9.83 per cent of the gross cropped area. (*Table 5.4 on next page*)

Table 5.4: Area under principal crops in andhra pradesh (2008-09)

(Area in Lakh Hectares)

Sl. No.	Crop	Khariff	Rabi	Total	Percentage to Total Cropped Area
1.	Rice	28.03	15.84	43.87	30.83
2.	Jowar	1.18	1.61	2.79	1.96
3.	Maize	4.98	3.54	8.52	5.99
4.	Bajra	0.50	0.09	0.59	0.14
5.	Greengram	2.07	1.13	3.20	2.25
6.	Blackgram	0.69	2.69	3.38	2.38
7.	Redgram	4.39	0.04	4.43	3.11
8.	Bengal gram	0.00	6.07	6.07	4.27
11.	Chillies	1.60	0.43	2.03	1.23
12.	Turmeric	0.63	0.00	0.63	0.44
13.	Sugar cane	1.96	0.00	1.96	1.37
14.	Onions	0.27	0.14	0.41	0.29
	Total food crops	**60.0**	**35.22**	**95.22**	**66.92**
15.	Cotton	13.99	0.00	13.99	9.83
17.	Groundnut	15.0	2.66	17.66	12.41
18.	Sunflower	0.89	3.30	4.19	2.94
19.	Castor	1.59	0.00	1.59	1.12
20.	Tobacco	0.0	1.71	1.71	1.20
Total non-food crops		**38.03**	**9.04**	**47.07**	**33.08**
Total cropped area		**98.03**	**44.26**	**142.29**	**100.00**

Source: Directorate of Economics and Statistics, Government of Andhra Pradesh, Hyderabad

Distribution of Land Possessions

Private individual owners in Andhra Pradesh almost exclusively carry out agriculture production. They have been categorized as per the size of their land possessions. Total land possessions and the land under agricultural operations are presented in Table 5.5. As per Statistical Abstract of Andhra Pradesh 2008-09, marginal holdings, which are less than one-hectare of area, constitute 61.49 per cent of the total holdings and control 22.69 per cent of the gross cultivated area. Small holdings with the size range of 1.0 to 2.00 hectares of area constitute 21.91 per cent of the total holdings and control 25.75 per cent of the cultivated area. In the total holdings, less than 2 hectares of area constitutes about 83.50 per cent and area operating is about 48.44 per cent of the cultivated area. Medium and semi-medium holdings in the size range of 2.0 to 10.0 hectares numbering about 19.31 lakh units constitute about 16.01 per cent in the total holdings and operate about 45.51 per cent of land under cultivation. Large holdings (above 10 hectares) constitute only 0.46 per cent in the total holdings and control 6.06 per cent of the area under cultivation.

Table 5.5: Size group-wise number of operational holdings and area operated for agriculture in andhra pradesh (2008-09)

Sl. No.	Size Group	Total No. of Holdings	% to Total Holdings	Total Operated Area (in hectares)	% to Total Area Operated	Average Holding Size
1.	Marginal (<1 hectare)	7417461	61.59	3287034	22.69	0.44
2.	Small (1.00-2.00 hectares)	2639110	21.91	3730303	25.75	1.41
3.	Semi-medium (2.00-4.00 hectares)	1444083	11.99	3835072	26.47	2.66
4.	Medium (4.00-10.00 hectares)	487423	4.05	2758745	19.04	5.66
5.	Large (>10.00 hectares)	56041	0.46	877734	6.06	15.66
	Total	**12044118**	**100.00**	**14488888**	**100.00**	**1.20**

Source: Directorate of Economics and Statistics, Government of Andhra Pradesh, Hyderabad

Economic Profile

The economy of Andhra Pradesh is predominantly an agriculture based economy and around 19 per cent (average contribution) of the state GDP is gained from agriculture. Agriculture sector in the state provides employment to around 65 per cent of the state's population. The state is one of the India's main rice-producing states. Eventhough the state GDP from agriculture has been getting declined since 1991, the population depending on this sector is still greater than the other sectors of the state.

Irrigation

Since independence, the Government of Andhra Pradesh has been initiating steps to extend irrigation facilities from coastal lands to interior dry lands by digging canals and constructing dams. Most of the rivers flowing through the state are highly seasonal and 90 per cent of their currents flow between June and December, and fluctuate from year to year. The Krishna and the Godavari are the major rivers in the state which irrigate about 6 million hectares of farmland. The major irrigation projects constructed on these rivers are Nagarjunsagar, Sriramsagar, Srisailam, Tungabhadra High level and Low Level Canals, Somasila, Vamsadhara and Yeleru etc. The Nagarjuna Sagar project on the Krishna constructed in 1960 is one of the largest irrigation projects in India. The canals under this project provide an irrigation system for rice and other crops that produce products for industries and processing agricultural products by flowing across about 800 km. (497 sq. miles).

The irrigation potential provided from surface water resources and ground water is estimated at 73 lakh hectares and 22 lakh hectares respectively. The source wise net irrigated area is presented in the Table 5.6. Canals, tanks tube wells and dug wells play a dominant role; 34.63 per cent of area is irrigated under canal irrigation; the area under tank irrigation is 6.48 lakh hectares which accounts for 13.44 per cent. The area under tube well and dug well irrigation is 23.23 lakh hectares, which accounts for 48.70 per cent in the year of 2008-09.

Table 5.6: Net area irrigated by different sources in andhra pradesh (2008-09)

(Area in Lakh Hectares)

Sl. No.	Source of Irrigation	Net Irrigated Area	Percentage to Total Net Irrigated Area
1.	Canals	16.69	34.63
2.	Tanks	6.48	13.44
3.	Tube wells and Dug wells	23.23	48.20
4.	Other sources	1.80	3.73
	Total	**48.20**	**100.00**

Source: Directorate of Economics and Statistics, Government of Andhra Pradesh, Hyderabad

The net and gross area irrigated during this period are about 38.81 and 49.87 lakh hectares respectively. The average irrigated land holding size in the state is 0.88 hectares while the average land holding size is 1.56 hectares. Tanks and wells (both open wells and tube wells) together provide a major portion of irrigation and account for 61.32 per cent of total net area irrigated, while canals irrigate about 34.63 per cent of net area irrigated during this period. This clearly explains that more than 50 per cent of cropped area is still under rainfed farming.

Crop-wise Irrigated Area

The area under irrigation by various crops during 2008-09 is presented in Table 5.7. Irrigation facilities in the state are available for nearly two-thirds of the cereal crops grown in the state and for more than half of the fruits and vegetables. Around 70 per cent of the irrigated area is under cereal crops. Among the cereal crops, rice is the predominant crop occupying more than half of the total irrigated area (63.04%). Other food crops, which include chillies, fruits and vegetables, cover 14 per cent of the irrigated area. Oil seeds cover 12 per cent of the irrigated area and the remaining irrigated area is placed by non-food crops such as tobacco, sugarcane and cotton. The share of total food crops and non-food crops in the gross cropped area is 86.41 per cent and 13.59 per cent respectively.

Table 5.7: Irrigated area under different crops in andhra pradesh (2008-09)

(Area in Lakh Hectares)

Sl. No.	Crop	Khariff	Rabi	Total	Percentage to Total Cropped Area
1.	Rice	26.65	15.84	42.49	63.04
2.	Jowar	0.06	0.19	0.25	0.40
3.	Maize	1.0	3.21	4.21	6.25
4.	Bajra	0.07	0.09	0.16	0.23
5.	Greengram	0.0	0.03	0.03	0.04
6.	Blackgram	0.0	0.03	0.03	0.04
7.	Bengalgram	0.0	0.13	0.13	0.20
8.	Fruit crops	2.90	0.41	3.31	4.91
9.	Vegetables	0.94	0.88	1.82	2.70
10.	Chillies	1.29	0.39	1.68	2.50
11.	Turmeric	0.60	0.0	0.60	0.89
12.	Sugarcane	1.82	1.36	3.18	4.72
	Total Food Crops	**35.39**	**22.85**	**58.24**	**86.41**
13.	Cotton	2.53	0.01	2.54	3.77
14.	Groundnut	0.39	2.55	2.94	4.36
15.	Sunflower	0.25	1.37	1.62	2.40
16.	Tobacco	0.01	0.46	0.47	0.70
Total Non-food Crops		**4.43**	**4.73**	**9.16**	**13.59**
Total Cropped Area		**39.82**	**27.58**	**67.40**	**100.0**

Source: Directorate of Economics and Statistics, Government of Andhra Pradesh, Hyderabad

Irrigation projects in the state have been divided into three categories based on the size of irrigated area. Major irrigation schemes contain command areas of more than 10,000 hectares, whereas medium irrigation projects have command areas ranging from 2,000 hectares to 10,000 hectares. Minor irrigation schemes comprise an area of less than 2000 hectares and usually include smaller irrigation schemes such as lift irrigation schemes, tanks, diversion weirs and open head channels. Traditionally minor irrigation schemes and ground water are under the control of Minor Irrigation Department, while the major and medium irrigation projects are under the Major Irrigation Department.

District-wise Rainfall and Cropping Pattern

The annual rainfall (district-wise) and potential of cropping systems in Andhra Pradesh during 2008-09 is shown in Table 5.8. The data clearly shows that the range of 600 mm to 800 mm rainfall is possible to cultivate inter cropping only in the districts of Ananthpur, Kadapa, Kurnool, Rangareddy, Hyderabad, Nalgonda, Mahaboobnagar and Prakasam. In such districts at least one of the component crops succeeds in producing economic yields during the drought situations.

Table 5.8: Rainfall and cropping pattern of 2008-09

Inter Cropping Districts	Rainfall (mm)	Double Cropping Districts	Rainfall (mm)	Other Cropping Districts*	Rainfall (mm)
Ananthpur	552	Nizamabad	1035	Chittor	933
Kadapa	699	Adilabad	1157	Nellore	1080
Kurnool	670	Karimnagar	968	Prakasam	871
Rangareddy	781	Warangal	993		
Hyderabad	779	Khammam	1124		
Nalgonda	752	Medak	873		
Mahaboobnagr	603	Guntur	853		
		Krishna	1033		
		West Godavari	1153		
		East Godavari	1217		
		Visakhapatnam	1202		
		Vizayanagaram	1131		
		Srikakulam	1162		

Source: Directorate of Economics and Statistics, Government of Andhra Pradesh, Hyderabad

* Other cropping Districts – some parts of the district having double croppingand some parts having mono cropping system.

The average rainfall of above 900 mm is possible to cultivate double cropping system successfully. This type of districts in Andhra Pradesh are thirteen, namely: *(i)* Nizamabad, *(ii)* Adilabad, *(iii)* Karimnagar, *(iv)* Warangal, *(v)* Khammam, *(vi)* Medak, *(vii)* Guntur, *(viii)* Krishna, *(ix)* West Godavari, *(x)* East Godavari, *(xi)* Visakhapatnam, *(xii)* Vizianagaram and *(xiii)* Srikakulam. Some of the districts in Andhra Pradesh follow double cropping and inter cropping systems. These districts are Chittore and Nellore. Double Cropping system is followed in the north regions of these two districts and inter-cropping system is followed in South Region.

District-wise Rainfed Area (2008-09)

The magnitude of rainfed agriculture varies significantly across in the districts as shown in Table 5.9. The percentage of rainfed area to net sown area is very high in the Districts of Ananthpur, Kurnool, Kadapa and Chittor of Rayalaseema region being constituted 87.54, 83.14, 66.01 and 57.53 per cent respectively. In the costal Andhra the share of rainfed area in the net sown area is very high in Prakasam district, accounting for 70.80 per cent followed by Visakhapatnam, Guntur, East Godavari, Srikakulam and Krishna districts with their respective percentages being 69.68, 56.79, 43.40, 42.11, 36.41, and 31.85. The share of rainfed area is very low in West Godavari district which is just 13.97 per cent. The costal Andhra region receives good rainfall and major rivers namely, the Krishna and the Godavari flow in the region. The share of rainfed area is very high in Mahabubnagar district of Telangana region which accounts for 83.58 per cent followed by Adilabad, Rangareddy, Medak, Nalgonda, Warangal, and Karimnagar districts respectively accounting for 78.57, 77.72, 70.51, 61.52, 55.62, 39.97, 29.30, and 27.56 per cent. The per cent of rainfed agriculture varies from region to region depending upon the quantum of rainfall, as it varies from region to region.

Table: 5.9: District-wise percentage of rainfed area (2008-09)

(Area in Hectares)

Districts	Net Sown Area	Net Irrigated Area	Net Un Irrigated Area	% to Rain Fed Area to Net	% to Net Irrigated Area
Anantapur	1092004	136048	955956	87.54	12.46
Mahbubnagar	882563	144910	737653	83.58	16.42
Kurnool	1005365	169490	835875	83.14	16.86
Adilabad	594216	127370	466846	78.57	21.43
Ranga Reddy	283658	63196	220462	77.72	22.28
Prakasam	652748	190625	462123	70.80	29.20
Medak	496185	146322	349863	70.51	29.49
Visakhapatnam	373139	113139	260000	69.68	30.32
Kadapa	397056	134941	262115	66.01	33.99
Nalgonda	635097	244384	390713	61.52	38.48
Chittoor	439183	186537	252646	57.53	42.47
Vizianagaram	333227	144003	189224	56.79	43.21
Khammam	496014	220124	275890	55.62	44.38
Guntur	657804	372329	285475	43.40	56.60
East Godavari	501427	290285	211142	42.11	57.89
Warangal	521046	312798	208248	39.97	60.03
Srikakulam	345894	219948	125946	36.41	63.59
Krishna	550828	375401	175427	31.85	68.15
Karimnagar	461813	326507	135306	29.30	70.70
Nizamabad	322652	233742	88910	27.56	72.44
Nellore	335699	269667	66032	19.67	80.33
West Godavari	492331	423556	68775	13.97	86.03
Andhra Pradesh	11869949	4845319	7024630	59.18	40.82

Source: Directorate of Economics and Statistics, Government of A. P., Hyderabad.

SECTION – II

District Profile

The profile of the Guntur district is discussed in this second sections. It includes the general features of the district, its demography and economy.

Guntur district spread over an area of 11391 square kms., with 57 revenue mandals divided into three revenue divisions. There are 729 revenue villages with 1024 *Grama Panchayats* and 10 municipalities. As per 2001 population census, the total population of the district is 44,65,144 and of this 71.2 per cent are living in rural areas. It is also observed that 42 per cent of total population was workers and literates constitute 55 per cent of the total population in the district, which is higher than both the State and National average. The density of population in the district is above 392 sq. kms.

District Map

Source: www.maps of India.com

Places of historical importance in Guntur District are: Amaravathi, Ponnur, Bhattiprolu, Vinukonda, Kotappakonda, Undavalli caves, Gurazala, Macherla, Kondavid fort and the archeological museum in Guntur.

Historical Background

The district derives its name from Guntur the headquarters town of the district. Various etymological explanations are given for the name of Guntur. The district abounds in paleolithic, microlithic, neolithic and megalithic sites scattered all over the district. The district occupies a very conspicuous and prominent part in the freedom struggle.

Guntur district was formed on 1st Oct 1904 with head quarters at Guntur after bifurcating Krishna and Nellore district. Prior to 1859, there was Guntur district with head quarters at Guntur but with a different jurisdiction. In 1904 Guntur district was constituted as a separate independent district including the areas of the while talukas of Ponnur, Tenali, Bapatla, Guntur, Sattenapalli, Narasaraopet, Vinukonda and Palnadu of old Krishna district and Ongole Taluk from Nellore district. Thus this district was formed in 1904 and was retained intact toll. Guntur district is part of Krishna delta. In 1970 while forming a new district with Ongole as its head quarters parts of Bapatla and Narasaraopet talukas and the whole of Ongole Taluk were taken to Prakasam district.

Location and Extent

Guntur district is a part of Krishna delta. The district extends approximately between 15° 18′ and 16° 50′ of North latitude and 79° 10′ and 80° 55′ of East longitudes. River Krishna bounds the district almost from three sides, Western, Northern and Eastern. The district occupies an area of 11391 sq. kms.

Soils and Rainfall

The black cotton and red loamy soils are predominant in the district 69 per cent of the total area of the district is black cotton while 24 per cent of that is the red loamy soils. The soils of the district are broadly divided into alluvial regar, red and arenaceous and are further subdivided into clayey, loamy and sandy. Of these alluvial soils occupy 7 per cent, while 53 per cent fall under regar series, 38 per cent under red and the remaining 2 per cent is covered by the arenaceous series. The district receives an average normal rainfall of about 814 mm., of which 499 mm., is of South West monsoon between June and September and remaining rainfall is of North east monsoon between October and December.

Rivers

The important rivers that pass through the district are: Krishna, Guntlakamma, the Musi, the Chandravanka and the Naguleru. The major irrigation project Nagarjunasagar dam is on the river Krishna and also a good number of minor irrigation projects are providing irrigation facilities to extent of 50 lake acres of the district.

Forests

The total forest area in Guntur is 161940 hectares, which constitutes about 14.30 per cent of the total area, which is less than the national minimum fixed by the government of India. About 90 per cent of the forest area in the district is spread out in the upland mandals in the west, while, 9 per cent is along sea cost in eastern part of the district.

Climate

The climate is generally warm in summer and heat is very serious in Rentachintala where the maximum temperature in the state is recorded. The year is mainly divided into four seasons. The summer season starts by about middle of February and continues till the first weak of June. Northeast monsoon breaks the hot spell and makes the weather bearable. The south monsoon season follows there after and extends up to the end of September, October and November constitutes the post monsoon season. The period from December to the middle of February is generally marked by fine weather.

Rainfall

Table 5.9 shows the seasonal wise rainfall (2008-09) in Guntur district. Rainfall in the district is generally decreases from east to west. The district gets the benefit from both southwest monsoon and northeast monsoon. While the rainfall in the monsoon seasons accounts for 71.78 per cent and 22.03 per cent of the total rain fall respectively.

Table 5.10: Season-wise rainfall distribution for 2007-08

Season	2007-08	Percentage to Total Rainfall
Southwest monsoon (June to September)	633.90	71.78
North west monsoon (October to December)	194.50	22.03
Winter period (January to February)	0	0
Hot weather period (March to May)	54.70	6.19
Total (June to May)	883.10	100

Source: Statistical Abstract of Andhra Pradesh, Hyderabad

Demographic Picture

A Comparative Picture of Population of Guntur District and Andhra Pradesh

Economic development of any region is influenced by its demographic aspects of the district considered. The district is predominantly rural with nearly 75 per cent of population inhabiting in the rural areas (Table 5.11). The population of the district increased from 28.5 lakhs to 44.05 lakhs by 2001, *i.e.,* a growth of 54.88 per cent which is less than that of the State (74.08% growth).

There is also difference in the rates of growth of rural and urban population of the districtduring 1971-2001. Sex-wise, while there is no much difference in the rates of growth in rural areas between male and female, but the rate of growth of females is higher than those of males. The district witnessed a remarkable growth in urban population. This is similar to the pattern observed at the state level. For instance, while urban population increased at 73.26 per cent during 1971-2001 at district level, it is 144.01 per cent in the State. However the district urban population growth rate is much lesser than that of State. This reflects basically on the rural urban migration character of the district with a growth in urbanisation.

Table 5.11: Population of guntur district and andhra pradesh 1971-2001

Region/ District	1971			1981		
	Total Persons	Males	Females	Total Persons	Males	Females Persons
1. Guntur District						
Rural	2133855 (75.01)	1081242 (75.03)	1052613 (75.00)	2489022 (72.47)	1261352 (72.44)	1227670 (72.49)
Urban	710638 (24.99)	359815 (24.07)	350818 (25.00)	945702 (27.53)	479750 (27.56)	465952 (27.51)
Total	2844488 (100.00)	1441057 (100.00)	1403431 (100.00)	3434724 (100.00)	1741102 (100.00)	1693622 (100.00)
2. Andhra Pradesh						
Rural	35100181 (80.69)	17698247 (80.41)	17401934 (80.96)	41062097 (76.68)	20697627 (76.35)	20364470 (77.01)
Urban	8402527 (19.31)	4310416 (19.59)	4092111 (19.04)	12487576 (23.32)	6411295 (23.65)	6076281 (22.99)
Total	43502708 (100.00)	22008663 (100.00)	21494045 (100.00)	53549673 (100.00)	27108922 (100.00)	26440751 (100.00)

Contd...

Region/ District	1991			2001			Percentage Change between 1971-2001		
	Total Persons	Males	Females	Total Persons	Males	Females Persons	Total Persons	Male	Females
1. Guntur District									
Rural	2920299 (71.11)	1484213 (71.20)	1436086 (71.00)	3174288 (72.05)	1602180 (72.16)	1572108 (71.94)	48.76	48.18	49.35
Urban	1186700 (28.89)	600267 (28.80)	586433 (29.00)	1231233 (29.00)	618125 (27.84)	613108 (28.06)	73.26	71.79	74.77
Total	4106999 (100.00)	2084480 (100.00)	2022519 (100.00)	4405521 (100.00)	2220305 (100.00)	2185216 (100.00)	54.88	54.07	55.71
2. Andhra Pradesh									
Rural	48620882 (73.10)	24591875 (72.91)	24029007 (73.30)	55223944 (72.92)	27852179 (72.75)	27371765 (73.11)	57.33	57.37	57.29
Urban	17887126 (26.90)	9132706 (27.09)	8754420 (26.70)	20503597 (27.08)	10434632 (27.25)	10068965 (26.89)	144.01	142.08	146.06
Total	66508008 (100.00)	33724581 (100.00)	32783427 (100.00)	75727541 (100.00)	38286811 (100.00)	37440730 (100.00)	74.08	73.96	74.19

Source: Census of India 1971, 1981, 1991, 2001, 2011, Series - 2, Andhra Pradesh General Population totals.

Table 5.12: Literacy levels - guntur district and andhra pradesh 1971-2001

Region/ District	1971			1981			1991			2001		
	Total Persons	Males	Females	Total Persons	Males	Females	Total Persons	Males	Females	Total Persons	Males	Females
1. Guntur District												
Rural	547068 (25.64)	367092 (33.95)	179976 (17.01)	767324 (30.83)	503441 (39.91)	263883 (21.50)	996111 (34.11)	639607 (43.10)	356504 (24.82)	1646940 (51.89)	957076 (59.74)	689864 (43.89)
Urban	326979 (46.01)	200825 (55.81)	126154 (35.96)	471080 (49.81)	284400 (61.03)	186680 (40.06)	624253 (52.60)	363523 (60.56)	26730 (44.46)	799964 (64.97)	440742 (71.30)	359222 (58.60)
Total	874047 (30.73)	567917 (39.41)	306130 (21.81)	1238404 (36.05)	787841 (45.24)	450563 (26.60)	1620364 (39.45)	1003130 (48.12)	617234 (30.52)	2446904 (55.54)	1397818 (62.96)	1049086 (48.00)
2. Andhra Pradesh												
Rural	7101832 (20.23)	5100264 (28.82)	1954023 (11.23)	9556230 (23.27)	6678341 (32.27)	2877889 (14.13)	14438253 (29.70)	9663607 (39.30)	4774646 (19.87)	26514952 (48.01)	15962354 (57.31)	10552598 (38.55)
Urban	3507168 (41.74)	2200036 (51.04)	1432077 (35.00)	6369431 (51.01)	3903904 (60.89)	2465527 (40.58)	10049306 (56.18)	5869082 (64.26)	4180224 (47.75)	13849813 (67.55)	7673723 (73.54)	6176090 (61.34)
Total	10609000 (24.39)	7300300 (33.17)	3386100 (15.75)	15925661 (29.74)	10582245 (39.04)	5343416 (20.21)	24487559 (36.82)	15532689 (46.05)	8954870 (27.32)	40364765 (53.30)	23636077 (61.73)	16728688 (44.68)

Source: Census of India 1971, 1981, 1991, 2001,2011, Series - 2, Andhra Pradesh General Population totals

State of Literacy

Data on literacy in Guntur district and Andhra Pradesh during 1971-2001 is given in Table 5.12. In respect of literacy, the district stood on a better footing with high percentage of literates in 2001. The literacy rate is increasing steadily from 30.73 per cent in 1971 to 55.54 per cent in 2001. This is higher than the State literacy rate (53.30%).

When we analyse the rate of literacy between males and females it is not surprising that male literacy rate is much higher than female literacy rate both at district and state levels. Anyhow 48 per cent of the female literacy rate speaks of the educational development of the district.

Agricultural Economy

Guntur district is well known for its commercial crops like: Chillies, Tobacco and Cotton etc. The district is one of the agriculturally advanced districts in the State. Agricultural economy of the district witnessed many changes. Guntur district occupies the foremost place in the state for cultivation in both food and non-food crops. The pre-dominant crops grown in the district are paddy, jowar and bajra among cereals, blackgram, greengram and redgram among pulses, cotton, chillies, turmeric and tobacco among non-food and commercial crops.

The advent of high yielding varieties, the increased use of fertilizers, pesticides and management practices have resulted in increased yield per acre. There has been increase in the yield of pulses also. But after 1990 the yield of crops especially cotton and chillies in a decreasing way. Virginia tobacco is very famous in Guntur district for a very long time. However with the release of Nagarjuna Sagar project water and with the change in cropping pattern the area has gone down in the district. The reputation of Guntur chillies is well known, cotton and that too sophisticated cotton of extra long staple has become popular in this district, which is, cultivated in 2.5 lakh acres. In this district Groundnut crop, which is only a rain fed crop previously, is now being cultivated in this district in the Nagarjuna sagar project Ayacut land also. For the last few decades the district has made great studies in agricultural production due to irrigation facilities, use of high yielding varieties, use of machines in farm operations, greater use of fertilizers and pesticides in the hands of enterprising farming community.

Land use Pattern

The land use pattern if the study area for the year 2008-09 is presented in Table 5.13. Table 5.13 describes that out of the total geographical area of 1152000 hectares nearly 601814 hectares are under cultivation which accounting for 52.17 per cent of the total geographical area. An area of 151 thousand hectares is cultivable wasteland, which accounted for 13.11 per cent of the total geographical area and more than 14.06 per cent of the total geographical area is under forest.

Table 5.13: Land use pattern pf the guntur district For 2008-09

Sl. No.	Land Use	Area in Acres (Area in 000 hect)	Percentage to Total Geographical Area
1.	Area under forests	162	14.06
2.	Barren and uncultivable land	41	3.56
3.	Cultivable waste land	151	13.11
	Land put to Non-Agricultural use	24	2.08
	Permanent Pastures and other Grazing lands	40	3.47
4.	Area under miscellaneous	34	2.95
5.	Land put to non agricultural use	37	3.21
6.	Other uncultivable land	42	3.65
7.	Net area sown	601	52.17
8.	Area sown more than once	20	1.74
9.	Total geographical area	1152	100.00

Source: District Statistical Officer, Guntur

Landholding Distribution

The number of operational holding and area operated according to size of the holdings of the study area is presented in the Table 5.14. Table 5.14 clearly shows that the land distribution is not uniform. Marginal farmers who constitute about 69.46 per cent of the total cultivators have owned 32.82 per cent of the total land. On the other hand big farmers cultivating households are less than 11.13 per cent more than 39.53 per cent of the total land holdings.

Table 5.14: Size-wise landholding distribution of guntur district

(Area in Acres)

Sl. No.	Land Holding Status	Number of Cultivators	Percentage to Total Cultivators	Total Area in Acres	Percentage to Total Area
1.	Marginal	487237	69.46	223559	32.82
2.	Small	136173	19.41	188422	27.66
3.	Large farmers	78060	11.13	269281	39.53
4.	**Total**	**701470**	**100.00**	**681262**	**100.00**

Source: District Statistical Officer, Guntur

Irrigation Facilities

The two Major irrigation projects in the district are: *(i)* Old Krishna Ayacut, now renamed as Prakasam Barrage with an ayacut of 2,02,032 hectares; and *(ii)* Nagarjuna Sagar Project with an ayacut of 2,54,583 hectares. Both the projects are constructed on the river Krishna. The total area irrigated by different source in Guntur district is presented in Table 5.15. The main sources of irrigation in the district is through canals, tanks and tube wells are accounting for 3,34,701 hectares, 4,660 hectares and 90,228 hectares of net area irrigated respectively during the year of 2007-08. The table clearly shows that the canals are the major source for irrigation contributing 73.90 per cent of the total irrigated area in the district. The net irrigated area of Guntur is 3,87,978 hectares in 2008-09. The lift irrigation share account to 3.47 and more than 17 per cent of the area depends up on ground water includes bore wells and tub wells.

Table 5.15: Net Irrigated area by different sources in guntur district 2007-08

(Area in Hectares)

Sl. No.	Source	Area in Kharif	Area in Rabi	Total	Percentage to the Total Irrigated Area
1.	Canals	304811	29890	334701	73.90
2.	Tanks	4105	555	4660	1.03
3.	Ground water	51727	38501	90228	19.92
4.	Lift irrigation	10806	4114	14920	3.29
5.	Other wells	4580	2070	6650	1.47
6	Other sources	1490	258	1748	0.39

Source: Statistical Abstract of Andhra Pradesh

Cropping Pattern

The total area under principle crops in Guntur district is shown in Table 5.16. Out of total geographical area of 11, 52,000 hectares nearly 6, 16,000 hectares are under cultivation. It is evident from Table 5.16 that the food crops occupied most important place in cropping pattern, occupying about 66.10 per cent of the gross cropped area. The most predominately cultivable crop with and area of 2,83,334 hectares was paddy followed by cotton 1,49,627 hectares, black gram 1,08,206 hectares, chilies 64,665 hectares in 2007-08. With in the food crops paddy has emerged as the most important food crop occupying about 36.75 per cent to the total cropped area. Cotton which has and important commercial crop of the area occupied an important place among non-food crops accounting for nearly 21.25 per cent of the total cropped area. The share of chilies accounts for 7.81 per cent of the total cropped area. The farmers have stated growing new crops like sugarcane and turmeric in place of maize, pulses (Red gram, Black gram and Bengal gram) and tobacco. Even though the area under these crops is very small, their place in the agro-business is significant.

Table 5.16: Season-wise cropping pattern of guntur district for 2008-09

(Area in 000 Hectares)

Sl. No.	Name of the Crop	Khariff	Rabi	Total	Percentages
1.	Paddy	282	5	287	36.75
2.	Jowar	0	5	5	0.64
3.	Maize	1	96	97	12.42
4.	Green gram	0	4	4	0.51
5.	Black gram	0	41	41	5.25
6.	Red gram	19	0	19	2.43
7.	Ground nut	0	5	5	0.64
8.	Costor	2	0	2	0.26
9.	Chillis	61	0	61	7.81
10.	Cotton	166	0	166	21.25
11.	Other crops	48	28	76	9.73
12.	Bengal gram	0	13	13	1.66
13.	Tobacco	0	5	5	0.64
	Total	**579**	**202**	**781**	**100.00**

Source: District Statistical Officer, Guntur

Yields of Principal Crops

The yields of principal crops during 1995-96 and 2008-09 are shown in Table 5.17. The yields of Rice, (9.13%), gren gram (37.30%), groundnut (11.86%), sugarcane (13.81%) and jowar (24.76%) have increased while that of pulses red gram (34.76%), balckgram (6.68%) sesamum (58.50%) and tobacco by 0.25 per cent witnessed a decline.

The district experienced commercialization of agriculture during 1995-96 and 2008-09 periods. This in turn transformed the nature of agricultural operations towards a greater degree of mechanization. The impact of agricultural prosperity of the district is also reflected in the growth of agro-based industries and development of tertiary sector as observed in the foregoing analysis.

Table 5.17: Yield per hectare of selected crops - guntur district 1995-96 – 2008-09

	Crop	1995-1996	1998-1999 (Kgs)	1999-2000 (Kgs)	2000-2001 (Kgs)	2008-2009 (Kgs)	% Change
1.	Rice	3109	3212	3316	3393	3770	9.13
2.	Redgram	607	763	580	396	1200	-34.76
3.	Blackgram	794	843	826	741	1000	-6.68
4.	Greengram	445	558	605	611	800	37.30
5.	Groundnut	1947	1550	2085	2178	1450	11.86
6.	Sesamum	559	381	442	232	625	-58.50
7.	Sugarcane	70163	70643	82001	79850	90000	13.81
8.	Tobacco	1572	1380	1911	1568	2630	-0.25
9.	Jowar	618	774	367	771	3300	24.76
10.	Chillies	–	3564	1878	2931	6000	-17.76

Source: District Statistical Officer, Guntur

Agricultural Implements and Machinery

The agricultural tools and implements form an integral part of the process of agricultural development. The major implements pertaining to agricultural usage are tractors, oil engines, electric motors and power sprayers etc., to have a better understanding about the agricultural machinery. Table 5.18 gives a vivid picture regarding the number of implements.

Table 5.18: Agricultural implements and machinery of guntur district for 2008-09

Sl. No.	Machinery	Number in Operation	Availability per 1000 Acre of N.S.A
1.	Tractors	6375	4
2.	Electric pump sets	13983	88
3.	Diesel	6105	4
4.	Iron ploughs	17692	112

Source: District Statistical Officer, Guntur

The Livestock Population

The livestock population plays an important role in the economic life of rural areas. They are treated as key stone of Indian farming since time immemorial as drought and milch. Data relating to live stock population as per 1999 and 2003 censes is presented in the Table 5.19. As seen from Table 5.19 the cattle population is decreased by 21.85 per cent during 2003 over 1999. But the buffalo population has increased by 0.010 per cent during the same period. The rate of increase in buffalo population and decrease in cattle population leads to reduce the per capita availability of milk and milk products to human population.

Table 5.19: Guntur district live-stock population of 1999 and 2003

Sl. No.	Category	1999	2003	Percentage Change
1.	Cattle	134908	132663	5.61
2.	Buffaloes	960932	1200166	50.72
3.	Sheep	483366	739229	31.24
4.	Goats	217029	250738	10.60
5.	Pigs	51703	17827	0.75
6.	Horse and pones	565	37	0.001

Source: Statistical abstract of A. P. 2005

SECTION – III

Profile of the Sample Mandal

Tenali is a town and a mandal in Guntur District of Andhra Pradesh, South India. It has a population of 149,839 (2001 census). It is located 16 miles east of Guntur City. Three canals of the Krishna River flow through Tenali making it a part of the rice bowl of Andhra Pradesh. One of the canals is navigable up to Nizampatnam port. Tenali is a major railway junction connecting Guntur, Vijayawada, Repalle and Chennai.

Overview

Tenali is known for its rich cultural and literary legacy. It is also very well known as Andhra Pradesh although the comparison sounds little dubious. It has produced many famous poets, theater artists, scholars, actors and academicians. The great Tenali Ramalinga (also known as Tenali Rama and Tenali Ramakrishna), who was a court-poet of Krishnadeva Raya of the Vijayanagara empire and well known for his wit and impressive Telugu poetry was born in Tumuluru near Tenali in the 16th century.

Tenali has contributed a major share of artists to Telugu stage drama. There are quite a few extraordinary artists who later moved on to film industry such as Savitri, Kanchanamala, Kongara Jaggayya, Gummadi Venkateswara Rao, Jamuna, Sarada, Prabha, Divvya Vani, Rajyalakshmi, Sivaparvathi, Mudigonda Lingamurty, Dr. Govindarajula Subba Rao, Vangara Venkata Subbaiah, Nalinikanth, Tenali Sakunthala, Meesala Bhaskar, Ghattamaneni Krishna, A V Satyarayana Rao (AVS) and writer Chinni Krishna.

The list of persons who contributed to culture, literature and knowledge includes:

1. Mylavarapu Sreenivasarao, Sanskrit scholor (Ramayana pravachanas).
2. Nori Narayana Murthy (Bhakthi programmes in TV).
3. Dr. P. Dakshina Murthy (Well known physician).
4. Chittineni Mrutyunjaya Rao.
5. Gummadi Basava Punnayya (ayurvedic doctor).
6. Burgula Gopala Krishna Murthy,
7. Modukuri Jhoson (chini writer) author and mentor for several poets and authors in and around Tenali.

Tenali also gave an excellent scientist to the nation in the form of Dr. Y. Nayudamma after whose name the prestigious NAYUDAMMA Award has been instituted. So far many eminent personalities in the country have been awarded with this prestigious award. The award presentation ceremony is held every year in Tenali.

Tenali is known for great food like Jilebi, Mirchi Masala, Grape juice at welcome soda fountain. Satyam Hotel in

Morrispet, Navayuga and Swatantra Vihar are some of the best places to eat delicious upma, karam idli, dosas, pooris and idlis.

Geography

Tenali is located at 16°14′N 80°39′E16.24°N 80.65°E. It has an average elevation of 11 metres (36 feet). Tenali is 25 km from Guntur City and 35 km., from Vijayawada City. All the three are in a triangular loop like structure at almost same distance and well connected by road and rail transport. One of the oldest town in Andhra Pradesh.

Transportation

Tenali town is well connected to all the nearby major cities through road and rail transport. It hardly takes 30 min by road and 20 min by train to Guntur city and takes 45 min by road and 30 min by train to Vijayawada city. Tenali is also well connected to State Capital (Hyderabad) and National Capital (New Delhi) through Railway. Tenali railway station has 5 platforms. Many trains were given halt in this station. It is the second biggest station in Guntur district. Tenali junction connects to four different routes like: *(i)* Guntur, *(ii)* Vijayawada, *(iii)* Chennai, and *(iv)* Repalle.

Climate

Tenali is located 30 km from the sea coast. It is generally hot and humid during summer with temperatures ranging between 32 and 45 C. Winters are milder with temperatures between 15 and 23 C. Heavy rains are experienced between July and November during monsoon time.

Population

As per 2001 Indian census, Tenali had a population of 149,839. Both males and females constitute equal share in the population. Tenali has an average literacy rate of 79 and which is higher than the national average of 59.5 and. About 10 and of the population in Tenali is under 6 years of age.

Table 5.20: Panchayat-wise population particulars mandal: tenali - census 2001

S. No.	Name of the Panchayat	House-holds	Population	Male	Female	S.C	S.T	S.C's Families	S.T's Families
1	2	3	4	5	6	7	8	9	10
1.	Kolakalur	3569	14057	7070	6987	3487	127	996.28	36.28
2.	Haafpet	417	1700	879	821				
3.	Nandivelugu	1712	6662	3311	3321	1239	136	354	38.85
4.	Gudivada	868	3078	1531	1547	2370	171	677.14	48.85
5.	Kopalle	494	1448	715	733				
6.	Yerukalapudi	221	1077	608	469				
7.	Sangamjagarlmudi	1416	5506	2705	2801	627	190	179.14	54.28
8.	Angalakuduru	2180	8134	4040	4094	1628	224	465.14	64.00
9.	Chava varipalem	256	946	461	485				
10.	Kattivaram	1307	4991	2501	2490	3446	27	984.57	7.71
11.	Somasundarapalem	368	1453	753	700				
12.	Kancherlapalem	429	1561	769	792				
13.	Telaprolu	636	2831	1463	1368				

Contd…

1	2	3	4	5	6	7	8	9	10
14.	Nelapadu	324	1297	688	609	606	4	173.14	1.14
15.	Burripalem	853	3203	1602	1601	969	71	276.85	20.28
16.	Jaggadaguntapalem	943	3669	1917	1752	54	119	15.42	34.00
17.	Pedaravuru	1796	6959	3438	3521	2599	184	742.57	52.57
18.	Mallepadu	415	1699	863	836	1340	86	382.85	24.57
Total		**18204**	**70271**	**35344**	**34927**	**18365**	**1336**	**5247.10**	**382.57**
	Tenali Town	36390	154740	77910	76830	19056	6386	5444.57	1824.57
Total		**54594**	**225011**	**113254**	**111757**	**37421**	**7725**	**10691.67**	**2214.85**

Source: Mandal Revenue Office - Tenali

Economy

The town thrives on trade and agriculture. The region around the town has fertile soil irrigated by the Krishna river and its canals. Major crops include: Lemons, Sugar Cane, Rice, Lentils, Sapota (Chickoo), Turmeric and Mango. Tenali is famous for pure gold, jewellery, wood and steel utensils. With its pivotal location between the commercial cities of Guntur and Vijayawada, many residents in and around Tenali mainly depend on them for livelihood. The town holds a huge middle class, making up more than 90 and of the total population. Major source of income is agriculture with two to three crops around the year.

List of Elected Members

1957,1962	–	Alapati Venkatramaiah
1967,1972 and 1978	–	Doddapaneni Indira
1983 and 1985	–	Annabathuni Satyanarayana
1989	–	Nadendla Bhaskara Rao
1994	–	Ravi Ravindranadh
1999	–	Gogineni Uma
2004	–	Nadendla Manohar
2009	–	Nadendla Manohar (Present Speaker of A.P Legislative Assemble)

Profile of the Sample Villages

Kolakaluru

Kolakalur is one of the sample village. This village is located on the road 6 kms., away to Tenali Mandal head quarter. In this village having famous for Lord Shiva Temple, a big chariot and Lord Vishnu Temple. Among the house holds in the village is 3569. Total population of the village is 14057 of which 7070 members are male, 6987 members are female population respectively. The total Scheduled Caste population of the village is 3487 and 127 members are belongs to Scheduled Tribe are ST population (2001 Census).

The village is having seven primary schools and three high schools in the village. The teacher, student's ratio is around 24.7 per cent. In this village have three libraries is this village. The Grama Panchayati providing five daily new papers and other magazines in the panchayati office and there is primary health centre in the village. Six RMPs are practitioner in the village. In case of emergency or chronic, people have to go to Tenali General Hospital, which is the nearest town to this village. At it is a private hospital, people may not afforded to get treatment at the high cost, so they need Government hospital near by the village. In that village had 252 self-help groups. This village two major political parties such as Congress and Telugu Desam have notable presence. BJP and CPM parties only play on impressive role in the village politics. The village panchayat of Kolakalur is divided into 16 wards. Out of 16 wards three wards are reserved for Scheduled Caste and three wards are reserved for BCs remaining ten wards are Other Castes. According to 73rd Constitutional Amendment Act 1993 in this panchayat sarpanch reserved for Scheduled Caste Women. In this village first Dalit Women sarpanch elected in the history of panchayat. So she belongs to Madiga Dalit Sub-Section.

Anaglakuduru

Angalakuduru is one of the sample village that comes on the road to Guntur City from Tenali 5 km., from Tenali. The village has a rich agricultural tradition. The three temples of Rama, Venugopala Swamy and Siva are ancient. It has another big temple complex for Anjaneya Swamy. Total population of the village is 8134 of which 4040 members are male and 4094 members are female. The total Scheduled Caste population is 1628 where as Scheduled Tribe population is 224. Anaglakuduru The village is having six primary schools and one high schools in the village. In this village have one library this village. The Grama Panchayati providing five daily new papers and other magazines in the panchayati office and there is primary health centre in the village. Two RMPs are practitioner in the village. In case of emergency or chronic, people have to go to Tenali General Hospital , which is the nearest town to this village. At it is a private hospital, people may not afforded to get treatment at the high cost, so they need Government hospital near by the village. In that village had 144 self help groups. This village two major political parties such as Congress and Telugu Desam have notable presence. The village panchayat of Angalakuduru is divided into 14 wards. Out of 14 wards six wards are reserved for Scheduled Caste and three wards are reserved for BCs remaining eight wards are Other Castes. According to 73rd Constitutional Amendment Act 1993 in this panchayat sarpanch reserved for Scheduled Caste General In this village panchayat sarpanch is elected Dalit Women in this history of panchayat. So she belongs to Madiga Dalit Sub-Section.

Pedaravuru

Pedaravuru is one of the sample Village 3 km., from Tenali. Srirama Navami Celebrations are very popular in that village. Both the temples, Sivalayam and Ramalayam in this village are very famous. In this village total house holds is 1796. Total population of the village is 6959 of which 3438 members are male, 3321 members are female population respectively. The total Scheduled Caste population of the village is 2599 and 184 members are belongs to Scheduled Tribe (2001 Census).

The village is having four primary schools and one high schools in the village. In this village have one libraries is this village. The Grama Panchayati providing five daily new papers in the panchayati office. In that village had 140 self-help groups. This village two major political parties such as Congress and Telugu Desam have notable presence. The village panchayat of Pedaravuru is divided into 14 wards. Out of 14 wards five wards are reserved for Scheduled Caste, three wards are reserved for BCs remaining six wards are Other Castes. According to 73rd Constitutional Amendment Act 1993 in this panchayat sarpanch reserved for Other Caste General.

Nandivelugu

Nandivelugu is one of the sample village. This village is located on the road 4 kms., away to Tenali Mandal head quarter. Among the house holds in the village is 1712. Total population of the village is 6662 of which 3321 members are male, 3321 members are female population respectively. The total Scheduled Caste population of the village is 1239 and 136 members are belongs to Scheduled Tribe are ST population (2001 Census).

The village is having four primary schools and one high school in the village. In this village have one libraries is this village. The Grama Panchayati providing five daily new papers in the panchayati office. In that village had 135 self-help groups. This village two major political parties such as Congress and Telugu Desam have notable presence. BJP and CPM parties only play on impressive role in the village politics. The village panchayat of Nandivelugu is divided into 14 wards. Out of 14 wards two wards are reserved for Scheduled Caste, two wards are reserved for Scheduled Tribe and two wards are reserved for BCs remaining seven wards are Other Castes. According to 73rd Constitutional Amendment Act 1993 in this panchayat sarpanch reserved for Scheduled Caste General. In this village first Dalit Women sarpanch elected in the history of panchayat. So he belongs to Mala Dalit Sub-Section.

Sangam Jagarlamudi

Located between Tenali and Guntur, is famous for its Lord Sangameswara Swamy (Siva) temple and Lemon crop. In this village total house holds is 1416. Total population of the village is 5506 of which 2705 members are male, 2801 members are female population respectively. The total Scheduled Caste population of the village is 627 and 224 members are belongs to Scheduled Tribe (2001 Census).

In this village is having milk diary form namely sangam diary and also having primary health centre. The village is having four primary schools and one high schools in the village. In this village have one libraries is this village. The Grama Panchayati providing five daily new papers in the panchayati office. In that village had 101 self-help groups. This village two major political parties such as Congress and Telugu Desam have notable presence. The village panchayat of Sangam Jagarlamudi is divided into 14 wards. According to 73rd Constitutional Amendment Act 1993 in this panchayat sarpanch reserved for Other Caste General.

Katevaram

Located at 2 km., from Tenali is famous for Lord Shiva temple built in 10th century and renovated during the Vijayanagara period and recently in 2009. Paddy, Turmeric and Lentils are the main crops harvested each year in this village. In this village total house holds is 1307. Total population of the village is 4991 of which 2501 members are male, 2490 members are female population respectively. The total Scheduled Caste population of the village is 2453 and 27 members are belongs to Scheduled Tribe (2001 Census).

The village is having four primary schools. In this village one library is available to all villages. The Grama Panchayati providing five daily new papers in the panchayati office. In that village had 111 self-help groups. This village has two major political parties such as Congress and Telugu Desam have notable presence. The village panchayat of Sangam Jagarlamudi is divided into 14 wards. According to 73rd Constitutional Amendment Act 1993 in this panchayat sarpanch reserved for Other Caste General.

6 RESEARCH METHODOLOGY

Dalit ('oppressed' or 'broken') is not a new word. Apparently it was used in the 1930's as a Hindi and Marathi translation of 'depressed classes'. The British used this term for what are now called the scheduled caste. Dr. Ambedkar chose the term 'broken men', as English translation of 'Dalit', to refer to the original ancestors of the untouchables. Dalit Panthers, the youth activists from Dalit community revived the term and in their 1973 manifesto expanded its reference to include the scheduled tribes, neo Buddhists, the working people, the landless and poor peasants, women and also those who are being exploited politically, economically in the name of religion (Omvedt cited in Webster, J, 1999).

Dalit Women

Dalit women are one of the most marginalized segments in the society. The condition of dalit women is more vulnerable than non-dalit women. Dalit women are suffering from multi-disadvantages:

(a) Being Dalit *i.e.,* socio-economically and culturally marginalized section.

(b) Being women and sharing the gender-based inequalities and sub-ordination Jogdand, 1995).

To explore these and other crucial issues concerning Dalit women there is a need to discuss some basic facts concerning the vulnerable situation of Dalit women. The Dalit women have to grapple with the discrimination due to the caste hierarchy and untouchability on the one hand and extreme economic deprivation and poverty on the other coupled with political, legal and religion-cultural discrimination. Dalit women continue to be illiterate, malnourished, in poor health, overworked, oppressed and victimised by a number of factors, including their own family and community. They make up the substance of the body of research, knowledge and information in the country displaying the poorest social indicators, dismal social and economic achievement. They lack access to resources including the natural resources they work with every day, although their labour enriches their masters.

Dalit women in India constitute 80 million or 48 per cent of the total Dalit population, 16.3 per cent of the total female population in India. 81.5 per cent of Dalit women live in rural areas. They, along with their male counterparts, constitute a sizeable social group-based discrimination and untouchability arising out of the caste system. Dalit women are particularly discriminated on the basis of their caste (which is lower than others – outcaste) poverty and gender. There are about 250 million Dalits in India. There is meager improvement in the socio-economic condition of Dalits in the past 50 years, which is not enough when compared to non-Dalits. Of course, much more needs to be done. The urgent need is to have a national sample survey on Dalits. Every fourth Indian is a dalit. There is no proper survey to give the correct number of Dalit women in India.

Socio-Cultural and Religious Factors

First and foremost Dalit women are victims of social, religious and cultural practices like: Devdasis and Jogins. In the name of these practices, village girls are married to God by their helpless parents. These girls are then sexually exploited by the upper caste landlords and rich men and directed into trafficking and prostitution. In his autobiography, Kale (1994) has described a ritual called 'chira'. The literal meaning of the word 'chira', is to cut or break. In this ritual when a girl from the lower caste community reaches the age of puberty, an elderly prestigious man from the higher caste breaks the hymen of the girl child by sexual act. This ritual is performed in a way to make the girl accept this fact as a routine practice. The 28th report of SC/ST commission reported that in February 1986 there were about ten thousand Jogins belonging to SC in Nizamabad district of Andhra Pradesh. The survey submitted by the district collector to Schedule Caste Finance Corporation revealed prevalence of 15,850 cases. Eighty per cent of these Jogins belonged to SC (Pal and Bhargav, 1999). This data is just an example of one district of the country. Practices such as Chira, Jogins, Devdasi which are prevalent even today are harmful and threaten the dignity of dalit women and violate their human rights (P. Sainath, 2003).

Dalit women not only grapple with the discrimination due to caste hierarchy and untouchability but they live in poverty coupled with political, legal and religio-cultural discrimination. Access to resources such as: land, water is out of reach to these women. Henceforth, Dalit women end up working as bonded agricultural labourers with low/under paid wages, inspite of their knowledge and skills in farming. The extreme perennial economic deprivation has also resulted in illiteracy, malnourishment, poor health conditions, besides this they are also overworked, oppressed and victimized by a number of factors, including patriarchal attitude within the family and community.

Dalit Women as Manual Scavengers

Thousands of women manual scavengers are forced to earn their living through scavenging, cleaning dry latrines, by using metal pans and a short broom to scoop up the night soil. The excreta is carried in baskets on their heads. The dehumanized practice has killed dignity of women at the same time these women believe that without this job they will be nowhere to their livelihoods.

Economic Deprivation of Dalit Women

Dalit Women are the most economically deprived section of Indian society.

- Dalit women labour force constitutes the backbone of Indian agriculture economy.
- 71 per cent of them are agricultural labourers.
- 90 per cent were cultivators (1991).
- 32.40 per cent of the household sector and large number of them employed in unorganized labour in urban areas.
- A large number of them employed in unclean occupation.
- They are denied just and equal wages, fair-share in economic distribution, maternity benefits, the security and protection.
- All most all the Dalit women enter the labour market before the age of 20.
- 31.6 of all girl children from Dalit communities are child labourers in Guntur District – Andhra Pradesh.

Dalit Women as Victims of Caste Hierarchy and Atrocities

Dalit Women's day-to-day struggle is one of existence, survival and justice. The everyday discrimination is dotted by mental and physical violence. Eternally, the principles of 'high and low', 'purity and pollution' has not left any scope for changing Dalit women's status. Thus any move by Dalit women to question the system, or challenge inequality to change the life situation has resulted in retaliation with abuses such as: beating, rape, naked parading, labeled as witches and harassed for murder. This further implicates in punishing the whole community by burning of houses, destruction of properties, valuables, crops etc. The crux of the Dalit Women's struggles for survival is rooted in her being at the lowest rung of the Caste hierarchy.

In this context the study would like to find out or inquiring into the over all development of Dalit women after independence. The study also examines how best the Dalit – Women have covered in the inclusive policy of the Government of India. The Review of literature, Objectives and Methodology of the study as follows.

Objectives of the Study

1. To study the improvement of Socio-Economic and Political conditions of the Dalit Women in Rural Area.
2. To study the Educational and Health aspects of the Dalit Women in Rural Area.
3. To study the impact of Developmental Programmes on the Dalit Women in Rural Area.
4. To make necessary suggestions for effective Empowerment of Dalit Women in Rural Area.

Hypotheses

1. Most of the Dalit Women are Poor.
2. Poor Dalit Women are Illiterates.
3. Most of the Dalit Women have less knowledge on Government Schemes.
4. Poor Dalit Women have less participation in Self-Help Groups (SHGs).
5. Poor Dalit Women have exposed to more Health Problems.

Area of the Study

The researcher wanted to study around 300 Dalit women of Six villages in the Tenali Mandal of Guntur District in Andhra Pradesh. The researcher selected the list on the basis of simple random sample survey. The list of the Scheduled Caste families was picked up from the Grama Panchayat Office. As the most of the Dalit women in the villages are illiterate, the researcher analysed them about the subject undertaken by him. On the bases of respondents' answers the questionnaire was filled.

Variables

As Dalit women are most down trodden in societal hierarchy, so researcher wanted to verify certain variables like: Poverty, Education, Socio-economic and political aspects, equality of life, Economic dependency, household circumstances and living conditions etc.

Research Design

To explore this study on Status of Dalit Women in Rural Area a tool descriptive research design was used.

Sampling

In this study the Research/Investigator selected 300 sample respondents in six villages by using a simple random sampling method. The selected villages are having significant proportion of socially disadvantaged group like: SCs, STs, BCs and other upper castes.

Tools for the Study

In this study the structured interview schedule consisting of 128 questions have prepared to measure the empowerment of Dalit women in Socio-Economic, educational and Political areas. Successful case studies of the groups of SHGs have also carriedout in this study to know how they are more successful than other groups.

Data Collection

The material required for the study was collected through primary and secondary source. The primary data was collected from respondent in the field survey. The techniques have used to collect the data like Interview schedule, discussion and participant observation to avoid ethnocentrism. A secondary source of Data was collected among the various official records in the villages and mandal level.

(A) Primary Sources

Primary data was taken from the 300 respondents of Dalit women by canvassing interview schedule. The Investigator directly interviewed all the respondents to enquiry about their socio-economic-political and educational, health and development programmes of Dalit women.

(B) Secondary Sources

A secondary source of Data was collected among the various official records. The secondary sources constitutes the studies conducted on Dalit women was taken and the data given by these studies also support this present study. The data collected in previous studies have also made use in this study. The information from the records in Mandal offices on dalit women have be gathered to emphasis this study. The study uses extensively the relevant secondary data available these sources consist of books, journals, Magazines, Reports prepared government agencies, Universities, Research institutions, NGOs and News papers... etc.

Field Work

For the field work, the scholar made visits according the suitable time of the Dalit women to collect the information. It was a difficult task for the scholar to fix to take interview with each respondent as all of them are going for work for their livelihood. So the investigator used to get the appointments in the early morning and evenings only. The scholar has collected the data for the present study in between the months of June 2010 to Nov-2010.

Pre-Test

The Interview schedule was pre-tested on 25 Dalit women and necessary modifications were made in the Interview schedule *i.e.,* regarding the personal, social, economic and political and various factors influencing for obstraction of their development. With the contribution of pre-test respondents some modification have made in the final interview schedule.

Scheme for the Study

The study is presented in Ten – chapters. Chapter – I Deals with Introduction. Chapter – II Deals with The Status of Women in India, Chapter – III Deals with Dalits and Dalit Women. In Chapter – IV Deals with Reviews of Literature. Profile of the study area presented in Chapter – V. Research Methodology deals with Chapter – VI. Data Interpretations and data analysis of the sample respondents deals with Chapter – VII. In Chapter – VIII deals with Results and Discussion of the sample respondents. Chapter – IX deals with Case Studies and Chapter X deals with Concluding Findings and Suggestions.

Data Interpretation and Data Analysis

In this study, univariate and bivariate tables had been prepared. Graphical representation, bar diagrams and pie diagrams have been made. The research/investigator have also used the SPSS package in this study.

7 DATA INTERPRETATION AND DATA ANALYSIS OF THE SAMPLE RESPONDENTS

Table 7.1, discussed Personal profile of the respondents. The data on Dalit Sub-Section of the respondents. Out of 300 sample respondents, 98 respondents *i.e.* 32.7 per cent are found from Mala Sub-Caste, followed by 193 respondents *i.e.* 64.3 per cent of them belong to Madiga Dalit sub-section and only meager *i.e.* 9 respondents which is about 3.0 per cent from Other Communities of Dalit sub-sections. The majority *i.e.* 41.6 per cent of the respondents are found in between 31-40 years of age group and followed by 32.0 per cent in between of the 41-50 years of age group, 22.6 per cent from 21-30 years of age group and only remaining 3.6 per cent are from less than the 20 years of age group respondents had been found. The data also revealed that the majority of the respondents *i.e.* 99.3 per cent are from Hindu religion and 0.7 per cent respondents are from Christian.

It is understood that the majority of the respondents have married *i.e.* 90.7 per cent, 7.7 per cent have Unmarried and only very meager *i.e.* 1.7 per cent were Widows. The data also revealed that the major chunck of the respondents *i.e.* 44.7 per cent have illiterates followed by Primary, Secondary, Inter, Degree.. Etc *i.e.* 18.7 per cent, 15.3 per cent, 10.3 per cent, 11.0 per cent from the total respondents. The data on annual income shows that the highest respondents *i.e.* 40.7 per cent are reported to be earning more than above Rs. 20,001/- and 34.3 per cent of the respondents annual income is in between

Table 7.1: Personal profile of the respondents

Variables	Frequency	Percentage
Dalit Sub-Section		
Mala	98	32.7
Madiga	193	64.3
Others	9	3.0
Age		
< - 20	11	3.7
21 - 30	68	22.6
31 - 40	125	41.6
41 - 50	96	32.0
Religion		
Hindu	298	99.3
Christian	2	.7
Marital Status		
Unmarried	23	7.6
Married	272	90.7
Widow	5	1.7
Educational Level		
Illiterates	134	44.7
Primary	56	18.7
Secondary	46	15.3
Inter	31	10.3
Graduate	33	11.0
Annual Income (in Rupees)		
< 5000	2	.7
5001 - 10000	21	7.0
10001 - 15000	17	5.7
15001 - 20000	103	34.3
20001 - >	122	40.7
Not Applicable	35	11.7

Note: N = 300

Source: Primary data

Rs. 15,001-20,000/-, 11.7 per cent of the respondents revealed that their annual income is not applicable, they are just house wives, 7.0 per cent of the respondents annual income is in between Rs. 5,001-10,000/-, 5.7 per cent of the respondents annual income in between Rs. 10,001-15,000/-. And only very meager *i.e.* 0.7 per cent of the respondents annual income falls less than Rs. 5000/-.

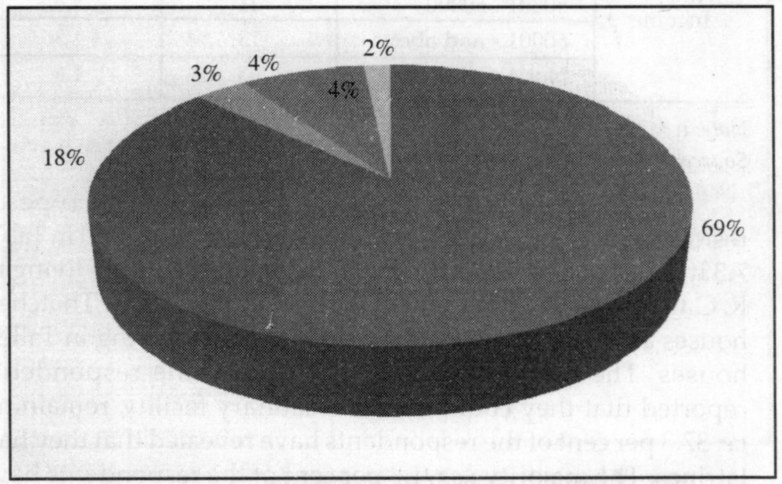

Fig. 7.1: Shows the Head of the Family Annual Income of the Respondents

Table 7.2 shows that the Head of the family annual income of the sample respondents. The majority 68.6 per cent of the respondents reported that their head of the family income is in between Rs. 20000-30000, followed by 18.3 per cent, 3.3 per cent, 3.6 per cent, 4.3 per cent, and 1.6 per cent of the respondents have revealed that their head of the family annual income is in between Rs. 300001-40000, Rs. 40001-50000, Rs. 50001-60000 and more than Rs. 60001 of the sample respondents. Among the 1.6 per cent of the respondents are revealed that they did not have applicable to the above all groups of annual income of the head of the family they may be widows.

Table 7.2: The table shows the head of the family annual income of the respondents

Variables Annual Income (in Rupees)		Frequency	Percentage
Head of the Family Annual Income	20000 - 30000	206	68.6
	30001 - 40000	55	18.3
	40001 - 50000	10	3.3
	50001 - 60000	11	3.6
	60001 - and above	13	4.3
	Not Applicable	5	1.6

Note: n = 300,
Source: Primary data

The distribution of the respondents by the type of residential accommodation and variable have presented in Table 7.3 It is found that 52.0 per cent of the respondents are living in R. C. C., houses; 42.3 per cent of the respondents in the Thatched houses and 5.7 per cent of the respondents are living in Tailed houses. The majority *i.e.* 62.7 per cent of the respondents reported that they could not have sanitary facility, remaining *i.e.* 37.3 per cent of the respondents have revealed that they had latrines. The majority *i.e.* 91.3 per cent of the respondents have reported that they are living as Nuclear family, while 8.0 per cent of the respondents have expressed that they are living with joint family, and very few reported to be *i.e.* 0.7 per cent of the respondents have told that they are living with extended family.

The Size of the family of respondents, it is found that the majority 74.0 per cent of the respondents the size of the family was in between 4-7 members. 18.3 per cent of the respondents were reported and the size of the family was in between 1-3 members, 7.3 per cent of the respondents have noticed that their size of the family is above 8 members. The majority of *i.e.* 56.0 per cent of the respondents occupation was presented that they are agricultural labourer; followed by the 7.7 per cent, 11.3 per cent, 2.3 per cent, 11.0 per cent 11.7 per cent of the respondents have informed that they are non-agricultural – labour, employed, business, any other, house wife of their occupation.

Table 7.3: The table showing the nature of house , sanitary facility, nature of family, size of family and occupation

S. No.	Variables	Frequency	Percentage
1.	Nature of House		
	RCC	156	52.0
	Tailed	17	5.7
	Thatched	127	42.3
2.	Sanitary Facility		
	Yes	112	37.3
	No	188	62.77
3.	Nature of Family		
	Joint family	24	8.0
	Nuclear Family	274	91.3
	Extended Family	2	0.7
4.	Size of Family		
	1-3	55	18.3
	4-7	223	74.3
	8 and >	22	7.3
5.	Occupation		
	Agricultural labour	168	56.0
	Non-Agricultural labour	23	7.7
	Employed	34	11.3
	Business	7	2.3
	House Wife	35	11.7
	Any other	33	11.0

Note: n = 300, *Source*: Primary data

Table 7.4: Table showing respondents age-*vs*-dalit women

Variables		Dalit-Sub-Section			Total
		Mala	Madiga	Others	
Age	< 20	4(4,1%)	7(3.6%)	0(.0%)	11(3.7%)
	21 - 30	17(17.3%)	49(25.4%)	2(22.2%)	68(22.7%)
	31 - 40	44(44.9%)	76(39.4%)	5(55.6%)	125(41.5%)
	41 - 50	33(33.7)	61(31.6%)	2(22.2%)	96(32.0%)
	Total	**98(100.0%)**	**193(100.0%)**	**9(100.0%)**	**300(100.0%)**

$X^2 = 3.501$, df = 6, $P < 0.744$, Not Significant

Figures in parenthesis indicate percentage

Source: Primary data

Data from Table 7.4 shows that the Age of the respondents and Dalit Sub-Section. It was found from Table 7.4 that 41.5 per cent of the respondents are in the age group of in between 31-40, while 32.0 per cent of the respondents are in the age groups of in between 41-50, followed by the 22.7 per cent, 3.7 per cent of the respondents are in the age group are in between 21-30, and less than 20 years of age group of the sample respondents.

Table 7.4 also shows that the age and Dalit sub-section of the respondents out of 300 respondents 98 respondents belongs to Mala Dalit sub section which is about 44.9 per cent of the respondents are in the age group between 31-40 years, followed by 33.7 per cent of the respondents are in the age group between 41-50, followed by 17.3 per cent, 4.1 per cent of the respondents are in the age group between 21-30 and less than 20 years of the respondents are in the same sub-section. A major *chunk i.e.* 193 respondents have informed that they are from the Madiga Dalit sub-section of the total respondents, out of which 39.4 per cent of the respondents are in the age group of in between 31-40, followed by 31.6, per cent, 3.6 per cent of the respondents are in the age group of in between 41-50, 21-30 and less than 20 years age of the respondents have found from the same sub section. Out of 300 respondents 9 respondents are from the other community of Dalit Sub-section, out of which 55.6 per cent of the respondents are in the age groups of in between 31-40. Among them 22.2 per cent of the respondents have found in the age group of in between 41-50, and in the same *i.e.* 22.2 per cent of the respondents are have found in the age group of in between 21-30. The generated chi-square value 3.501 is found to be not significant, because it is less than the table value. As per the statistical calculation there is no significant association in between the age of the respondents and the Dalit Sub-Section.

Table 7.5 shows that the Occupation of the Dalit Women of the respondents. The majority 56.0 per cent of the respondents reported that their occupation is agricultural labour, followed by 7.7 per cent, 11.3 per cent, 2.3 per cent, 11.7 per cent, 11.0 per cent of the respondents have noticed that their occupation is non-agricultural labour, employed, business, house wife of the Dalit women.

Table 7.5: Table showing occupation *vs.* dalit women of the respondents

Variables		Dalit-Sub-Section			Total
		Mala	Madiga	Others	
Occupation	Agricultural labour	55(56.1%)	108(56.0%)	5(55.6%)	168(56.0%)
	Non-Agricultural labour	9(9.2%)	13(6.7%)	1(11.1%)	23(7.7%)
	Employed	8(8.2%)	25(13.0%)	1(11.1%)	34(11.3%)
	Business	4(4.1%)	3(1.3%)	0(0%)	7(2.3%)
	House Wife	13(13.3%)	22(11.4%)	0(0%)	35(11.7%)
	Any Other	9(9.2%)	22(11.4%)	2(22.2%)	33(11.0 %)
	Total	**98(100.0%)**	**193(100.0%)**	**9(100.0%)**	**300(100.0%)**

$X^2 = 6.593$; df = 10; $P < 0.076$; Not Significant
Figures in parenthesis indicate percentage
Source: Primary data

It can be seen from Table 7.5 that the occupation of the respondents among the different sub-castes from the Dalit Women, out of 300 respondents 98 respondents belongs to Mala Dalit sub-section of which 56.1 per cent of the respondents have reported that their occupation is as agricultural labour. Whereas 9.2 per cent of the respondents reveal that their occupation is non-agricultural labour, followed by 8.2 per cent, 4.1 per cent 9.2 per cent, 13.3 per cent of the respondents reported that their occupation is employed, business, house wives and any other work of the respondents.

Of the total sample 193 respondents are from Madiga Dalit sub-section of which 56.0 per cent of the respondents have informed that their occupation is agricultural labour. Among them 6.7 per cent of the respondents are reported that their occupation is non-agricultural labour, followed by the 13.0 per cent, 1.3 per cent, 11.4 per cent, 11.4 per cent of the respondents that their occupations are employed, business, house wives and any other work. It is noticed that the other community of the Dalit sub-section, out of 300 respondents 9 respondents have found out of which 55.6 per cent of the respondents have revealed that their occupation is agricultural labour, followed by 11.1 per cent, 11.1 per cent, 22.2 per cent of the respondents reported that their occupation is non-agricultural, employed, house wives and any other work of the respondents. The generated chi-squire value 6.593 is found to be not significant, because it is less than the table value. This indicates that there is no significant association in between Occupation of the respondents and the Dalit Sub-Section.

Table 7.6 shows that the annual income of Dalit Women. It is evident that majority *i.e.* 40.7 per cent of the respondents are reported that their annual income is more than Rs. 20,001. Whereas 34.3 per cent of the respondents reported that their annual income is in between Rs. 15,001-20,000, As regards to 11.7 per cent of the respondents have noticed that they did not applicable to annual income may be because they are house wives, followed by 7.0 per cent, 5.7 per cent, 0.7 per cent of the respondents noticed that their annual income is in between Rs. 5,001-10,000, Rs. 10,001-15,000, and less than Rs. 5000 rupees of the sample respondents.

Table 7.6: Table showing respondent's annual income *vs* dalit women

Variables		Dalit-Sub-Section			Total
		Mala	Madiga	Others	
Annual Income	< - 5000	1(1.0%)	1(.5%)	0(.0%)	2(.7%)
	5001 - 10000	7(7.1%)	8(4.1%)	6(66.7%)	21(7.0%)
	10001 - 15000	2(2.0%)	12(6.2%)	3(33.3%)	17(5.7%)
	15001 - 20000	44(44.9%)	59(30.6%)	0(.0%)	103(34.3%)
	20001 - >	38(38.8%)	84(43.5%)	0(.0%)	122(40.7%)
	Not Applicable	6(6.1%)	29(15.0%)	0(.0%)	35(11.7%)
	Total	**98(100.0%)**	**193(100.0%)**	**9(100.0%)**	**300(100.0%)**

$X^2 = 250.716$; df = 10; $P < 0.000$, 0.5% Significant

Figures in Parenthesis indicate Percentage

Source: Primary data

Table 7.6 also shows that the annual income of the respondents in the different sub-caste from Dalit women. Out of the 300 respondents 98 respondent reported that they belong to Mala Dalit sub-section, of which 44.9 per cent of the respondents have reported that their annual income is in between Rs. 15,001-20,000 whereas 38.8 per cent of the respondents are reported that their annual income is more than Rs. 20001. Followed by 7.1 per cent, 6.1 per cent, 2.0 per cent, 1.0 per cent of the respondents reveals that their annual income is between Rs. 5,001-10,000, Not applicable, Rs. 10001-15000, and less than Rs. 5000. Regarding Madiga dalit sub-section of the total sample 193 respondents have found and out of which 43.5 per cent of the respondents annual income is more than Rs. 20001. It is noticed that 30.6 per cent of the respondents annual income is between Rs. 15001-20000, whereas 15 per cent of the respondents are not applicable to annual income as they are house wives, followed by 6.2 per cent, 4.1 per cent, 0.5 per cent of the respondents annual income is in between Rs. 10,001-15000, Rs. 5,001-10,000 and less than Rs. 5,000 rupees. Among the other community of the Dalit sub sections out of 300 respondents only 9 respondents have found, of which 66.7 per cent of the sample respondent's annual income is in between Rs. 5001-10000, remaining 33.3 per cent of the respondents annual income is in between Rs. 10001-15000 rupees. Generated the Chi-Square table value 250.716 is found to be significant it is more than the table value. The statistical calculation indicates that there is a significant association in between Annual Income of the respondents and of the Dalit Sub-Section. The hypothesis formulated in this study as to findout the association of the development of Dalit Women and economic background is proved to be true as the chi-square statistical results are proved to be significant.

Table 7.7 shows that the nature of the house the respondents are living and Dalit Women. Of the total respondents majority *i.e.* 52.0 per cent of the respondents have reported that they are living in RCC houses, where as 42.3 per cent of the respondents revealed that they are living in Thatched houses and remaining 5.7 per cent of the respondents have noticed that they are in Tiled houses.

Table 7.7: The table shows the nature of house and dalit women of the respondents

Variables		Dalit-Sub-Section			Total
		Mala	Madiga	Others	
Nature of the House	RCC	59(60.2%)	97(50.3%)	0(0.0%)	156(52.0%)
	Tiled	7(7.1%)	9(4.7%)	1(11.1%)	17(5.7%)
	Thatched	32(32.7%)	87(45.1%)	8(88.9%)	127(42.3%)
	Total	**98(100.0%)**	**193(100.0%)**	**9(100.0%)**	**300(100.0%)**

$X^2 = 14.372$ df = 4; $P < 0.006$ significant
Figures in parenthesis indicate percentages
Source: Primary data

It was also revealed that the nature of residence and of the different Dalit sub-section of the respondents. Out of 300 respondents 98 respondents belongs to Mala Dalit sub-section out of which 60.2 per cent of the respondents are reported that their nature of house is RCC houses. Among the 32.7 per cent of the respondents revealed that their nature of house Thatched houses and remaining 7.1 per cent of the respondents have noticed that their nature of house Tiled houses. Regarding Madiga Dalit subsection, out of the total 300 respondents 193 respondents have found, of which 50.3 per cent of the respondents nature house was RCC, followed by 45.1 per cent, 4.7 per cent of the respondents have noticed that their nature of house was Thatched and Tiled. As regards to the other community it is very meager *i.e.* 9 respondents have found to be of which 88.9 per cent of the respondent presented that their nature of house was Thatched, and remaining 11.1 per cent of the respondents are reported that their houses are tiled. The generated Chi-Square table value 14.372 is found to be not significant as it is less than table value. This indicates that there is no significant association is found in between the Nature of the house and Dalit Sub-Section.

Table 7.8 shows that the Assets of the sample respondents. Out of 300 respondents 270 respondents *i.e.* 90.0 per cent of the respondents reported that they have been living in their own house, followed by the 7.3 per cent, 2.6 per cent of the respondents have noticed that they had been living in rented and other houses. Of the total respondents 276 respondents which is about 92.0 per cent of the respondents reported that their house has been having electrification facility and remaining 8.0 per cent of the respondents have informed that their house is did not have electrification facility. Of the total respondents 280 respondents which is about 93.3 per cent of the respondents have reported that they have television and very meager *i.e.* 6.7 per cent of the respondents have noticed that they did not have television. Out of the 300 respondents 219 respondents, which is about 73.0 per cent of the respondents stated that they did not have any cycle, followed by the 20.3 per cent, 6.7 per cent of the respondents reported that they have cycle, and motor cycle. Of the total respondents 241 respondents, which is about 80.3 per cent of the respondents said that they have milk animals and remaining 19.7 per cent of the respondents have revealed that they did not have any milk animals.

Table 7.8: Table showing assets of the respondents

S. No.	Variables	Frequency	Percentage
1.	Status of home		
	Own	270	90.0
	Rented	22	7.3
	Other	8	2.6
2.	Your house electrification		
	Yes	276	92.0
	No	24	8.0
3.	Do you have Television		
	Yes	280	93.3
	No	20	6.7
4.	Do you have your family any cycle or motor cycle		
	Cycle	61	20.3
	Motor cycle	20	6.7
	Not cycles	219	73.0
5.	Do you have milk animals		
	Yes	59	19.7
	No	241	80.3

Note: n = 300, *Source* Primary data

Table 7.9 shows that the education of the Dalit Women and their sub section. It is observed that the 44.7 per cent of the respondents are reported to be illiterates. As regards to 18.7 per cent of the respondents have expressed that they studied upto primary education, followed by 15.3 per cent, 11.0 per cent, 10.3 per cent of the respondents have informed that they were educated upto Secondary, Intermediate and Graduate level of education of Dalit women.

Table 7.9: Table showing education *vs* dalit women of the respondents

Variables		Dalit-Sub-Section			Total
		Mala	Madiga	Others	
Education	Illiterate	42(42.9%)	84(43.5%)	8(88.9%)	134(44.7%)
	Primary	21(21.4%)	35(18.1%)	0(.0%)	56(18.7%)
	Secondary	15(15.3%)	31(16.1%)	0(.0%)	46(15.3%)
	Inter	13(13.3%)	18(9.3%)	0(.0%)	31(10.3%0
	Graduate	7(7.1%)	25(13.0%)	1(11.1%)	33(11.0%)
	Total	**98100.0%**	**193100.0%**	**9100.0%**	**300100.0%**

$X^2 = 11.555$; df = 8; $p < 0.172$ Not Significant
Figures in Parenthesis indicate percentages
Source: Primary data

To study across the total respondents 98 respondents have reported that they are belongs to Mala Dalit sub section, out of which 42.9 per cent of the respondents reported that they were illiterates. Whereas 21.4 per cent of the respondents reveal that their education level is primary, followed by 15.3 per cent, 13.3 per cent, 7.1 per cent of the respondents expressed that they have studied upto Secondary, Intermediate and Graduate level of education respectively. Regarding Madiga Dalit sub-section of the total respondents 193 have been found, out of which 43.5 per cent of the respondents have noticed that they have illiterates. Among 18.1 per cent of the respondents have revealed that they studied primary level of education. Across the total respondents, very meager 9 respondents have from other community of Dalit sub-section, out of which 88.9

per cent of the respondents are reported that they were illiterates and only 11.1 per cent of the respondents revealed that they studied upto Graduate level of education.

According to this study, it is revealed that a significant *i.e.* 44.7 per cent of total Dalit-Women and 42.9 per cent, 43.5 per cent, 88.9 per cent have reported from among the cross sections of Mala, Madiga and Other sub-section have found to be illiterates. So in this connection Government should take necessary action to improve the literacy level among the Dalit-Women.

Table 7.10 shows that the occupation and educational level of the respondents. Out of the 300 respondents 168 respondents have informed that they are working as agriculture labour under different education levels of which major *chunk i.e.* 122 have found from illiterates and the lowest only one respondent is found from graduate education. The highest *i.e.* 35 respondents from the total sample have reported as house wives in different educational background of which 14 respondents reported that they have studied upto secondary level and very low *i.e.* 4 respondents have reported to be illiterate.

Out of the total respondents 134 respondents have informed as illiterate and working in different occupation of which a major *chunk i.e.* 122 have reported which is about 91.0 per cent were agriculture labour and nil was found in the occupation of business. Out of the total respondents 56 respondents reported that they are from primary level of education and working in different occupation of which a majority revealed to be 35 *i.e.* 62.5 per cent respondents from agricultural labour and very meager *i.e.* 7.1 per cent of the respondents have found in the occupation is business. Of the total respondents 46 respondents have informed that they were upto secondary level of education and working in different occupations out of which 30.4 per cent of the respondents occupation reported to be house wives and only very meager *i.e.* 2.2 per cent of the respondents reported that

Table 7.10: Table showing occupation *vs* education of the respondents

Variables		Education					Total
		Illiterate	Primary	Secondary	Intermediate	Graduate	
Occupation	Agricultural labour	122(91.0%)	35(62.5%)	8(17.4%)	2(6.5%)	1(3.0%)	168(56.0%)
	Non-Agricultural labour	3(2.2%)	1(1.8%)	13(28.3%)	6(19.4%)	0(.0%)	23(7.7%)
	Employed	1(.7%)	3(5.4%)	3(6.5%)	8(25.8%)	19(57.6%)	34(11.3%)
	Business	0(.0%)	4(7.1%)	1(2.2%)	2(6.5%)	0(.0%)	7(2.3%)
	House Wife	4(3.0%)	5(8.9%)	14(30.4%)	6(19.4%)	6(18.2%)	35(11.7%)
	Any other	4(3.0%)	8(14.3%)	7(15.2%)	7(22.6%)	7(21.2%)	33(11.0%)
	Total	**134(100.0%)**	**56(100.0%)**	**46(100.0%)**	**31(100.0%)**	**33(100.0%)**	**300(100.0%)**

$X^2 = 250.716$, df = 20, $P < 0.000$ Significant 0.5%

Figures in Parenthesis indicate percentages

Source: Primary data

their occupation was business. Out of the total respondents, 31 respondents reported to be stuidied upto Intermediate and working in different occupations of which a major chunk reported to be *i.e.* 25.8 per cent employed in Government or Private sector, and followed by 22.6 per cent, 19.4 per cent, 19.4 per cent, 6.5 per cent, 6.5 per cent have reported to be other than the mentioned, housewives, Non-agriculture, agriculture and business. Out of 300 respondents 33 respondents have reported to be upto graduate level of education and they are working in different occupations of which 57.6 per cent have found to be employed and only 3.0 per cent of the respondents have reported that their occupation is agricultural labour. As generated in the chi-squire value 250.716 is found to be significant because it is more than table value. This indicates that there is a significant association between Education and Occupation. It also revealed the higher the illiterate and high percentage of agriculture labourers and at the same time it is noticed that those who studied upto graduation they could get employment either in the Government or private employment.

Table 7.11 shows that the awareness of the respondents on education, it is noticed from the data *i.e.* 93.3 per cent of the respondents were reported that their villages have the Government schools. 51.6 per cent of the respondents have revealed that they satisfied with standards of the education in the government schools. Of the total respondents 100 each *i.e.* 33.3 per cent have reported that 3 or 4 members of their family are studying in school and 80 respondents *i.e.* 26.6 per cent have informed that 5 of their family members are studying in school. As regards the environment of the school that 40 per cent have reported as good and 37.3 per cent have reported to be very good. In connection with awareness of reservation of seats in the educational institutions 66.3 per cent have reported to be they have got awareness and 39.7 per cent informed that they have no awareness. Highest percentages of respondents *i.e.* 99 per cent have informed to be encouraging for the education.

Table 7.11: Table showing awareness regarding educational facilities in the village of the respondents

S. No.	Variables	Frequency	Percentage
1.	Is there any Government School in your Village		
	Yes	280	93.3
	No	20	6.6
2.	Are you satisfied with standards of the education in the government school		
	Yes	155	51.6
	No	145	48.3
3.	Your Family Members studied/ Studying		
	1	10	3.3
	2	10	3.3
	3	100	33.3
	4	100	33.3
	More the 5	80	26.6
4.	What about your school environment		
	Very good	112	37.3
	Good	127	42.3
	Average	50	16.8
	Poor	11	3.7
5.	Awareness of reservation of the seats in educational institutions		
	Yes	199	66.3
	No	101	33.6
6.	Are you encouraging for education in your family members, relatives or neighbors		
	Yes	297	99.0
	No	3	1.0

Note: n = 300,
Source: Primary data

It can be seen from Table 7.12 that the opinion of the respondent on family status in relation of education. Majority *i.e.* 95.3 per cent of the respondents were reported that their family status has been increased through education. It is evident that 62.0 per cent of the respondents are reported to be equal status of the Dalit women with other women because of their education. The majority *i.e.* 75.3 per cent of the respondents reported that their personality development has improved through education. While 41.7 per cent of the respondents have noticed that they have acquiring knowledge through education and 56.3 per cent of the respondents informed that the earning capacity can be more because of education.

Table 7.12: The table shows the opinion of the respondents change regarding their family status through education

S. No.	Variables	Frequency	Percentage
1.	Status of your family increased		
	Yes	286	95.3
	No	14	4.7
2.	Equal status of dalit women with other women		
	Yes	186	62.0
	No	114	38.0
3.	Personal development		
	Yes	226	75.3
	No	74	24.7
4.	Acquiring Knowledge		
	Yes	125	41.7
	No	175	58.3
5.	Earning capacity can be more because of your education		
	Yes	131	43.7
	No	169	56.3
6.	Getting job through education		
	Yes	34	11.3
	No	266	88.7

Note: n = 300, *Source*: Primary data

Where as 88.7 per cent of the respondents were reported that they know they will be getting job through education. Only 11.3 per cent of the respondents revealed that they had got job through education.

It can be seen from Table 7.13 shows the utilisation of reservation that the majority *i.e.* 74.7 per cent of the respondents reported that their admission for education is not through the reservation, because they have lack of awareness on the reservation of seats of educational institutions, and remaining 25.3 per cent of the respondents reported that they have got admission for education through reservation. Out of 300 respondents 18 respondents which is about 6.0 per cent of the respondents revealed that they have got jobs through reservation facilities. Of the total respondents 282 respondents which is 94.0 per cent of the respondents reported that they have not utilised reservation facilities because they are illiterates and lack of awareness on reservation facilities. Through these figures it can be said lack of awareness of reservation provided by the constitution. They could not make use of the reservation facility in both educational institutions and jobs.

Table 7.13: Table shows reservation facilities utilised by respondents

S. No.	Variables	Frequency	Percentage
1.	Admission for education through reservation		
	Yes	76	25.3
	No	224	74.7
2.	Have you got job through reservation facilities		
	Yes	18	6.0
	No	282	94.0

Note: n = 300,
Source: Primary data

Table 7.14 shows that the educational facilities utilised for the jobs, the majority *i.e.* 87.3 per cent of the respondents are reported that they have not taken any type of free coaching providing by the government. Only 12.6 per cent of the respondents are revealed that they have taken free coaching for getting jobs in state government services. Out of 300 respondents 38 respondents, which is about 36.84 per cent of the respondents have reported that they had taken free coaching for Bank exams, followed by the 13.15 per cent, 5.26 per cent, 15.78 per cent, 26.31 per cent, 2.63 per cent of the respondents noticed that they had been taken free coaching for *i.e.* APPSC, DSC, SSC, RRB, Other exams of the sample respondents.

Table 7.14: Table shows the educational facilities utilised by the respondents

S. No	Variables	Frequency	Percentage
1.	Do you get benefit of any Government free coaching for getting job		
	Yes	38	12.6
	No	262	87.3
2.	What type of services n = 38		
	APPSC	5	13.15
	DSC	2	5.26
	SSC	6	15.78
	RRB	10	26.31
	Bank	14	36.84
	Other	1	2.63

n = 300, n = 38,
Source: Primary data

Table 7.15 shows that the education of the sample respondents and annual income. It is observed that 44.7 per cent of the respondents are reported to be illiterates and 18.7 per cent of the respondents have expressed that they studied upto primary education, followed by 15.3 per cent, 11.0 per cent, 10.3 per cent of the respondents have informed their education is Secondary, Intermediate and Graduate level of education of those Dalit women.

Table 7.15: The table shows education *vs* annual income of the respondents

Variable		Annual Income						Total
		< 5000	5001 - 10000	10001 - 15000	15001 - 20000	20001 >	Not Applicable	
Education	Illiterate	1(50.0%)	11(52.4%)	7(41.2%)	69(67.0%)	26(21.3%)	20(57.1%)	134(44.7%)
	Primary	1(50.0%)	5(23.8%)	3(17.6%)	19(18.4%)	23(18.9%)	5(14.3%)	56(18.7%)
	Secondary	0(.0%)	3(14.3%)	5(29.4%)	9(8.7%)	26(21.3%)	3(8.6%)	46(15.3%)
	Inter	0(.0%)	2(9.5%)	0(.0%)	2(1.9%)	23(18.9%)	4(11.1%)	31(10.3%)
	Graduate	0(.0%)	0(.0%)	2(11.8%)	4(3.9%)	24(19.7%)	3(8.6%)	33(11.3%)
	Total	**2(100.0%)**	**21(100.0%)**	**17(100.0%)**	**103(100.0%)**	**122(100.0%)**	**35(100.0%)**	**300(100.0%)**

$X^2 = 72.416$; df = 20; $p<0.000$, Significant 0.5%

Figures in Parenthesis indicate percentages,

Source: Primary data

Table 7.16 shows that the education of the respondent in the different annual income. Out of 300 respondents 2 respondents reported that their annul income is less than Rs. 5000, of which 50.0 per cent each of the respondents have noticed that their level of education is illiterates and primary. Regarding the annual income is in between Rs. 5001-10000 of the total respondents 21 respondents of which 52.4 per cent of the respondents are illiterates and 9.5 pre cent of the respondents are reported that their level of education is Intermediate. Among the annual income in between Rs. 10001-15000 of the sample respondents out of 300 respondents 17 respondents have noticed, of which 41.2 pre cent of the respondents are reported that they are illiterates, followed by 17.6 per cent, 29.4 per cent, 11.8 per cent of the respondents *i.e.* primary, secondary, graduate level of education respectively. Whereas the annual income is in between Rs. 15001-20000 of the total respondents 103 respondents have found, of which 67.0 per cent of the respondents are reported that their level of education is illiterates and very meager 1.9 per cent of the respondents revealed that their education upto Intermediate. It is noticed that the annual income is above Rs. 20,001, out of 300 respondents 122 respondents have found, of which 21.3 per cent of the respondents noticed that their education is illiterates and secondary, followed by 18.9 per cent, 19.7 per cent of the respondents presented that their education is primary, intermediate and graduates. Of the total respondents 35 respondents have not reported regarding to their annual income because they may be house wives. The calculated chi-square value is 72.416 is found to be significant because it is more than the table value. This indicates that there is a significant association between the education and annual income of the respondents. According to this table the higher the education, higher the income and almost nil have found in the lower income group *i.e.* > 5000 and in between 5001-10000. Most of them those who had higher education could be found in the higher income groups *i.e.* 19.7 per cent have from Rs. 20001 and above and at the same time the illiterates have found in all income groups.

Table 7.16: Awareness regarding health facilities in the village of the respondents

S. No.	Variables	Yes	No
1.	Any primary health centre is there in your village	291 (97.0%)	9 (3.0%)
2.	Any qualified MBBS doctors in your village	108 (36.0%)	192 (64.0%)
3.	Are you satisfied with the medical services in your village provided by Government	273 (91.0%)	27 (9.0%)
4.	Do you aware the help rendering by Government to pregnant women until the delivery in the Government hospitals	288 (96.0%)	12 (4.0%)
5.	Are you aware of nutrition food	277 (92.3%)	23 (7.7%)
6.	Do you know 108 medical ambulance services	300 (100.0%)	–
7.	Do you know about 104 medical mobile services for your village	300 (100.0%)	–
8.	Do you know about Rajeev Arogyasri Scheme	288 (96.0%)	12 (4.0%)
9.	Are you aware about HIV/AIDS	297 (99.0%)	3 (1.0%)

Note: n = 300,
Source: Primary data

Table 7.16 explains about the awareness of health facilities provided by the Government in the village. It is evident from the table that about 97.0 per cent of the respondents were reported that the villages having primary health centres and 64.0 per cent of the respondents have informed that there are having no qualified M.B.S.S Doctors in their primary health centres. As regards 91.0 per cent of the respondents have revealed that they have satisfied with the medical services providing by the government in there villages. The Majority *i.e.* 96.0 per cent of the respondents are noticed that they have awareness about the help rendering by government to the pregnant women for the delivery in the government hospital. About 92.3 per cent of the respondents have said that they had awareness about the nutrition food. While 100 per cent of the respondents have stated that they are aware about 108 and 104 medical services in their villages provided by the government. These services have been providing by the Government of Andhra Pradesh for any emergencies in every village. The patient will be picked up by just telephone call to the nearest primary health centre.

As regards to 96.0 per cent of the respondents have revealed that they had knowledge about the Rajeev Arogyasri scheme, remaining 4.0 per cent of the respondents did not aware about Rajeev Arogyasri scheme. The majority 99.0 per cent of the respondents have reported that they have awareness about HIV/AIDS. By and large the results of the study provide that the Dalit Women had good awareness on medical facilities provided by the Government.

Whether the respondents had utilised health facilities or not was presented in Table 7.17. Out of 300 respondents 267 respondents, which is about 89.0 per cent of the respondents stated that they have undergone family planning. Of the total respondent 33 respondents which is about 11.0 per cent of the respondents have reported that they did not undergo family planning. Further it is observed that 88.7 per cent of the respondents families are having Rajeev Arogyasree cards.

Table 7.17: Table showing government provisions of health facilities utilised by the respondents

S. No.	Variables	Yes	No
1.	Have you undergone family planning	267(89.0%)	33(11.0%)
2.	Do your family got Rajeev Arogyasri Card	266(88.7%)	34(11.3%)
3.	Any member in your family get treated under Rajeev Arogyasri Scheme	27(9.0%)	273(91.0%)

Note: n = 300
Source: computed field survey

The majority 91.0 per cent of the respondents have reported that they did not get the treatment under Rajeev Arogyasree scheme. It should be noted here that though they have Rajeev Arogyasree card, they could not made use of them as they may not know the procedure.

It is found from Table 7.18 that the awareness level of the respondents on Primary Health centre in their village. Out of 300 respondents 291 respondents are reported that they had awareness about the primary health centre in their village, out of which 44.3 per cent of them illiterates respondents have reported that they had awareness about the primary health centre in their village, followed by the 19.2 per cent, 14.8 per cent, 10.7 per cent, 11.0 per cent of the respondents revealed that they had awareness about the primary health centre in their village at primary, secondary, intermediate, graduate level education respectively. Out of total respondents, only 9 respondents have reported that they did not aware about the primary health centre in their villages of which 55.6 per cent of the respondents were from illiterate group, where as 33.3 per cent of them were from secondary level of education. Calculated the chi-squire table value. 4.893 is found to be not significant because it is less than the table value. This indicates that there is no significant association between level of education and knowledge on primary health centre in their villages.

Table 7.18: Table showing awareness evel of the respondents *vs* on primary health centre in the village

Variables		Any Primary Health Centre in your Village		Total
		Yes	No	
Education	Illiterate	129(44.3%)	5(55.6%)	134(44.7%)
	Primary	56(19.2%)	0(.0%)	56(18.7%)
	Secondary	43(14.8%)	3(33.3%)	46(15.3%)
	Inter	31(10.7%)	0(.0%)	31(10.3%)
	Graduate	32(11.0%)	1(11.1%)	33(11.0%)
	Total	**291(100.0%)**	**9(100.0%)**	**300(100.0%)**

$X^2 = 4.893$; df = 4; $P < 0.298$ Not significant
Figures in Parenthesis indicate Percentage
Source: Primary data

Table 7.19 shows that the level of education and the family planning of the respondents. It is observed among the total respondents that in 44.7 per cent of them are illiterates, 18.7 per cent of the respondents reported that they have studied upto primary education, followed by 15.3 per cent, 11.0 per cent, 10.3 per cent of the respondents have informed their education is Secondary, Intermediate and Graduate level of education of the respondents respectively.

Table 7.19: Table showing education level of the respondents *vs* family planning

Variables		Have you undergone Family Planning		Total
		Yes	No	
Education	Illiterate	130(48.7%)	4(12.1%)	134(44.7%)
	Primary	53(19.9%)	3(9.1%)	56(18.7%)
	Secondary	40(15.0%)	6(18.2%)	46(15.3%)
	Inter	25(9.4%)	6(18.2%)	31(10.3%)
	Graduate	19(7.1%)	14(42.4%)	33(11.0%)
	Total	**267(100.0%)**	**33(100.0%)**	**300(100.0%)**

$X^2 = 46.307$; df = 4; $p < 0.000$; 0.5% Significant

Figures in Parenthesis indicate Percentage

Source: Primary data.

Out of 300 respondents 267 respondents are reported that they had underwent the family planning of which majority of them have reported to be illiterate *i.e.* 48.7 per cent, followed by the 19.9 per cent, 15.0 per cent, 9.4 per cent, 7.1 per cent of the respondents have primary, secondary, intermediate, graduate educators reported to be undergone family planning respectively. Of the total respondents 33 respondents have reported that they did underwent family planning, of which 18.2 per cent, 18.2 per cent, 12.1 per cent, 9.1 per cent of the respondents have studied upto Secondary, intermediate, illiterates and primary education of the respondents have stated that they did not undergo family planning. Generated the chi-square table value 46.307 is found to be a significant because it is more than table value. This indicates that there is a significant association between level of education and undergone family planning of respondents.

It is interested to note that higher the education of the respondents *i.e.* graduation have undergone family planning and less percentage *i.e.* 7.1 per cent and the highest percentage *i.e.* 48.7 of respondents have reported that they have illiterates and had undergone family planning. It made it as contradicting that the impression of public that the more of the illiterates and less undergone family planning. As they just believe that the god has given children and the same god will look after them. Another reason is that the less educated and poor are also have an impression that if they have more children, they will be looked after at their oldage. But in this study it is revealed that the both the impressions of above have proved to be irrelevant and the illiterates were in the forefront in under going family planning.

Distribution of the respondents by whether they have awareness about the HIV/AIDS to different Dalit Sub-Sections presented in Table 7.20. The majority 99.0 per cent of the respondents have revealed that they had awareness about the HIV/AIDS, remaining 1.0 per cent of the respondents have noticed that they did not awareness about the HIV/AIDS.

Table 7.20: Table showing awareness regarding HIV/AIDS *vs* dalit women

Variables		Dalit-Sub-Section			Total
		Mala	Madiga	Others	
Are you Aware about HIV/AIDS	Yes	98(100.0%)	190(98.4%)	9(100.0%)	297(99.0%)
	No	0(.0%)	3(1.6%)	0(.0%)	3(1.0%)
	Total	**98(100.0%)**	**193(100.0%)**	**9(100.0%)**	**300(100.0%)**

$X^2 = 1.680$; df = 2 $P < 0.432$ Not Significant

Figures in Parenthesis indicate Percentage

Note: n = 300,

Source: Primary data

Out of the 300 respondents 98 respondents belongs to Mala Dalit sub-section of which 100 per cent of the respondents reported that they had awareness about the HIV/AIDS. Of the total respondents 193 respondents belong to Madiga dalit sub-section of which 98.4 per cent of the respondents reported that they have awareness about the HIV and AIDS. And very meager *i.e.* 1.6 per cent of women stated that they did not aware about the HIV/AIDS. The 100 per cent of the Others of dalit sub-section said they had aware about the HIV/AIDS. Calculated the chi-squire table value. 1.680 is found to be not significant because it is less than table value. This indicates that there is no significant association between awareness about HIV/AIDS and Dalit Sub-Sections.

Table 7.21 shows that the nutrition food for pregnant women and Dalit women. 91.7 per cent of the total sample respondents are reported that Anganawadi centres have been providing the nutrition food for pregnant women and remaining 8.3 per cent of the respondents have revealed that the others giving nutrition food for pregnant women.

Table 7.21: Table showing nutrition food for pregnant women *vs* dalit women

Variables		Dalit-Sub-Section			Total
		Mala	Madiga	St	
Who give the nutrition food for pregnant women	Anganawadi	84 (85.7%)	182 (94.3%)	9 (100.0%)	275 (91.7%)
	Others	14 (14.3%)	11 (5.7%)	0 (.0%)	25 (8.3%)
	Total	**98 (100.0%)**	**193 (100.0%)**	**9 (100.0%)**	**300 (100.0%)**

X^2 = 7.116 df = 2 P<= 0.28 Not significant
Figures in Parenthesis indicate percentage
Note: n = 300,
Source: Primary data

Table 7.21 also shows that the nutrition food for pregnant women and Dalit sub-section. Out of 300 respondents 98 respondents belong to Mala Dalit sub-section of which 85.7

per cent of the respondents stated that the nutrition food had given by Anganawadi and 14.3 per cent of the respondents are noticed that the nutrition food had given by others. Of the total respondents 193 respondents belong to Madiga Dalit sub-section out of which 94.3 per cent of the respondents reported that the Anganawadi has been providing nutrition food for pregnant women and 5.7 per cent of the respondents reported that the nutrition food for pregnant women had been given by other than Anganawadi. Of the total respondents 9 respondents belongs to other community of dalit sub section of which 100 per cent of the respondents have revealed that the anganawadi has been given nutrition food for pregnant women. Calculated the chi-square table value 7.116 it is found to be not significant because it is less than the table value. There is no significant association between nutrition food for pregnant women and Dalit Sub-Section.

Table 7.22: Table showing the levels of education *vs* satisfaction with medical services provided by government to the respondents in the village

Variables		Are you Satisfied with the Medical Services in your Village Provided by Government		Total
		Yes	**No**	
Education	Illiterate	122(44.7%)	12(44.4%)	134(44.7%)
	Primary	52(19.0%)	4(14.8%)	56(18.7%)
	Secondary	40(14.7%)	6(22.2%)	46(15.3%)
	Inter	29(10.6%)	2(7.4%)	31(10.3%)
	Graduate	30(11.0%)	3(11.1%)	33(11.0%)
	Total	**273(100.0%)**	**27(100.0%)**	**300(100.0%)**

Note: $X^2 = 1.924$; df = 2, P< = 0.382 Not significant

Figures in parentheses indicate percentage

Source: Primary data.

Table 7.22 shows that the levels of Education of the respondents and the medical services provided by Government in the villages of the respondents. In this study they have expressed different views on the medical services provided to the respondents. Out the total respondents, 273 respondents have reported that they have had satisfaction on medical services providing by the government, of which it is observed from the table that the highest percentage of the illiterate respondents stated that they had satisfaction on medical services providing by the government *i.e.* 44.7, followed by the Primary, Secondary, Intermediate, and Graduate *i.e.* 19.0 per cent, 14.7 per cent, 10.6 per cent, 11.0 per cent of the respondents respectively reported that they have satisfied with the medical services in their village providing by the government. Of the total respondents only 27 respondents *i.e.* 44.4 per cent of the illiterate respondents have reported that they did not have satisfaction on medical services providing by the government, followed by the 18.7 per cent, 15.3 per cent, 10.3 per cent, 11.0 per cent *i.e.* Primary, Secondary, Intermediate and Graduate respectively. Generated the chi-squire value 1.924, is found to be not significant, because it is less than the table value. The results reveal that there is no significant association between education of the respondents and satisfaction of medical services providing by the government.

Table 7.23 shows that the awareness on rendering in pre-natal services to pregnant women until the delivery in the government hospitals and Dalit sub-sections. Out of the total respondents 288 respondents of which 96.0 per cent of the Dalit sub-section respondents are noticed that they have awareness on rendering pre-natal services to pregnant women until the delivery in the government hospitals. Whereas 12 respondents of which 4.0 per cent of the respondents reported that they did not have awareness on rendering pre-natal services to pregnant women until the delivery in the government hospitals.

Table 7.23: Table showing the awareness on the services to pregnant women until the delivery in the government hospital *vs* dalit sub-section

Variables		Dalit-Sub-Section			Total
		Mala	Madiga	Others	
Do you aware of the help rendering by government to pregnant women until the delivery in the Government hospitals	Yes	92 (93.9%)	187 (96.9%)	9 (100.0%)	288 (96.0%)
	No	6 (6.1%)	6 (3.1%)	0 (0.0%)	12 (4.0%)
	Total	**98 (100.0%)**	**193 (100.0%)**	**9 (100.0%)**	**300 (100.0%)**

Note: X^2 = 1.924; df = 2 P< = 0.382 Not significant
Figures in parentheses indicate percentage
Source: Primary data

Among the different Dalit sub-caste categories, Out of the total respondents 98 respondents belongs to Mala Dalit sub-section of which 93.9 per cent of the respondents stated that they have got awareness about services rendering by government to pregnant women until the delivery in the government hospitals. Where as remaining 6.1 per cent of the respondents revealed that they did not have awareness of the services provided by Government for pre-natal care. Out of the 300 respondents 193 respondents are belongs to be Madiga Dalit sub-section of which 96.9 per cent of the respondents reported that they had awareness, where as 3.1 per cent of the respondents stated that they did not have aware. Regarding other communities very meager of the total respondents *i.e.* 9 respondents, of which 100 per cent respondents revealed that they have aware of the services rendering to pregnant women until the delivery in the government hospitals. Calculate the Chi-squire table value 0.382 is found to be not significant because it is less than the table value. The result reveals that there is no significant association between awareness of the services rendering by government to pregnant women until the delivery in the government hospitals and Dalit Sub-Castes.

Table 7.24 shows that the annual income and occupation of the respondents. It is evident that the majority of 40.7 per cent of the respondents reported that their annual income is above Rs. 20,001, followed by the 34.3 per cent, 11.75 per cent, 7.0 per cent, 5.7 per cent and 0.7 per cent of the respondents noticed that their annual income is in between Rs. 15001-20000. Some of the respondents reported the annual income is not applicable to annual income because they are house wives, Rs. 5001-10000, Rs. 10001-15000 and Rs. Less than 5000 of the sample respondents.

Out of the total respondents 168 respondents were agricultural labour of which 48.8 per cent of the respondents have reported that their annual income is in between is 15001-20000, followed by the 25.0 per cent, 12.5 per cent of the respondents noticed that their annual income is in between above Rs. 20,001. Some respondents reported that the income is not applicable to annual income because they are house wives. Of the total respondents 23 respondents were non-agricultural labour of which 69.6. per cent of the respondents have revealed that their annual income was more than Rs. 20,001, where as the 13.0 per cent of the respondents stated that their annual income is in between Rs. 15,001-20,000. Out of the total respondents 34 respondents have reported that their occupation was employment of which 79.4 per cent of the respondents revealed that their annual income is more than Rs. 20001, followed by the 8.7 per cent, 5.9 per cent of the respondents have noticed that their annual income is not applicable, Rs. 15,001-20,000. Among the total respondents very meager *i.e.* 7 respondents have reported that their occupation is business of which 42.9 per cent of the respondents presented that their annual income is in between Rs. 5,001-10,000. Out of the total respondents 33 respondents occupation reported to be any other of which 48.5 per cent of the respondents reported that their annual income is more than Rs. 20,001. Out of the total respondents 35 respondents are reported that their occupation is house wives of which 54.3 per cent reported that their annual income is above

Table 7.24: Table showing annual income *vs* occupation of the respondents

Variables		Occupation						Total
		Agricultural Labour	Non-Agricultural Labour	Employed	Business	House Wife	Any Other	
Annual Income	< 5000	1(.6%)	0(0.0%)	0(.0%)	1(14.3%)	0(0.0%)	0(0.0%)	2(0.7%)
	5001-10000	11(6.5%)	1(4.3%)	2(5.9%)	3(42.9%)	1(2.9%)	3(9.1%)	21(7.0%)
	10001-15000	11(6.5%)	1(4.3%)	0(0.0%)	0(0.0%)	2(5.7%)	3(9.1%)	17(5.7%)
	15001-20000	82(48.8%)	3(13.0%)	2(5.9%)	0(0.0%)	7(20.0%)	9(27.3%)	103(34.3%)
	20001->	42(25.0%)	16(69.6%)	27(79.4%)	2(28.6%)	19(54.3%)	16(48.5%)	122(40.7%)
	Not applicable	21(12.5%)	2(8.7%)	3(8.8%)	1(14.3%)	6(17.1%)	2(6.1%)	35(11.7%)
	Total	**168(100.0%)**	**23(100.0%)**	**34(100.0%)**	**7(100.0%)**	**35(100.0%)**	**33(100.0%)**	**300(100.0%)**

Note: $X^2 = 96.272$; df = 25; P< = 0.000, 0.5% Significant

Figures in parentheses indicate percentage

Source: Primary data

Rs. 20,000 thousand rupees. Calculate the chi-squire table value 96.272 is found to be significant because it is more than the table value, the results revealed a significant association in between annual income and occupation of the respondents. The hypotheses formulated in the study as to enquiry of association of the development of Dalit women and economic background is proved to be true as the chi-square statistical results are proved to be significant.

Table 7.25 shows that the land holding of the respondents. It is evident that the majority 90.0 per cent of the respondents reported that they did not have land, followed by 6.6 per cent, 2.0 per cent, 0.6 per cent of the respondents are revealed that they have 0.5 acre, 0.5-1 acre, 1-1.5 acres, and 1.5-2 acres of land holding of the sample respondents. Therefore the majority of the respondents have reported that they did not have agri-land holding. The results of the data revealed that whole land is totally under control of other then the Dalits. Though Government is declaring that the land was also distributed to the weaker section whish was not all done as according to the findings of the study.

Table 7.25: The table shows the land holding of the respondents

Variables (in Acres)		Frequence	Percentage
Land Holding	< - 0.5	20	6.6
	0.5-1	6	2.0
	1-1.5	2	0.6
	1.5-2	2	0.6
	No land	270	90.0
	Total	**300**	**100.0%**

Note: n = 300,

Source: Primary data

Figure 7.2, Table 7.26 The majority 83.7 per cent of the respondents presented husband and wife have been taking care of financial responsibility of their family. Where as 5.7 per cent of the respondents reported that the husband only takes care of financial responsibility of their family. Followed by the 4.7 per cent, 4.3 per cent of the respondents reported that their family financial responsibility had taken by the respondents themselves and their fathers.

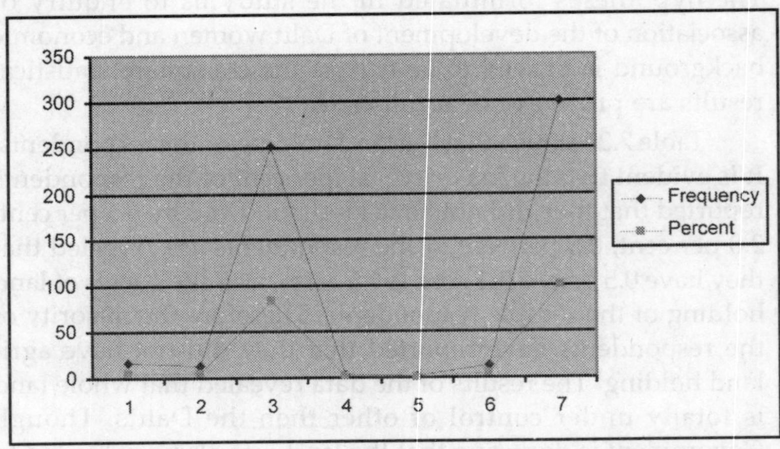

Fig. 7.2: Figure Showing Financial Responsibility of the Respondents

Table 7.26: The table showing financial responsibility of the respondents

Variable		Frequency	Percentage
Financial Responsiblity	Husband	17	5.7
	Your self	14	4.7
	Husband and wife	251	83.7
	Father in law	4	1.3
	Mother in law	1	.3
	Father	13	4.3
	Total	**300**	**100.0%**

Note: n = 300,

Source: Primary data

The Figure 7.3, Table 7. 27 shows that the awareness of the respondents on the wages paying to the labour in their village. The majority 47.3 per cent of the respondents reported that the wages are given in between Rs. 50-100 per day work. Where as 27.0 per cent of the respondent informed that the wages in their villages is in between Rs. 101-150 rupees per day. As regards to 17.0 per cent of the respondents reported that the wages in their village in between Rs. 151-200 rupees per day work.

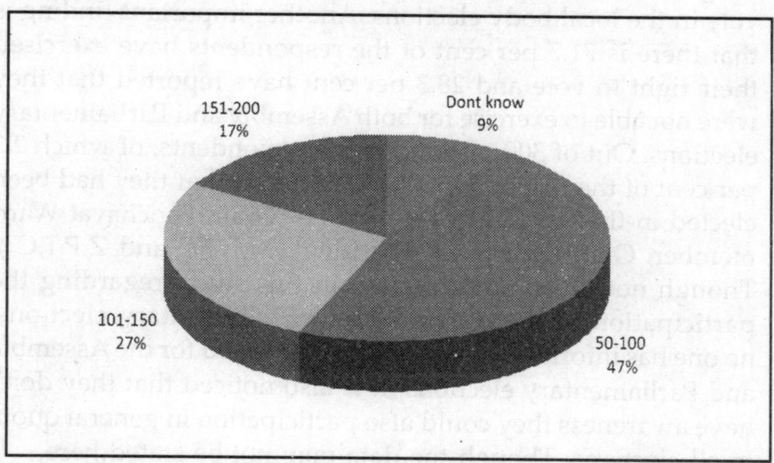

Fig. 7.3: The Awareness of the Respondents on the Wages giving to the Labour in your Village

Table 7.27: The table shows the awareness of the respondents on the wages giving to the labour in your village

Variable (Per-day)	Frequency	Percentage
Don't Know	27	9.0
50 - 100	142	47.3
101 - 150	81	27.0
151 - 200	50	16.7
Total	**300**	**100.0%**

Note: n = 300,
Source: Primary data

Table 7.28 discloses that the respondents exercising their right to vote for local body elections (Gram Panchayat, MPTC,

ZPTC) and Assemble and Parliamentary elections. It is also elicits from the respondents regarding the participation in the elections. In this study it is revealed that 89.7 per cent of the respondents have exercised their right to vote for local body elections (Gram Panchayat, MPTC, ZPTC) and also very insignificant *i.e.* 10.3 per cent have not exercised their right to vote in the local body elections. Another important finding is that there is 71.7 per cent of the respondents have exercised their right to vote and 28.3 per cent have reported that they were not able to exercise for both Assembly and Parliamentary elections. Out of 300 respondents 7 respondents, of which 2.3 per cent of the respondents have revealed that they had been elected in the local body election *i.e.* (Gram Panchayat Ward member, Gram Panchayat President, M.P.T.C and Z.P.T.C). Though not given any question in this study regarding the participation in the Assembly and Parliamentary elections, no one has informed that they have contested for the Assemble and Parliamentary elections. It is also noticed that they don't have awareness they could also participation in general quota in all elections. Though the data may not be stated here.

Table 7.28: The table shows the excrise of vote and participation in elections of the respondents

S. No.	Variables	Yes	No
1.	Have you exercised your vote for Gram Panchayat Elections, MPTC, ZPTC	269 (89.7%)	31 (10.3%)
2.	Have you exercised your vote for Assembly or Parliamentary Elections	215 (71.7%)	85 (28.3%)
3.	Have you elected ward member, president, MPTC, ZPTC	7 (2.3%)	293 (97.7%)

Note: n = 300,

Source: Primary data

Table 7.29 shows that the awareness of the respondents on political parties in the village level. The majority of 83.7 per cent of the respondents reported that their village President, MPTC, ZPTC belongs to the Congress party and remaining 16.3 per cent of the respondents stated that their village

President, MPTC, ZPTC are belongs to Telugu Desam Party. As regards to 53.0 per cent of the respondents participated voting more then three times of gram panchayat elections. Followed by the One time, Two times, Three times *i.e.* 2.0 per cent, 10.3 per cent, 32.0 per cent of the respondents respectively have reveled that they had participated in voting to grama panchayat elections and remaining 2.7 per cent of the respondents reported that they did not participate in voting to gram panchayats elections. The majority *i.e.* 88.3 per cent of the respondents informed that they did not have membership of any political party. About 9.7 per cent of the respondents reported that they have a membership in Congress political party. Where as 2.0 per cent of the respondents presented that they have membership in Telugu Desam political party.

Table 7.29: Table showing awareness on political parties and participation of voting elections of the respondents

S. No.	Variables	Frequency	Percentage
1.	Do you aware which party of your village president, MPTC, ZPTC		
	Congress	251	83.7
	TDP	49	16.3
2.	How many times participated in voting Gram Panchayat Elections		
	Not participated	8	2.7
	1 Time	6	2.0
	2 Times	31	10.3
	3 Times	96	32.0
	More than 3 Times	159	53.0
3.	Have you got membership of any political party		
	Congress	29	9.7
	TDP6	2.0	
	No membership	265	88.3

Note: n = 300

Source: Primary data

Table 7.30 shows that the education levels of respondents and awareness on reservation of seats for SCs, STs in the Panchayati Raj Institutions according to 73rd Constitutional Amendment Act. Out of the total respondents, 59 respondents have reported that they had awareness of the 73rd constitutional amendment Act for reservation of seats for SCs, STs, in the Panchayats of which 52.5 per cent who studied upto graduation, followed by the 18.6 per cent, 13.6 per cent of the respondents informed that they have intermediate, secondary and primary level of education respectively. Of the total respondents 241 respondents have reported that they did not have awareness about the 73rd constitutional amendment Act for reservation of seats for SCs, STs, in the Panchayats, of which 53.5 per cent of the respondents who were illiterates, followed by the 21.6 per cent, 15.8 per cent, 8.3 per cent, 0.8 per cent of the respondents who were studied upto primary, secondary, intermediate and graduate level of education.

Table 7.30: Table showing education levels vs awareness of the reservation of seats for SC, ST according to the 73rd constitutional ammendment

Variables		Awareness on Reservation of Seats for SC, ST According to the 73rd, Constitutional Amendment Act		Total
		Yes	No	
Education	Illiterate	5(8.5%)	129(53.5%)	134(44.7%)
	Primary	4(6.8%)	52(21.6%)	56(18.7%)
	Secondary	8(13.6%)	38(15.8%)	46(15.3%)
	Inter	11(18.6%)	20(8.3%)	31(10.3%)
	Graduate	31(52.5%)	2(0.8%)	33(11.0%)
	Total	**59(100.0%)**	**241(100.0%)**	**300(100.0%)**

$X^2 = 147.382$, df = 4, P< 0.000 Significant 0.05%

Figures in parenthesis indicate percentage,

Note: n = 300,

Source: Primary data

Calculated the chi-squire table value 147.382 , it is found to be significant because it is more than table value. The results reveal a significant association between levels of education and awareness about the reservation of seats for SCs, STs, according to the 73rd constitutional amendment Act. In this table it can be said that the higher the education level of respondents, the higher awareness and the illiterate have reported to be that they did not have awareness on 73rd constitutional amendment Act. The hypotheses formulated in this study as to enquiry of association of the awareness of the Dalit women and educational background is proved to be true as the chi-square statistical results are proved to be significant.

Table 7.31: Table showing occupation of the respondents *vs* participation in gram panchayat elections

Variables		Participated Gram Panchayats Elections		Total
		Yes	No	
Occupation	Agriculture	151 (56.1%)	17 (54.8%)	168 (56.0%)
	Non-Agriculture Activities	20 (7.4%)	3 (9.7%)	23 (7.7%)
	Employed both Government and Private	32 (11.9%)	2 (6.5%)	34 (11.3%)
	Business in	7 (2.6%)	0 (0.0%)	7 (2.3%)
	House wife	31 (11.5%)	4 (12.9%)	35 (11.7%)
	Other than the above	28 (10.4%)	5 (16.1%)	33 (11.0%)
	Total	**269 (100.0%)**	**31 (100.0%)**	**300 (100.0%)**

$X^2 = 2.596$; df = 5, $P < 0.762$ Not significant

Figures parenthesis indicate percentage

Note: n = 300,

Source: Primary data

Table 7.31 shows that the occupation of the respondents and their participation in the gram panchayat elections have disclosed here. It is evident that the most of the respondents *i.e.* 56.0 per cent have reported that their occupation is agricultural labour, followed by 7.7 per cent, 11.3 per cent, 2.3 per cent, 11.7 per cent, 11.0 per cent of the respondents respectively informed that their occupation is non-agricultural labour, employed, business, house wives of the dalit sub-section.

Out of the total respondents 269 respondents have reported that they had participated in voting to the grama panchayats elections of which 56.1 per cent of the respondents expressed that they have participated in voting in the grama Panchayat elections their occupation is agricultural labour, followed by the non-agricultural, employed, business, house wives, other activities, *i.e.* 7.4 per cent, 11.9 per cent, 2.6 per cent, 11.5 per cent, 10.4 per cent, of the respondents have expressed that they did not participate in Gram panchayat elections. Of the total respondents 31 respondents, of which 54.8 per cent of the respondents were from the agricultural labourers, followed by the 9.7 per cent, 6.5 per cent, 0.0 per cent, 12.9 per cent, 16.1 per cent, of the non-agricultural labour, employed, business, house wives, other activities. In calculation of testing of the chi-squire table value 2.596, it is found to be not significant because it is lees than the table value. The result reveals that there is no significant association in between the occupation and participation in the gram panchayats elections of the respondents.

Table 7.32 shows that the education levels and utilisation of right to vote of the respondents. The majority 44.7 per cent of the respondents are reported to be illiterates. As regards to 18.7 per cent of the respondents are expressed that they studied upto primary education, followed by 15.3 per cent, 11.0 per cent, 10.3 per cent of the respondents have informed that their education upto Secondary, Intermediate and Graduate level the of Dalit women.

Table 7.32: Table showing education levels of the respondents *vs* their utilisation of right to vote

Variables		Utilisation of Right to Vote		Total
		Yes	No	
Education	Illiterate	130(44.5%)	4(50.0%)	134(44.7%)
	Primary	56(19.2%)	0(0.0%)	56(18.7%)
	Secondary	43(14.7%)	3(37.5%)	46(15.3%)
	Inter	31(10.6%)	0(0.0%)	31(10.3%)
	Graduate	32(11.0%)	1(12.5%)	33(11.0%)
	Total	**292(100.0%)**	**8(100.0%)**	**300(100.0%)**

$X^2 = 5.087$, df = 4, P < = 0.279 Not Significant
Figures parentheses indicate percentage
Note: n = 300,
Source: Primary data.

Out of the total respondents 292 respondents have reported that they had utilised their right to vote of which 44.5 per cent were illiterates, followed by the primary, secondary, intermediate, graduate educators *i.e.* 19.2 per cent, 14.7 per cent, 10.6 per cent, 11.0 per cent, As regards of the total respondents, only a few *i.e.* 8 respondents of which 50.0 per cent of the illiterates respondents did not utilise right to vote, followed by the 37.5 per cent, 12.5 per cent of the of the respondents studied upto secondary, graduate levels of educators. Calculating the chi-squire table value 5.087 it was found to be not significant because it is less than the table value. The results have did not find any significant association in between education and utilisation of right to vote of the respondents.

Though it may not be found a significant association, higher the exercise of their right to vote been found in the illiterates and the less exercised their vote of right *i.e.* 50 per cent have also found from the same group.

Table 7.33 presented that the awareness about Gram Panchayat activities of the respondents. Out of 300 respondents 257 respondents which is about 85.7 per cent of the respondents reported that they had awareness about Gram

Panchayat activities in the development of the village. Of the total respondents 43 respondents which is about 14.3 per cent of the respondents reported that they did not aware of the Gram Panchayat activities for developing their villages. As regards the 82.0 per cent of the respondents are reported that they know about the role of the ward members in the development activities of the village, remaining 18.0 per cent of the respondents have expressed that they did not know about the role of ward members in the village. The majority of 80.3 per cent of the respondents have reported that they did not aware about the reservation of seats in Gram Panchayats according to 73rd constitutional amendment Act. About 19.7 per cent of the respondents revealed that they had awareness about reservation of seats in Gram Panchayats according 73rd constitutional amendment Act. The majority of 97.3 per cent of the respondents had utilised the right to vote. Where as 2.7 per cent of the respondents have reported that they did not utilised the right to vote. About 98.3 per cent of the respondents have reported that they did not participated voting in co-operative society elections and remaining 1.7 per cent of the respondents reported that they have participated voting in co-operatives society elections.

Table 7.33: Table showing awareness on panchayat activities of the respondents

S. No.	Variables	Yes	No
1.	Regarding Gram Panchayat activities for development of village	257 (85.7%)	43 (14.3%)
2	Regarding ward members role in developing village	246 (82.0%)	54 (18.0%)
3.	Regarding the reservation of seats for SC, ST according to the 73rd constitutional amendment Act	59. (19.7%)	241 (80.3%)
4.	Utilisation of right to vote	292 (97.3%)	8 (2.7%)
5.	Have you participated in Co-Operative Society Elections	5 (1.7%)	295 (98.3%)

Note: n = 300,
Source: Primary data

Table 7.34 shows on awareness about Gram Panchayats activities for development of the village and Dalit sub-castes. The majority 85.7 per cent of the respondents expressed that they had awareness in the grama panchayat activities for development of the village, whereas 14.3 per cent of the respondent revealed that they did not had awareness of the gram panchayats activities development of village.

Table 7.34: Table showing about the awareness on dalit sub-caste in gram panchayat development activities

Variables		Dalit-Sub-Section			Total
		Mala	Madiga	Others	
Dalit Sub-Caste in Gram Panchayat activities for development of village	Yes	89 (90.8%)	166 (86.0%)	2 (22.2%)	257 (85.7%)
	No	9 (9.2%)	27 (14.0%)	7 (77.8%)	43 (14.3%)
	Total	**98 (100.0%)**	**193 (100.0%)**	**9 (100.0%)**	**300 (100.0%)**

$X^2 = 31.638$, df = 2, P < = 0.000 Significant 0.5%

Figures parentheses indicate percentage

Note: n = 300

Source: Primary data

The distribution of different Dalit sub-Castes, Out of 300 respondents 98 respondents belongs to Mala Dalit sub-section of which 90.8 per cent of the respondents have reported that they had awareness about the gram Panchayat activities in the development of village. Regarding 9.2 per cent of the respondents have revealed that they did not awareness of the gram panchayats activities in the development of the village. Of the total respondents, 193 respondents belongs to Madiga Dalit sub-section, of which 86.0 per cent of the Madiga Dalit sub-Caste reported that they had awareness about the Gram Panchayats activities in the development of their villages, remaining 14.0 per cent of the respondents Madiga Dalit sub-Caste reported that they did not have awareness about the Gram Panchayats activities in the development of their villages. Of the total respondents 9 respondents belongs to other communities of Dalit sub-section of which 77.8 per cent *i.e.* STs respondents reported that they did not aware about Gram Panchayat activities in the development of their villages, remaining 22.2 per cent of the respondents have reported that they got awareness on Gram Panchayat activities in the development of their villages. Generated the chi-squire table value *i.e.* 31.638, is found to be significant because it is more than table value. The results revealed a significant association in between the Dalit sub-Castes of the respondents and their activities in the Gram Panchayat development. It implied that the majority STs do not have awareness that they can participate in the activities of the development of their villages.

Table 7.35 shows that the awareness of the respondents on the role of the ward members in the developing their villages and dalit sub-sections was trying to findout. The majority *i.e.* 82.0 per cent of the Dalit sub section respondents reveled that they have awareness about their ward member in the developing their villages, remaining 18.0 per cent of the respondents have informed that they did not had awareness of the ward member role in the developing village.

Table 7.35: Table showing the awareness on the ward members role in developing their villages *vs* dalit sub-caste

Variables		Dalit-Sub-Section			Total
		Mala	Madiga	STs	
Awareness of the respondents on the ward members role in developing their villages	Yes	85 (86.7%)	159 (82.4%)	2 (22.2%)	246 (82.0%)
	No	13 (13.3%)	34 (17.6%)	7 (77.8%)	54 (18.0%)
	Total	**98 (100.0%)**	**193 (100.0%)**	**9 (100.0%)**	**300 (100.0%)**

$X^2 = 23.297$, df = 2, P < = 0.000 Significant 0.5%

Figures parentheses indicate percentage,

Note: n = 300

Source: Primary data

Among the different Dalit sub-sections, Out of 300 respondents, 98 respondents belongs to Mala Dalit sub-section, of which 86.7 per cent of the respondents stated that they had aware of the role played by the ward members in developing their villages. About 13.3 per cent of Mala Dalit sub-caste do not know about the role of the ward members in the developing their villages. Of the total respondents, 193 respondents belongs to Madiga Dalit sub-section of which 82.4 per cent of the Madiga dalit sub-caste respondents have revealed that they know about the role of the ward members in the developing their villages, remaining *i.e.* 17.6 per cent of the Madiga Dalit sub-caste informed that they did not know about the role of the ward members in the development of their villages. Out of the total respondents *i.e.* 9 respondents of which 77.8 per cent of the Others of the Dalit sub-section respondents have reported that they did not know about the role of the ward members in the development of their village and remaining 22.2 per cent of the respondents stated that they know the role of the ward members in the developing of their villages. Generated the chi-squire table value *i.e.* 23.297 is found to be significant as it is more than the table value. The results reveal that a significant association was established in between the role of ward members in their development of their villages and Dalit sub-Caste of the respondents. Higher the percentage *i.e.* 77.8 per cent of respondents reported that they have found that the other then the Dalit sub-Caste *i.e.* Sts did not know the role of ward members role in their development activities of their villages.

Table 7.36 shows the age and joining in the SHGs. Out of the total sample of the respondents 248 respondents have joined in SHGs (Self-Help Groups) of which *i.e.* 47.2 per cent of the respondents age group is in between 31-40 followed by the 31.9 per cent, 20.2 per cent of the respondents have joined in SHGs, their age groups is in between 41-50, 21-30 of the respondents. Out of the 300 respondents 52 respondents have not joined in SHGs, of which 34.6 per cent of the respondents in the age group were between 21-30. Calculated the chi-squire table value *i.e.* 46.322 was found to be significant, because it is more than the table value. The results revealed that a significant association was found in between the age and joining in self-help groups (SHGs). Very less *i.e.* 0.8 per cent have reported in between < 20 years of their age and majority of their *i.e.* 47.2 per cent have found to be joined in between the age group of 31-40 years of their age.

Table 7.36: Table showing age *vs* joining in self-help groups (SHGs) of the respondents

Variables		Have you Joined in SHGs		Total
		Yes	No	
Age	< 20	2(0.8%)	9(17.3%)	11(3.7%)
	21 - 30	50(20.2%)	18(34.6%)	68(22.7%)
	31 - 40	117(47.2%)	8(15.4%)	125(41.7%)
	41 - 50	79(31.9%)	17(32.7%)	96(32.0%)
	Total	**248(100.0%)**	**52(100.0%)**	**300(100.0%)**

$X^2 = 46.322$; df = 3, $P < 0.000$; Significant 0.5%

Figures parentheses indicate in the percentage

Note: n = 300

Source: Primary data

Table 7.37 shows that the Age and reasons for joining in self-help groups (SHGs). Out of the 300 respondents 52 respondents have reported that they did join in the self help groups, of which 34.6 per cent of respondents were in between the age group of 21-30. Of the total sample respondents 50 respondents have informed that they have joined in the SHGs for getting loans, of which 56.0 per cent in between the age group of 31-40. Regarding the 188 respondents revealed that they had joined in the self-help group promoting savings of which 45.7 per cent of respondents in their age group in between 31-40. As regards to 3 respondents have stated that they had joined in the self-help group for their social status of which 66.7 per cent of the respondents in between the age group of 41-50 years, followed by 57.1 per cent of the respondents have reported that they have joined in SHGs for domestic needs in the age group of in between 41-50. Calculated chi-squire table value *i.e.* 53.995 is found to be significant as it is more than the table value. The results revealed a significant association in between the age and reasons in joining SHGs.

Table 7.37: Table showing age of the respondents *vs* the reasons for joining the self-help groups (SHGs)

Variables (in Years)		Reasons for Join in SHGs					Total
		Not Applic-able	For Getting Loans	Promoting Savings	Social Status	Domestic Needs	
Age	< 20	9 (17.3%)	0 (0.0%)	2 (1.1%)	0 (0.0%)	0 (0.0%)	11 (3.7%)
	21-30	18 (34.6%)	8 (16.0%)	41 (21.8%)	1 (33.3%)	0 (0.0%)	68 (22.7%)
	31-40	8 (15.4%)	28 (56.0%)	86 (45.7%)	0 (0.0%)	3 (42.9%)	125 (41.7%)
	41-50	17 (32.7%)	14 (28.0%)	59 (31.4%)	2 (66.7%)	4 (57.1%)	96 (32.0%)
	Total	**52 (100.0%)**	**50 (100.0%)**	**188 (100.0%)**	**3 (100.0%)**	**7 (100.0%)**	**300 (100.0%)**

X^2 = 53.995 df = 12 P < 0.000 Significant 0.5%
Figures parentheses indicate in the percentage
Note: n = 300
Source: Primary data

The reporting of the respondents have noticed 66.7 per cent in between the age group of 41-50 years have joined in SHGs is only for their social status followed by 57.1 per cent, 56 per cent in between 41-50 years of age and 31-40 of the age have reported that the reason for joining SHGs is for domestic needs and for getting loans. The general impression and the basic purpose of SHGs are for their financial help in their need and for inculcating the habits of saving, but it is very important finding through SHGs was that the highest majority in the age group of in between 41-50 have expressed that they can attain good social status in their village.

Table 7.38 shows that the awareness on SHGs management of the respondents. The highest 60.3 per cent of the respondents reported that they are having an habit of the saving and

Table 7.38: Table showing respondents awareness on self-help groups (SHGs) management

S. No.	Variables	Frequency	Percentage
1	2	3	4
1.	Do you have an habit of saving		
	Yes	181	60.3
	No	119	39.7
2.	Is your groups confined to one caste or all castes (n = 248)		
	One Caste	239	96.3
	All Castes	9	3.6
3.	How many members have joined in your group (n = 248)		
	0-5	8	3.2
	50-10	199	80.2
	10-15	41	16.6
4.	How much monthly saving of the beneficiaries (n = 248)		
	Rs. 00-50	131	52.8
	Rs. 50-100	102	41.1
	Rs. 100-150	7	2.8
	Rs. 150-200	8	3.2
5.	Do you maintaining attendance register in your group (n = 248)		
	Yes	247	99.59
	No	1	0.40
6.	Do you maintaining group meetings regularly, (n = 248)		
	Yes	246	99.19
	No	2	0.80
7.	Do your group collect the monthly saving (n = 248)		
	Yes	248	100.0
	No	0	0.0

Contd...

1	2	3	4
8.	Have you maintaining minutes books, (n = 248)		
	Yes	246	99.2
	No	2	0.8
9.	Have you taken revolving fund, (n = 248)		
	Yes	84	33.8
	No	164	66.1
10.	How much amount of loan taken from revolving fund (n = 248)		
	Not taken	164	66.1
	Rs. 10000.00	77	31.0
	Rs. 15000.00	7	2.8

Source: Primary data

remaining 39.7 per cent of the respondents stated that they did not have the habit of the saving. As regards the 96.3 per cent of the respondents expressed that they had confined their group to one caste, while 3.6 per cent of the respondents stated that their group consists of all castes. It can be learned that about drawn from the 80.2 per cent of the respondents have reported in their group they were in between 5-10 members have formed. Where as 52.8 per cent of the respondents informed that their monthly saving was Rs. 50 rupees per month.

Majority *i.e.* 99.19 per cent of respondents informed that they have been maintaining attendance registers. About 99.19 per cent of the respondents revealed that they have been conducting group meetings regularly. Cent per cent of the respondents have been collecting the monthly savings in the meetings group. Where as 99.2 per cent of the respondents informed that they have been maintaining minutes books. About 66.1 per cent of the respondents, they could not taken revolving fund and remaining 33.8 per cent of the respondents had been taking revolving fund. About 31.0 per cent of the respondents reported that they have been taking as loan Rs. 10000.00 from revolving fund.

Table 7.39 shows the borrowing of loans from the SHGs by the respondents. The Self-Help Group concept is more impressive or attractive for the development of women in the villages, in this study majority *i.e.* 82.33 per cent of the respondents had reported that they have taken loan from SHGs. Around 35.0 per cent of the respondents revealed that they had been taken less than Rs. 5000, rupees. Where as 21.33 per cent of the respondents revealed that they have taken more than Rs. 20000 rupees. The majority of *i.e.* 48.38 per cent of respondents have informed that they have taken for the loan for the purpose of their children education.

Table 7.39: The table showing borrowing loans from the SHGs by the respondents

S. No.	Variables	Frequency	Percentage
1.	Have you taken loan from SHGs		
	Not Applicable	52	17.33
	Yes	248	82.33
2.	How much amount of loan taken (n = 248) (in Rupees)		
	< 5000	87	35.0
	5001 - 10000	48	19.3
	10001 - 15000	17	6.8
	15001 - 20000	32	12.9
	20001 - >	64	25.8
3.	What purpose did you take loan		
	Consumption	18	7.25
	Income-generated Project	30	12.09
	Agricultural investment	35	14.11
	House construction	45	18.14
	Education of the children	120	48.38

Note: n = 300

Source: Primary data

According to this study, it was found that there is a good significance in investing money for their children's education which was barrowed from SHGs and also found the changing attitude of Dalit Women for educating their children.

Table 7.40 shows that the management of banking transaction by the respondents. It is evident that 93.3 per cent of the respondents revealed that they have an idea on banking transactions after joining in SHGs, remaining 6.6 per cent of the respondents have reported that they don't have an idea about banking. As regards the opinion on banking it was found that 62.0 per cent respondents reported that they feel less interest and easy installments for the money barrowed from the banks. Followed by the getting loans, beneficial to the rich people, beneficial to the poor people and needy etc.. *i.e.* 16.7 per cent, 7.3 per cent, and 14.0 per cent of the respondents have found from the data. The data on individual bank passbooks, the majority 51.33 per cent of the respondents revealed that they have been maintaining individual bank passbooks. Where as 48.7 per cent of the respondents did not maintain individual pass books. Because of the joining as a member in the SHGs they have got good knowledge on banking transactions and major chunk of the respondents have been maintaining bank passbooks.

Table 7.40: Table showing management of bank transactions by the respondents

S. No.	Variables	Frequency	Percentage
1.	Do you have an idea about banking		
	Yes	280	93.3
	No	20	6.6
2	What is your opinion on banking services		
	Getting loans	50	16.7
	Beneficial to rich people	22	7.3
	Beneficial to the poor people and needy	42	14.0
	Less interest and easy installments	183	62.0
3.	Do you maintain individual bank passbook		
	Yes	154	51.3
	No	146	48.7

Note: n = 300

Source: Primary data

It is also noticed the installments payments are more easy for them to repay loans and the interest is also very comfortable for them.

Table 7.41 shows taking loans from the Banks by the SHGs members. It is understood the majority *i.e.* 35.4 per cent of the respondents reported that their group had taken loan upto Rs. 50,000 rupees. Followed by the group Rs. 50,001-1,00,000; Rs. 1,00,001-1,50,000; Rs. 1,50,001-2,00,000 and above Rs. 2,00,001 *i.e.* 18.9 per cent, 6.8 per cent, 12.9 per cent, and 25.8 per cent of the respondents had taken loans. The majority *i.e.* 96.7 per cent of the respondents reported that they have paying interest @ 25 paisa for every Rs. 100/- Anyway it is very interesting to note that in this present days it is rarely heard about the interest rate of 25 paisa, but the members of SHGs have a good pride in enjoying at the cheaper rate.

Table 7.41: The table showing the taking loans from the bank by the SHGs members

S. No.	Variables	Frequency	Percentage
1.	How much amount loan the bank is given to your group (n = 248)		
	Rs. 50000	88	35.4
	Rs. 50001 - 100000	47	18.9
	Rs. 100001 - 150000	17	6.8
	Rs. 150001 - 200000	32	12.9
	Above 200000	64	25.8
2.	Do you now how much interest is collected on every Rs. 100/- on your borrowing		
	90 paisa	7	2.8
	25 paisa	240	96.7
	50 paisa	1	0.4

Note: n = 248

Source: Primary data

Table 7.42: Table showing awareness on the government programmes for the development of villages as well as the respondents

S. No.	Variables	Frequency	Percentage
1.	Do you know Government Programmes (n = 300)		
	Yes	280	93.3
	No	20	6.6
2.	Which type of Government Programmes do you know (n = 300)		
	DWCRA/MGNREGS	278	92.6
	PMRY	10	3.3
	CMEY	12	4.0
3.	Have you MGNREGS job card in your family (n = 300)		
	Yes	219	73.0
	No	81	27.0
4.	How many days work providing in Gram Panchayat in one year (n = 219)		
	Not Apply for work	35	1539
	0-25	58	26.4
	26-50	46	21.0
	51-75	3	1.3
	76-100	7	3.1
	Not providing	70	31.9
5.	How much money earning through MGNREGS works per day (n = 114)		
	Rs. 50 - 75	19	16.6
	Rs. 75 - 100	75	65.78
	Rs. 100 - Above	20	17.54

Source: Primary data

Table 7.42 shows that the awareness of the Government Programmes providing for the development both villages as well as the sample respondents. The majority *i.e.* 93.3 per cent of the respondents reported that they had awareness of the Government programmes, where as 6.6 per cent of the respondents have revealed that they did not know the Government programmes. About 92.6 per cent of the respondents have reveled that they know the different programmes organizing by Government like DWCRA/ MGNREGS programmes, followed by the 3.3 per cent, 4.0 per cent of the respondents have stated that they know the PMRY, CMEY. Among the 73.0 per cent of the respondents have reported that their family is having MGNREGS job card, where as 27.0 per cent of the respondents have noticed that their family did not have MGNREGS job card.

It is understood that the majority of the respondents are *i.e.* 31.9 per cent of the sample respondents revealed that the gram Panchayat did not provide work, followed by the 26.7 per cent, 21.0 per cent, 15.9 per cent, 3.0 per cent and 1.3 per cent of the respondents revealed that the grama Panchayat is providing for 0 -25 days of work, not apply for work, for 26-50 days of work, for 51-75 days of work, and for 76-100 days of work. Among the 65.78 per cent of the respondents reported that they have been earning per day work was in between Rs. 75-100, followed by the 17.54 per cent of the respondents have revealed that they have been earning per day more than Rs. 100 per head.

8 RESULTS AND DISCUSSION

Personal Profile of the Respondents

- *The Analysis on the Respondents of the Dalit Sub-Section:* Out of 300 respondents 98 respondents which is about 32.7 per cent are found from Mala Sub-Caste, followed by 193 respondents *i.e.* 64.3 per cent of them belong to Madiga dalit sub-section and only meager *i.e.* 9 respondents, which is about 3.0 per cent are from other Communities of Dalit sub-sections have found. The majority *i.e.* 41.6 per cent of the respondents have found in between 31-40 years of age group and followed by 32.0 per cent in between of the 41-50 years of age group, 22.6 per cent fall in 21-30 years of age group and only remaining 3.6 per cent are less than the 20 years of age group. The data also revealed that the majority of the respondents *i.e.* 99.3 per cent are from Hindu religion and 0.7 per cent respondents are from Christian religion.

It is found that the majority of the respondents *i.e.* 90.7 per cent have got married, 7.7 per cent were Unmarried and only very meager *i.e.* 1.7 per cent were Widows. The data also revealed that the major chunck of the respondents *i.e.* 44.7 per cent are illiterates followed by Primary, Secondary, Inter and Degree.. etc *i.e.* 18.7 per cent, 15.3 per cent, 10.3 per cent and 11.0 per cent respectively from the total respondents. The data on annual income showed that the highest respondents *i.e.*

40.7 per cent have reported that they were earning more than Rs. 20,001/- and 34.3 per cent of the respondents annual income is in between Rs. 15,001-20,000/- and 11.7 per cent of the respondents have reported that their annual income is not applicable since they are house wives, 7.0 per cent of the respondents annual income is in between Rs. 5,001-10,000/-, 5.7 per cent of the respondents annual income is in between Rs. 10,000-15,000/-. And only very meager *i.e.* 0.7 per cent of the respondents annual income fellin below Rs. 5000/-.

- *Annual Income of the Head of the Family of the Respondents:* The majority *i.e.* 68.6 per cent of the respondents have reported that their head of the family income was in between Rs. 20,000-30,000, followed by 18.3 per cent, 3.3 per cent, 3.6 per cent, 4.3 per cent, and 1.6 per cent of the respondents respectively have reported that their heads of the families annual income was in between Rs. 30001-40000, Rs. 40001-50000, Rs. 50001-60000 and more than Rs. 60001 respectively of the respondents. Among them 1.6 per cent of the respondents have reported that they were do not fellin one of the above mentioned (not applicable for all the above) groups of annual income of the head of the family, and they were widows.
- *Analyses on the Type of Residence of the Respondents:* It was found that 52.0 per cent of the respondents were living in R. C. C., houses; 42.3 per cent of the respondents were living in the Thatched houses and 5.7 per cent of the respondents were living in Tailed houses. The majority 62.7 per cent of the respondents have reported that they have no sanitary facility and remaining *i.e.* 37.3 per cent of the respondents have reported that they have sanitary facilities. The majority of the respondents *i.e.* 91.3 per cent have reported that their family was Nuclear family, where as 8.0 per cent of the respondents have reported that there is a joint family, and very few *i.e.* 0.7 per cent of the respondents have reported that theirs was an extended family.

- *The Size of the Family of Respondents:* It was found that the majority *i.e.* 74.0 per cent of the respondents family size was in between 4-7 members. 18.3 per cent of the respondents were reported that their family size was in between 1-3 members, 7.3 per cent of the respondents have expressed that their size of the family was above 8 members. The majority of *i.e.* 56.0 per cent of the respondents occupation was agricultural labourer, followed by the 7.7 per cent, 11.3 per cent, 2.3 per cent, 11.0 per cent and 11.7 per cent of the respondents have informed that they are non-agricultural – labour, employed, business, house wife and any other respectively of their occupation.
- *Analysis on the Dalit Sub-Section Respondents Age*: It was found from the data that 41.5 per cent of the respondents were in the age group of in between 31-40, while 32.0 per cent of the respondents are in the age groups of in between 41-50, followed by the 22.7 per cent and 3.7 per cent of the respondents were in the age group in between 21-30, and less than 20 years of age group respectively of the sample respondents.

Age of the Dalit sub-section respondents have expressed through this study that out of 300 respondents 98 respondents are belong to Mala Dalit sub section, which was about 44.9 per cent of the respondents were in the age group of in between 31-40 years, followed by 33.7 per cent of the respondents are in the age group of in between 41-50, followed by 17.3 per cent and 4.1 per cent of the respondents were in the age group of in between 21-30 and less than 20 years of the respondents were in the same sub-section. A major *chunk i.e.* 193 respondents have informed that they were from the Madiga Dalit sub-section, of the total respondents, out of which 39.4 per cent of the respondents were in the age group of in between 31-40, followed by 31.6, per cent and 3.6 per cent of the respondents are in the age group of in between 41-50, 21-30 and less than 20 years age of the respondents were found from the same sub section. Out of 300 respondents 9 respondents were from the other communities of Dalit sub section, of the total respondents, out of which 55.6 per cent of the respondents were in the age groups of in between 31-40. Among them 22.2 per cent of the respondents were found in the age group of in between 41-50, and in the same *i.e.* 22.2 per cent of the respondents were have found in the age group of in between 21-30. The generated chi-square value 3.501 was found to be not significant, because it is less than the normac value. As per the statistical calculations there is no significant relation in between the age of the respondents and the Dalit Sub-Section.

- *The Occupation of the Dalit Women of the Respondents:* The majority 56.0 per cent of the respondents have reported that their occupation is agricultural labour, followed by 7.7 per cent and 11.3 per cent, 2.3 per cent, 11.7 per cent and 11.0 per cent of the respondents have noticed that their occupation is non-agricultural labour, employed, business, house wife of the dalit women respectively.

It can be seen from this study that the occupation of the respondents among the different sub-castes from the Dalit Women, out of 300 respondents 98 respondents are belongs to Mala Dalit sub-section out of which 56.1 per cent of the respondents have reported that their occupation is an agricultural labour. Where as 9.2 per cent of the respondents reported that their occupation is non-agricultural labour, followed by 8.2 per cent, 4.1 per cent 9.2 per cent and 13.3 per cent of the respondents reported that their occupation is employed, business, any other and house wives respectively.

Of the total sample 193 respondents are from Madiga Dalit sub-section of which 56.0 per cent of the respondents have informed that their occupation is agricultural labour. Among them 6.7 per cent of the respondents are reported that their occupation is non-agricultural labour, followed by the 13.0 per cent, 1.3 per cent and 11.4 per cent, 11.4 per cent of the respondents have reported that their occupation is employed, business, house wives and any other respectively. It is noticed that the other community of the dalit sub-section, out of 300 respondents 9 respondents of which 55.6 per cent of the respondents have reported that their occupation is agricultural labour, followed by 11.1 per cent, 11.1 per cent and 22.2 per cent of the respondents reported that their occupation is non-agricultural, employed, any other and house wives respectively.

- *Annual Income of the Dalit Women Respondents:* It is found that majority of the respondents *i.e.* 40.7 per cent are reported that their annual income is more than Rs. 20001. Where as 34.3 per cent of the respondents reported that their annual income is in between Rs. 15001-20000, and 11.7 per cent of the respondents have noticed that they did not applicable to annual income may be because they are house wives. Followed by 7.0 per cent, 5.7 per cent and 0.7 per cent of the respondents noticed that their annual income is in between Rs. 5001-10000, Rs. 10001-15000, and less than Rs. 5000 rupees respectively.
- *The Annual Income of the Respondents in the Different Sub-Caste from Dalit Women:* Out of the 300 respondents 98 respondents reported that they belong to Mala Dalit sub-section, of which 44.9 per cent of the respondents have reported that their annual income is in between Rs. 15001-20000, where as 38.8 per cent of the respondents reported that their annual income is more than Rs. 20001. Followed by 7.1 per cent, 6.1 per cent, 2.0 per cent and 1.0 per cent of the respondents reported that their annual income is in between Rs. 5001-10000, Not applicable, Rs. 10001-15000, and less than Rs. 5000 respectively. Regarding Madiga Dalit sub-section of the total sample 193 respondents *i.e.* 43.5 per cent of the respondent's annual income is more than Rs. 20001. It is noticed that 30.6 per cent of the respondent's annual income is in between Rs. 15001-20000, where as 15 per cent of the respondents are not applicable to annual income category as they are house wives, followed by 6.2 per cent, 4.1 per cent and 0.5 per cent of the respondent's annual income is in between Rs. 1001-15000, 5001-10000 and less than Rs. 5000 rupees. Among the other community of

the dalit sub section out of 300 respondents, only 9 respondents are found, out of which 66.7 per cent of the sample respondent's annual income is in between Rs. 5001-10000, remaining 33.3 per cent of the respondent's annual income is in between Rs. 10001-15000 rupees.

- *Nature of the House of the Dalit Women:* Of the total respondents majority *i.e.* 52.0 per cent of the respondents have reported that they are living in RCC houses, where as 42.3 per cent of the respondents reported that they are living in Thatched houses and remaining 5.7 per cent of the respondents have noticed that they are living in Tiled houses.
- *The Nature of Residence and of the Different Dalit Sub-Section of the Respondents:* Out of 300 respondents 98 respondents belong to Mala Dalit sub-section out of which 60.2 per cent of the respondents reported that their nature of house in which living in is RCC house. Among the 32.7 per cent of the respondents revealed that their nature of house in which they are living in is Thatched house and remaining 7.1 per cent of the respondents have noticed that their nature of house was Tiled house. Regarding Madiga Dalit sub-section, out of the total 300 respondents 193 respondents have reported that out of which 50.3 per cent of the respondents nature of house was RCC, followed by 45.1 per cent and 4.7 per cent of the respondents have noticed that their nature of house is Thatched and Tiled respectively. As regards to the other community very meager *i.e.* 9 respondents of which 88.9 per cent of the respondents reported that their nature of house is Thatched, and remaining 11.1 per cent of the respondents reported that their nature of house is tiled.
- *The Assets of the Sample Respondents*: Out of 300 respondents 270 which is about 90.0 per cent of the respondents reported that they are living in their own houses, followed by the 7.3 per cent and 2.6 per cent of the respondents have noticed that they are living in rented and other houses respectively. Of the total respondents 276 which

is about 92.0 per cent of the respondents has reported that their house has electrification facility and remaining 8.0 per cent of the respondents have informed that their house did not have electrification facility. Of the total respondents 280 respondents which is about 93.3 per cent of the respondents have reported that they have television and very meager *i.e.* 6.7 per cent of the respondents have noticed that they did not have television. Out of the 300 respondents 219 respondents, which is about 73.0 per cent of the respondents stated that they did not have any cycle, followed by the 20.3 per cent and 6.7 per cent of the respondents reported that they have cycle, and motor cycle respectively. Of the total respondents 241 respondents, which is about 80.3 per cent of the respondents said that they have milk animals and remaining 19.7 per cent of the respondents have reported that they did not have any milk animals.

Educational Status of Dalit Women

- *Educational Status of the Dalit Women and their Sub-Section:* It is observed that the 44.7 per cent of the respondents are reported that they are illiterates. Around to 18.7 per cent of the respondents have expressed that they studied upto primary education, followed by 15.3 per cent, 11.0 per cent and 10.3 per cent of the respondents have informed that they studied upto the Secondary, Intermediate and Graduate levels respectively.
- *Literacy Levels of the Dalit Sub-Section of the Total Respondents:* 98 respondents have reported that they belong to Mala Dalit sub section, out of which 42.9 per cent of the respondents have reported that they are illiterates. Where as 21.4 per cent of the respondents reported that their education level is primary, followed by 15.3 per cent, 13.3 per cent and 7.1 per cent of the respondents expressed that they have studied upto the Secondary , Intermediate and Graduate level respectively. Regarding Madiga Dalit sub-section of the total respondents 193 out of which 43.5 per cent of the respondents have noticed that they

are illiterates. Among them 18.1 per cent of the respondents have reported that they studied upto primary level, followed by 16.1 per cent, 13.0 per cent and 9.3 per cent of the respondents reported that their educational status is Secondary, Graduate and Intermediate levels respectively. Across the total respondents very meager 9 respondents are from other community of Dalit sub section, out of which 88.9 per cent of the respondents have reported that they were illiterates, and only 11.1 per cent of the respondents have reported that they studied upto Graduation level.

According to the present study it is revealed from the respondents that a significant *i.e.* 44.7 per cent of total Dalit-Women and 42.9 per cent, 43.5 per cent and 88.9 per cent of the cross sections of Mala, Madiga and Other sub-section respectively are found to be illiterates. So in this connection there is necessity for the Government to take improve the literacy levels among Dalit women.

- *Occupation and Educational Levels of the Respondents:* Out of the 300 respondents 168 respondents have informed that they are working as agriculture labour under different education levels of which major *chunk i.e.* 122 are found illiterates and the lowest only one respondent is found from graduation education level. The highest *i.e.* 35 respondents from the total sample have reported as house wives, in different educational background of which 14 respondents reported that they have studied upto secondary level and very low *i.e.* 4 respondents are reported illiterates.

Out of the total respondents 134 respondents have informed as illiterate and working in different occupations of which a major chunk *i.e.* 122 which is about 91.0 per cent have reported that they are agriculture labour and nil was found in the occupation of business. Out of the total respondents 56 respondents reported that they are from primary level of education and working in different occupation of which a majority revealed to be 35 *i.e.* 62.5 per cent respondents are from agricultural labour and very meager *i.e.* 7.1 per cent of the respondents have reported that their the occupation is business. Of the total respondents 46 respondents have informed that they studied upto the secondary level and working in different occupations, out of which 30.4 per cent of the respondents occupation reported to be house wives and only very meager *i.e.* 2.2 per cent of the respondents reported that their occupation was business. Out of the total respondents, 31 respondents reported to be stuidied upto Intermediate and working in different occupations of which a major chunk reported to be *i.e.* 25.8 per cent employed in Government or Private sector, and followed by 22.6 per cent, 19.4 per cent, 19.4 per cent, 6.5 per cent and 6.5 per cent have reported to be other than the mentioned, housewives, Non-agriculture, agriculture and business respectively. Out of 300 respondents 33 respondents have reported to be upto graduate level of education and they are working in different occupations of which 57.6 per cent have found to be employed and only 3.0 per cent of the respondents have reported that their occupation is agricultural labour. It also revealed that the higher the illiterate, the high percentage of agriculture labourers and at the same time it is noticed that those who have studied upto graduation level they have got employment either in the Government or in the private sector.

- *Awareness of the Respondents on Education:* It is found from the data of 93.3 per cent of the respondents that their villages have the Government schools. 51.6 per cent of the respondents have reported that they have satisfied with standards of the education in the government schools. Of the total respondents 100 each *i.e.* 33.3 per cent have reported that 3 or 4 members of their family are studying in schools and 80 respondents *i.e.* 26.6 per cent have informed that 5 of their family members are studying in schools. As regards the environment of the school that 40 per cent have reported as good and 37.3 per cent have reported to be very good. In connection with awareness of reservation of seats in the educational institutions 66.3 per cent have reported that they have got awareness and 39.7 per cent informed that they have not got awareness. Highest percentage of respondents *i.e.* 99 per cent have informed to be encouraging for the education.

- *The Opinion of the Respondents on the Family Status in Relation to Education:* Majority *i.e.* 95.3 per cent of the respondents were reported that their family status has been increased through education. It is evident that 62.0 per cent of the respondents have reported to be equal status of the Dalit women with other women because of their education. The majority *i.e.* 75.3 per cent of the respondents reported that their personality development has improved through education. While 41.7 per cent of the respondents have noticed that they have acquired knowledge through education and 56.3 per cent of the respondents informed that the earning capacity increased because of education. Where as 88.7 per cent of the respondents have reported that they know that they will get job through education. Only 11.3 per cent of the respondents reported that they had got job through education.
- *Utilisation of Reservation:* The majority *i.e.* 74.7 per cent of the respondents reported that their admission for education was not through reservation, because of the lack of awareness on the seats reservation in the educational institutions, and remaining 25.3 per cent of the respondents reported that they have got admission through reservation. Out of 300 respondents 18 respondents which is about 6.0 per cent of the respondents reported that they have got jobs through reservation facility. Of the total respondents 282 respondents which is 94.0 per cent reported that they have not utilised reservation facility because they were illiterates and lack of awareness on reservation facility.
- *Educational Facilities Utilised for the Jobs:* The majority *i.e.* 87.3 per cent of the respondents reported that they have not taken any type of free coaching provided by the government. Only 12.6 per cent of the respondents have

reported that they have taken free coaching for getting their jobs in the state government sector. Out of 300 respondents 38 respondents, which is about 36.84 per cent of the respondents have reported that they had taken free coaching for Bank exams, followed by the 13.15 per cent, 5.26 per cent, 15.78 per cent, 26.31 per cent and 2.63 per cent of the respondents have noticed that they had been taken free coaching for *i.e.* APPSC, DSC, SSC, RRB and for Other exams respectively.

- *The Educational Qualifications of the Respondents and their Annual Income:* It is observed that the 44.7 per cent of the respondents have reported to be illiterates and 18.7 per cent of the respondents have expressed that they have studied upto primary education, followed by 15.3 per cent, 11.0 per cent and 10.3 per cent of the respondents have informed that their educational qualifications are Secondary, Intermediate and Graduate level respectively.
- *The Education Level of the Respondent and their Annual Income:* Out of 300 respondents 2 respondents have reported that their annul income is less than Rs. 5000 of which 50.0 per cent each of the respondents have noticed that their level of education is illiterates and primary. Regarding the annual income, in between Rs. 5001-10000 of the total respondents 21 respondents of which 52.4 per cent of the respondents are illiterates and 9.5 pre cent of the respondents are reported that their level of education is intermediate. Among the annual income in between Rs. 10001-15000 of the sample respondents, out of 300 respondents 17 respondents have noticed, of which 41.2 pre cent of the respondents have reported that they are illiterates, followed by 17.6 per cent, 29.4 per cent and 11.8 per cent of the respondents are *i.e.* in primary, secondary, graduate levels of education. Where as the annual income is in between Rs. 15001-20000 of the total respondents 103 respondents have found, of which 67.0 per cent of the respondents have reported that their level of education is illiterate and very meager *i.e.* 1.9 per cent

of the respondents reported that their education is upto intermediate. It is noticed that the annual income is above Rs. 20001, out of 300 respondents 122 respondents have found, of which 21.3 per cent of the respondents noticed that their education is illiterates and secondary, followed by 18.9 per cent, 19.7 per cent of the respondents presented that their education is primary, intermediate and graduates. Of the total respondents 35 respondents have not reported regarding to their annual income because they are house wives. According to the present observation the higher the education are in the higher in the income and almost nil have found in the lower income group *i.e.* less 5000 and in between 5001-10000. Most of them those who had higher education found in the higher income groups *i.e.* 19.7 per cent have from Rs. 20001 and above and at the same time the illiterates have found in all income groups.

Health Conditions of Dalit Women

- *Awareness of Health Facilities Provided by the Government in the Villages.* It is evident from the study that about 97.0 per cent of the respondents have reported that the villages having primary health centres and 64.0 per cent of the respondents have informed that they are not qualified M.B.S.S Doctors in their primary health centres. As regards 91.0 per cent of the respondents have revealed that they have satisfied with the medical services provided by the government in there villages. The Majority 96.0 per cent of the respondents have noticed that they have awareness about the help rendering by the government to the pregnant women for the delivery in the government hospital. About 92.3 per cent of the respondents have said that they had aware about the nutrition food. While 100 per cent of the respondents have stated that they are aware about 108 and 104 medical services in their villages provided by the government. These services are availed/ provided by the Government of Andhra Pradesh for any emergencies in every villages. The patient will be picked up by just telephone call to the nearest primary health centre at finet with these 108 and 104 facility.

As regards to 96.0 per cent of the respondents have revealed that they had knowledge about the Rajeev Arogyasree scheme, remaining 4.0 per cent of the respondents did not aware about Rajeev Arogyasree scheme. The majority 99.0 per cent of the respondents have reported that they have awareness about HIV/AIDS. By and large the results of the study provide evidence to consider that the Dalit Women had fetter awareness on medical facilities provided by Government.

- *Whether the Respondents had Utilised Health Facilities or Not:* Out of 300 respondents 267 respondents, which is about 89.0 per cent of the respondents stated that they have undergone family planning. Of the total respondent 33 respondents which is about 11.0 per cent of the respondents have reported that they did not undergone family planning. Further it is observed that 88.7 per cent of the respondents families are having Rajeev Arogyasree cards. The majority 91.0 per cent of the respondents have reported that they did not get any treatment under the Rajeev Arogyasree scheme. It should be noted here that though they have Rajeev Arogyasree card, they could not know made use of them as they may not know the procedure to set benefit by it.
- *The Education Level of the Respondents and Awareness of the Primary Health Centre in their Village:* Out of 300 respondents 291 respondents are reported that they had awareness about the primary health centre in their village, out of which 44.3 per cent of them are illiterate respondents have reported that they had awareness about the primary health centre in their village, followed by the 19.2 per cent, 14.8 per cent, 10.7 per cent and 11.0 per cent of the respondents have reported that they had awareness about the primary health centre in their village *i.e.* primary, secondary, intermediate, graduation levels respectively. Out of the total respondents, only 9 respondents have reported that they were not aware

about the primary health centres in their villages of which 55.6 per cent of the respondents are from illiterate group, where as 33.3 per cent of them are from secondary level of education.

- *The Study Reveals that the Level of Education and the Family Planning of the Respondents.* It is observed among the total respondents that 44.7 per cent are illiterates, 18.7 per cent of the respondents reported that they have studied upto primary education, followed by 15.3 per cent, 11.0 per cent and 10.3 per cent of the respondents have informed that that their education is Secondary, Intermediate and Graduate levels respectively.

Out of 300 respondents 267 respondents have reported that they had underwent the family planning of which majority of them have reported to be illiterate *i.e.* 48.7 per cent, followed by the 19.9 per cent, 15.0 per cent, 9.4 per cent and 7.1 per cent of the respondents have primary, secondary, intermediate, graduation qualifications respectively, reported to be undergone family planning. Of the total respondents 33 respondents have reported that they did underwent family planning, of which 18.2 per cent, 18.2 per cent, 12.1 per cent and 9.1 per cent of the respondents have studied upto Secondary, intermediate, illiterates and primary education of the respondents have stated that they did not undergone family planning.

It is interested to note that the higher the education of the respondents *i.e.,* graduation have undergone family planning have shown less percentage *i.e.* 7.1 per cent and the highest percentage *i.e.* 48.7 of respondents have reported that they are illiterates and had undergone family planning. Which made it as contradicting that the impression of public that the more of the illiterates and less undergone family planning. As they just believe that the God has given children and the same God will look after them. Another reason is that the less educated and poor are also have an impression that if they have more children, they will be looked after at their oldage. But in this study it is revealed that the both impressions and hypothesis above are proved to be irrelevant and the illiterate were in the forefront in under going family planning.

- *Distribution of the Respondents of Different Dalit Sub-Sections by Whether they have Awareness about the HIV/AIDS:* The majority 99.0 per cent of the respondents have revealed that they had awareness about the HIV/AIDS, remaining 1.0 per cent of the respondents have noticed that they did not have awareness about the HIV/AIDS.

Out of the 300 respondents 98 respondents belong to Mala Dalit sub-section of which 100 per cent of the respondents reported that they had awareness about the HIV/AIDS. Of the total respondents 193 respondents are belong to Madiga Dalit sub-section of which 98.4 per cent of the respondents reported that they have awareness about the HIV and AIDS. And very meager *i.e.* 1.6 per cent of women stated that they did not aware about the HIV/AIDS. The 100 per cent of the Others of Dalit sub-section noticed that they are aware of the HIV/AIDS.

- *Nutrition Food for Pregnant Women and Dalit Women:* 91.7 per cent of the total sample respondents have reported that the Anganawadi centres have been providing the nutrition food for pregnant women and remaining 8.3 per cent of the respondents have reported that the others giving nutrition food for pregnant women.
- *The Nutrition Food for Pregnant Women and Dalit Sub-Section:* Out of 300 respondents 98 respondents are belong to Mala Dalit sub-section of which 85.7 per cent of the respondents stated that the nutrition food had given by Anganawadi and 14.3 per cent of the respondents have noticed that the nutrition food had given by others. Of the total respondents 193 respondents are belongs to Madiga Dalit sub-section, out of which 94.3 per cent of the respondents reported that the Anganawadi has been providing nutrition food for pregnant women and 5.7 per cent of the sample respondents reported that the nutrition food for pregnant women had been given by other than Anganawadi. Of the total respondents 9 respondents belongs to other community of Dalit sub section of which 100 per cent of the respondents are reported that the Anganawadi has been giving nutrition food for pregnant women.

- *The Levels of Education of the Respondents and the Medical Services Provided by Government in the Villages:* The present study they have expressed different views on the medical services provided to the respondents. Out of the total respondents, 273 respondents have reported that they have had satisfaction on medical services providing by the government, of which it is observed from the table that the highest percentage of the illiterate respondents stated that they had satisfaction on medical services that the government is providing, *i.e.* 44.7, followed by the Primary, Secondary, Intermediate, and Graduate *i.e.* 19.0 per cent, 14.7 per cent, 10.6 per cent and 11.0 per cent of the respondents reported that they have satisfied with the medical services in their village providing by the government. Of the total respondents only 27 respondents of which 44.4 per cent of the illiterate respondents have reported that they are not have satisfied by the medical services providing by the government, followed by the 18.7 per cent, 15.3 per cent, 10.3 per cent, 11.0 per cent *i.e.* Primary, Secondary, Intermediate and Graduate levels respectively.
- *Awareness on Rendering in Pre-natal Services to Pregnant Women until the Delivery in the Government Hospitals vs. Dalit Sub-Sections:*. Out of the total respondents 288 respondents of which 96.0 per cent of the Dalit sub-section respondents have noticed that they have awareness on rendering pre-natal services to pregnant women until the delivery in the government hospitals. Where as 12 respondents of which 4.0 per cent of the respondents reported that they did not have awareness on rendering pre-natal services to pregnant women until the delivery in the government hospitals.

Among the different Dalit sub-caste categories, the expressed the total respondents, 98 respondents belongs to Mala Dalit sub-section of which 93.9 per cent of the respondents stated that they have got awareness about services rendering by government to pregnant women until the delivery in the government hospitals. Where as remaining 6.1 per cent of the respondents have reported that they did not have awareness of the services provided by Government in the pre-natal. Out of the 300 respondents 193 respondents belong to Madiga dalit sub-section of which 96.9 per cent of the respondents reported that they had awareness, where as 3.1 per cent of the respondents stated that they did not have awareness. Regarding other communities very meager of the total respondents *i.e.* 9 respondents, of which 100 per cent respondents have reported that they have awareness of the services rendering to pregnant women until the delivery in the government hospitals.

Economic Status of Dalit Women

- *Annual Income and Occupation of the Respondents:* It is evident that the majority the respondents *i.e.* 40.7 per cent of the respondents reported that their annual income is above Rs. 20001, followed by the 34.3 per cent, 11.75 per cent, 7.0 per cent, 5.7 per cent and 0.7 per cent of the respondents have noticed that their annual income is in between Rs. 15001-20000, not applicable to annual income because they are house wives, Rs. 5001-10000, Rs. 10001-15000 and Rs. Less than 5000 respectively.

Out of the total respondents 168 respondents are agricultural labours of which 48.8 per cent of the respondents have reported that their annual income is in between 15001-20000, followed by the 25.0 per cent, 12.5 per cent of the respondents have noticed that their annual income is in between above Rs. 20001 and not applicable to annual income because they were house wives. Of the total respondents 23 respondents are non-agricultural labour of which 69.6 per cent of the respondents have reported that their annual income was more than Rs. 20001 rupees, where as the 13.0 per cent of the respondents stated that their annual income is in between Rs. 15001-20000. Out of the total respondents 34 respondents have reported that their occupation was employment of which 79.4 per cent of the respondents reported that their annual income is more than Rs. 20001, followed by the 8.7 per cent and 5.9 per cent of the respondents have noticed that their annual income *i.e.*

not applicable to Rs. 15001-20000. Among the total respondents very meager 7 respondents have reported that their occupation is business of which 42.9 per cent of the respondents presented that their annual income is in between Rs. 5001-10000. Out of the total respondents 33 respondents have occupation has reported to be any other, of which 48.5 per cent of the respondents reported that their annual income is more than Rs. 20001. Out of the total respondents 35 respondents are reported that their occupation is house wives of which 54.3 per cent have reported that their annual income is above Rs. 20,000 thousand rupees.

- *Land Holding of the Respondents:* It is evident that the majority 90.0 per cent of the respondents reported that they did not have land, followed by 6.6 per cent, 2.0 per cent and 0.6 per cent of the respondents have reported that they have 0.5 acre, 0.5 - 1 acre, 1 - 1.5 acres, and 1.5 - 2 acres of land holding of the sample respondents. Therefore the majority of the respondents have reported that they did not have agri-land. The results of the data revealed that the whole land is totally under the control of other than the Dalits. Though Government is declaring that the land was distributed to the weaker sections was not found similar according to the findings of the study.
- *Financial Responsibility of the Respondents:* The majority 83.7 per cent of the respondents have reported husband and wife has been taking care of financial responsibility in their family. Where as 5.7 per cent of the respondents have reported that the only husband is taking care of financial responsibility of their family. Followed by the 4.7 per cent, 4.3 per cent of the respondents have noticed that their family financial responsibility had taken by the respondents themselves and also by their Father.

Awareness of the respondents on the wages paying to the labour in their village have found through this study. The majority 47.3 per cent of the respondents have reported that their wages are in between Rs. 50-100 rupees per day work. Where as 27.0 per cent of the respondent informed that the wages in their villages are in between Rs. 101-150 rupees per day. As regards the 17.0 per cent of the respondents reported the wages in their village is in between Rs. 151-200 rupees per day work.

Political Status of Dalit Women

- *Discloses that the Respondents Exercising their Right to Vote for Local body Election (Gram Panchayat, MPTC, ZPTC) and Assemble and Parliamentary Elections:* It also elicited from the respondents regarding the participation in the elections. In the present study it is reported that 89.7 per cent of the respondents have exercised their right to vote for local body elections (Gram Panchayat, MPTC, ZPTC) and also very insignificant *i.e.* 10.3 per cent have not exercised their right to vote in the local body elections. Another important finding is that 71.7 per cent of the respondents have exercised their right to vote and 28.3 per cent have reported that they could not able to exercise for both Assemble and Parliamentary elections. Out of 300 respondents 7 respondents, of which 2.3 per cent of the respondents have revealed that they had been elected in the local body elections *i.e.* (Gram Panchayat Ward member, Gram Panchayat President, M.P.T.C and Z.P.T.C). Though not given any question an contest in this study regarding the participation in the Assembly and Parliamentary elections, no one has informed that they have contested for the Assemble and Parliamentary elections. It is also noticed that they don't have awareness that they too could also participate under the general quota in all the elections.
- *The Awareness of the Respondents on Political Parties at the Village Level:* The majority *i.e.* 83.7 per cent of the respondents have reported that their village President, MPTC, ZPTC are belong to Congress party and remaining 16.3 per cent of the respondents stated that their village President, MPTC, ZPTC are belong to Telugu Desam Party. As regards to 53.0 per cent of the respondents have voted more than three times in gram panchayat elections.

Followed by the One time, Two times, Three times *i.e.* 2.0 per cent, 10.3 per cent and 32.0 per cent of the respondents have reported that they had participated in voting to grama panchayat elections and remaining 2.7 per cent of the respondents reported that they did not participated in voting to gram panchayats elections. The majority *i.e.* 88.3 per cent of the respondents informed that they did not have membership of any political party. About 9.7 per cent of the respondents reported that they have a membership in Congress political party. Where as 2.0 per cent of the respondents have reported that they have membership in Telugu Desam political party.

- *Education Levels of Respondents and Awareness on Reservation of Seats for SCs, STs in the Panchayati Raj Institutions According to 73rd Constitutional Amendment Act 1993.* Out of the total respondents, 59 respondents have reported that they had awareness of the 73rd constitutional amendment Act 1993 for reservation of seats for SCs, STs, in the Panchayats of which 52.5 per cent who studied upto graduation, followed by the 18.6 per cent and 13.6 per cent of the respondents informed that they have intermediate, secondary and primary level of educational qualifications. Of the total respondents 241 respondents have reported that they were not aware of the 73rd constitutional amendment Act for reservation of seats for SCs, STs, in the Panchayats, of which 53.5 per cent of the respondents who were illiterates, followed by the 21.6 per cent, 15.8 per cent, 8.3 per cent and 0.8 per cent of the respondents who have studied upto primary, secondary, intermediate and graduation levels of education respectively. The higher the awareness and the illiterate have reported that they were not aware of 73rd constitutional amendment Act. The hypotheses formulated in the present study as to enquiry of association of the awareness of the Dalit women and educational background is proved to be true as the chi-square statistical results are proved to be significant.

The study disclosed the occupation of the respondents and their participation in the gram panchayat elections have disclosed here. It is evident that the most of the respondents *i.e.* 56.0 per cent have reported that their occupation is agricultural labour, followed by 7.7 per cent, 11.3 per cent, 2.3 per cent, 11.7 per cent and 11.0 per cent of the respondents informed that their occupation is non-agricultural labour, employed, business, house wives of the Dalit sub-section respectively.

Out of the total respondents 269 respondents have reported that they had participated in voting to the gram panchayat elections of which 56.1 per cent of the respondents have expressed that they have participated in voting in the gram Panchayat elections who have reported their occupation as agricultural labour, followed by the non-agricultural, employed, business, house wives and other activities, *i.e.* 7.4 per cent, 11.9 per cent, 2.6 per cent, 11.5 per cent and 10.4 per cent, of the respondents respectively have expressed that they did not have participated in Gram panchayat elections. Of the total respondents 31 respondents, of which 54.8 per cent of the respondents are from the agricultural labourers, followed by the 9.7 per cent, 6.5 per cent, 0.0 per cent, 12.9 per cent and 16.1 per cent, of the non-agricultural labour, employed, business, house wives, other activities respectively.

- *Education Levels and Utilisation of Right to Vote of the Respondents:* The majority *i.e.* 44.7 per cent of the respondents have reported to be illiterates. As regards to 18.7 per cent of the respondents have expressed that they have studied upto primary education, followed by 15.3 per cent, 11.0 per cent and 10.3 per cent of the respondents have informed that their education is upto Secondary, Intermediate and Graduation level respectively of the Dalit women.

Out of the total respondents 292 respondents have reported that they had utilised their right to vote, of which 44.5 per cent were illiterates, followed by the primary, secondary, intermediate, graduate educators *i.e.* 19.2 per cent,

14.7 per cent, 10.6 per cent and 11.0 per cent respectively. As regards of the total respondents only very few *i.e.* 8 respondents of which 50.0 per cent of the illiterate respondents were not utilised their right to vote, followed by the 37.5 per cent and 12.5 per cent of the respondents were studied upto secondary and graduation level.

Though it may not be found a significant association, higher the exercise of their right to vote been found in the illiterates and the less of them have exercised their right to vote of *i.e.* 50 per cent have also found from the same group.

- *Awareness about Gram Panchayat Activities of the Respondents:* Out of 300 respondents 257 respondents which is about 85.7 per cent of the respondents have reported that they had awareness about Gram Panchayat activities in the development of the village. Of the total respondents 43 respondents, which is about 14.3 per cent of the respondents have reported that they were not aware of the Gram Panchayat activities for in developing their villages. As regards the 82.0 per cent of the respondents have reported that they know about the role of the ward members in the developmental activities of the village, remaining 18.0 per cent of the respondents have expressed that they did not know about the role of ward members in the village. The majority of which 80.3 per cent of the respondents have reported that they did were aware about the seats reservations in Gram Panchayats according to 73rd constitutional amendment Act. About 19.7 per cent of the respondents have reported that they had awareness about reservation of seats in Gram Panchayats according 73rd constitutional amendment Act. The majority *i.e.* 97.3 per cent of the respondents had utilised the right to vote. Where as 2.7 per cent of the respondents have reported that they did not utilised their right to vote. About 98.3 per cent of the respondents have reported that they did not participated in Co-operative society elections and remaining 1.7 per cent of the respondents have reported that they have participated voting in the Co-operative society elections.

- *Awareness about Gram Panchayat Activities for the Development of the Village and the Dalit Sub-Castes:* The majority of the respondents *i.e.* 85.7 per cent have expressed that they had awareness in the gram panchayat activities for the development of the village, where as 14.3 per cent of the respondents reported that they were not aware of the grama panchayats activities for the development of the village.
- *The Distribution of different Dalit sub-Castes:* Out of 300 respondents 98 respondents belong to Mala Dalit sub-section of which 90.8 per cent of the respondents have reported that they had awareness about the gram Panchayat activities in the development of the village. Regarding 9.2 per cent of the respondents have reported that they did not have awareness of the gram panchayat activities in the development of the village. Of the total respondents, 193 respondents belongs to Madiga Dalit sub-section, of which 86.0 per cent of the Madiga Dalit sub-Caste have reported that they had awareness about the Gram Panchayats activities in the development of their villages, remaining 14.0 per cent of the respondents Madiga Dalit sub-Caste have reported that they did not have awareness about the Gram Panchayat activities in the development of their villages. Of the total respondents 9 respondents are belong to other communities of Dalit sub-section of which 77.8. per cent *i.e.* STs respondents have reported that they were not aware about Gram Panchayat activities in the development of their villages, remaining 22.2 per cent of the respondents have reported that they had awareness on Gram Panchayats activities in the development of their villages. It implied that the majority of the STs do not have awareness that they too can participate in the activities for the development of their villages.
- *The Awareness of the Respondents on the Role of the Ward Members in Developing their Villages in Relation Dalit Sub-Sections:* The majority *i.e.* 82.0 per cent of the Dalit sub

sections respondents have reported that they had awareness about the ward member role in developing of their villages, remaining 18.0 per cent of the respondents have informed that they were not aware of the ward member role in developing their village.

- *Among the Different Dalit Sub-Sections:* Out of 300 respondents, 98 respondents belong to Mala Dalit sub-section, of which 86.7 per cent of the respondents stated that they are aware of the role played by the ward members in developing their villages. About 13.3 per cent of Mala Dalit sub-caste do not know about the role of the ward members in the developing their villages. Of the total respondents, 193 respondents belong to Madiga Dalit sub-section of which 82.4 per cent of the Madiga Dalit sub-caste respondents have reported that they are aware of the role of the ward members in developing their villages, remaining *i.e.* 17.6 per cent of the Madiga Dalit sub-caste have informed that they did not know about the role of the ward members in developing their villages. Of the total respondents very meager 9 respondents of which 77.8 per cent of the Others of the Dalit sub-section respondents have reported that they did not know about the role of the ward members in developing their village, and remaining 22.2 per cent of the respondents have stated that they know the role of the ward members in developing their villages. The higher percentage *i.e.* 77.8per cent of the respondents have reported that the Dalit sub-Caste *i.e.* STs did not know the role of ward members role in their developing of their villages.

Impact of Development Programmes

- *Age and Joining in the Self-Help Group (SHGs):* Out of the total sample of the respondents 248 respondents have joined in SHGs (Self-Help Groups) of which *i.e.* 47.2 per cent of the respondents in between 31-40 age group, followed by the 31.9 per cent, 20.2 per cent of the respondents have joined in SHGs, their age groups are in between 41-50, 21-30 of the respondents. Out of the

300 respondents 52 respondents have not joined in SHGs, of which 34.6 per cent of the respondents in the age group were in between 21-30. Very less *i.e.* 0.8 per cent have reported in between less than 20 years of their age and majority of their *i.e.* 47.2 per cent have found to be joined in between the age group of 31-40 years of their age.

- *Age and Reasons for Joining in Self-Help Groups (SHGs):* Out of the 300 respondents 52 respondents have reported that they have joined in the self-help groups, of which 34.6 per cent of the respondents are in between the age group of 21-30. Of the total sample respondents 50 respondents have informed that they have joined in the SHGs for getting loans, of which 56.0 per cent in between the age group of 31-40. Regarding the 188 respondents have reported that they had joined in the self help group for promoting savings of which 45.7 per cent of respondents in their age group in between 31-40. As regards to 3 respondents have stated that they had joined in the self help groups to improve their social status, of which 66.7 per cent of the respondents in between the age group of 41-50 years, followed by 57.1 per cent of the respondents have reported that they have joined in SHGs for meeting/ fulfilling their domestic needs in the age group of in between 41-50.

The respondents have reported out of which 66.7 per cent in between the age group of 41-50 years have joined in SHGs only for improving their social status followed by 57.1 per cent, 56 per cent in between 41-50 years of age and 31-40 of the age have reported the reason for joining SHGs is to satisfy their domestic needs by getting loans. The general impression and the basic purpose of SHGs are for the financial support in their need and for inculcating the habit of saving, but it is surprising to find the highest majority in the age group of in between 41-50 who have expressed that they are attaining good social status in their village through SHGs.

- *The Awareness of the Respondents on the SHGs Management:* The highest *i.e.* 60.3 per cent of the respondents have reported that they have the habit of saving and remaining 39.7 per cent of the respondents stated that they did not have the habit of the saving. As regards the 96.3 per cent of the respondents have expressed that they had confined their group to one particle caste, while 3.6 per cent of the respondents have stated that their group consists of all castes. It can drawn from the 80.2 per cent of the respondents, Who have reported that they have formed the group with 5-10 members. Where as 52.8 per cent of the respondents have informed that their monthly saving was Rs. 50 rupees per month.

Majority *i.e.* 99.19 per cent of the respondents have informed that they had been maintaining attendance registers. About 99.19 per cent of the respondents have reported that they have been conducting group meetings regularly. The total respondents have been collecting every monthly in their group meetings to save money. Where as 99.2 per cent of the respondents informed that they have been maintaining minutes book. About 66.1 per cent of the respondents, they have not take revolving fund and remaining 33.8 per cent of the respondents have been taking revolving fund. About 31.0 per cent of the respondents have reported that they have been taking Rs. 10000.00 as loan from the revolving fund.

- *Barrowing of Loans from the SHGs by the Respondents have Expressed*: The Self-Help Group concept is more impressive or attractive for the development of women in the villages, in this study majority *i.e.* 82.33 per cent of the respondents had reported that they have taken loan from SHGs. Around 35.0 per cent of the respondents have reported that they had been taken less than Rs. 5000 rupees. Where as 21.33 per cent of the respondents have reported that they have taken more than Rs. 20000 rupees. The majority of *i.e.* 48.38 per cent of the respondents have informed that they have taken the loan for the purpose of their children education.

According to the present study, it was found that there is a significant in investing money for their children's education which was barrowed from SHGs and also found the changing in the attitude of the Dalit Women for educating their children.

- *Management of Banking Transaction by the Respondents:* It is evident that 93.3 per cent of the respondents reported that they have an idea on banking transactions after joining in SHGs, remaining 6.6 per cent of the respondents have reported that they don't have an idea about banking. As regarding the opinions on banking it was found that 62.0 per cent of the respondents have reported that they have less interest and easy installments for the money barrowed from the banks. Followed by the getting loans, beneficial to the rich people, beneficial to the poor people and needy etc.. *i.e.* 16.7 per cent, 7.3 per cent, and 14.0 per cent of the respondents have found respectively from the data. The data on individual bank passbooks, the majority 51.33 per cent of the respondents reported that they have been maintaining individual bank passbooks. Where as 48.7 per cent of the respondents did not maintain individual pass books. Because of their membership in the SHGs they have got good knowledge on banking transactions and major chunk of the respondents have been maintaining bank passbooks. It is also noticed the installment payments are more easy for them to clear the loans at the lowest interest rate. That makes them fell comfortable.
- *Taking Loans from the Banks by the SHGs Members:* It was understood that the majority *i.e.* 35.4 per cent of the respondents have reported that their group had taken loan upto Rs. 50,000 rupees. Followed by the group Rs. 50,001-1,00,000; Rs. 1,00,001-1,50,000; Rs. 1,50,001-2,00,000 and above Rs. 2,00,001 *i.e.* 18.9 per cent, 6.8 per cent, 12.9 per cent, and 25.8 per cent of the respondents respectively had taken loans. The majority *i.e.* 96.7 per cent of the respondents have reported that they are paying interest @ 25 paisa for every Rs. 100/-. Anyway it is very interesting to note that in these present days it was rarely heard about such an lowest interest rate of 25

paisa, but the members of SHGs have a good pride for in enjoying money at the cheaper interest rate.

- *Awareness of the Government Programmes for the Development of both Villages as well as the Sample Respondents:* The majority *i.e.* 93.3 per cent of the respondents reported that they had awareness of the Government programmes, where as 6.6 per cent of the respondents have reported that they did not know the Government programmes. About 92.6 per cent of the respondents have reported that they know the different programmes conducted by the Government like DWACRA/MGNREGS programmes, followed by 3.3 per cent and 4.0 per cent of the respondents have stated that had a know the PMRY, CMEY. Among the 73.0 per cent of the respondents have reported that their family has MGNREGS job card, where as 27.0 per cent of the respondents have noticed that their families did not have MGNREGS job card.

It is found that the majority of the respondents *i.e.* 31.9 per cent of the sample respondents have reported that the gram Panchayat did not providing any work, followed by the 26.7 per cent, 21.0 per cent, 15.9 per cent, 3.0 per cent and 1.3 per cent of the respondents have reported that the grama panchayat is providing work for 0 -25 days, not apply for work, for 26-50 days of work, for 51-75 days of work, and for 76-100 days of work respectively. Among the 65.78 per cent of the respondents have reported that they have been earning per day work was in between Rs. 75-100, followed by the 17.54 per cent of the respondents have reported that they have been earning per day more than Rs. 100 per head.

9 CASE STUDIES

Case Study – 1 Manorama

Manorama was awarded The Right Livelihood Award in 2006. Considered the alternative Noble Prize and the world's premier award for personal courage and social transformation, it got her the recognition as the sub-continent's most effective organizer and advocate for Dalit women. She was also one among the thousand nominees for the 1,000 Peace women for Nobel Peace Prize in 2005.

As General Secretary of Women's Voice Karnataka, an organization working for the rights of women of poorer sections, women living in the slums and working in the unorganized sector, she has never hesitated to take up their issues. During the 1980s and the 90s, she was in the forefront of mass struggles against eviction and Operation Demolition by the State Government of Karnataka and organized massive processions and fought legal cases on their behalf. She also enjoys the distinction of establishing the first trade union in the country in 1987 for domestic workers in Bengaluru and strived for inclusion in the Minimum Wages.

One among the numerous key offices Manorama holds is president of the National Alliance of Women. Pointing to the fact that it all begins at home, Manorama believes that the situation in some families is not a very happy one, with a level playing field still a distant dream.

"Many women do not enjoy autonomy. They are vulnerable and dependent on male partners who make all the decisions. Although it looks as if women are progressing on many fronts, in terms of power relations, it is still unequal. Our law application is unequal and our laws are patriarchal. One women become widowed, they are left to their own defence. Property is taken away. This scenario extends to public life and politics".

If one is looking for solutions, Manorama spells out a blue-print for that. "How do people gain power? It is political power that gives you social power and economic power. Women miss to get into politics in order to acquire power not for themselves but for a whole lot of people. It was thought that through the Constitution, women will automatically get power and men will be out. The Panchayati Raj system, no matter however flawed, has its merits. Women make decisions and offer resistance. Democracy without women is non democracy without women is no democracy. I am not talking of politics for making money. Our generating is not for garnering wealth but for reclamation of the human spirit. Women have better brain capabilities and if it is put to use have such bright women, imagine what can be achieved".

Manorama's vision for the future is to start a Political academy. She has already prepared the ground through specific capacity building exercises and has been instrumental in training around 300 women in the country to equip them for community action and leadership positions at the Panchayat, Zilla Perished and State level.

Manorama is the president of the National Federation of Dalit Women. She "Grew up in a fairly progressive atmosphere with Christian values where you gave freely and treated people with respect". Theirs was an open house and her parents extended all kinds of support to visitors from helping to fill out job applications, money order forms and for a consultation on sundry matters. Her parents' lifestyle and dedication inspired Manorama, and the upbringing she received reminded her that whatever she did, she had to serve the poor.

Early Days

Initially Manorama wanted to become a doctor or a collector. While in Chennai she worked in slum, squatter settlements and realised that working for the urban poor could be her vocation. At her father's suggestion she enrolled for a Master in Social Work. Later she moved to villages, understood caste structures, land patterns and the problems of Dalits.

Right from the beginning of her foray into the social sector she set about organizing oppressed people, getting them to claim their rights and become stake holders in development. '*I grew up on that kind of pitch*', she says.

Manorama closes with a pointer. "The situation of Dalits can't be changed by Dalits themselves. Dalits must lead and other progressive people must join in this struggle. As Indian citizens we have a role to play in transforming pains into power".

Case Study – 2 Nalukurthi Vijaya

She was president of Angalakuturu Grama Panchayati. This Grama Panchayati is reserved for Scheduled Caste General according to 73rd Constitutional Amendment Act 1993. She studied upto 5th class only. She got membership of Telugu Desam Political Party. She participated in Co-operative Society elections and she expressed she has exercised of her right to vote in all elections.

She is member in Self-Help Group (SHG) and expressed that reason for join in SHGs is in promoting savings. In her SHGs group she had 10 members. She has an idea about banking before joining SHGs members. She was saving Rs. 50/- per every month. Her group was taken revolving fund for Rs. 10,000/-. Her groups is taken a loan Rs. 1,00,000/-. Her group is maintaining attendance register, minutes books, group meetings are conducting every month and monthly savings are collecting in group meeting. The installments for repayment is in between 10 to 20 months was fixed. She expressed that she is using the money taken form SHGs for her childerns education.

Nalukurthi Vijaya is in between 41-50 years age group. She is one of the sample respondent Dalit women. She belongs to Madiga Dalit Sub-Section. She is living R.C.C. House and Nuclear family. She stays with her three children, husband and her occupation is as an agricultural labour. She is participating in their community activities of their village like community festival, cultural programmes and agricultural and other works. According to the information given by her that the village streets have arranged according to their caste. She expressed that she has been participating in all community functions, festivals and other meetings along with other caste people. She reeled that there is no discrimination in entering temples and water tanks and she reported no untouchability practice is there in their village. She expressed that the inter caste marriages will certainly bring changes in the society. She has accepted equal recognaization to Dalit women and other women. She never faced discrimination on the name of the caste in their village.

She was aware about MGNREGS and having MGNREGS job card her family. She told had undergone Family planning and encouraged good number of women. She had awareness about the help rendering by Government to pregnant women until the delivery in the Government Hospitals and she informed that she aware about 108, 104 medical services in their villages provided by the government. She expressed that these services have been providing by the Government of Andhra Pradesh for any emergencies in every village. The patient will be picked up by just telephone call to the nearest primary health centre.

Case Study – 3: Drakshapali Dhevamani

Drakshapali Dhevamani is in between 31-40 years age group she was one of the sample respondent of Kativaram village. She belongs to Mala Dalit Sub-Section. She was living thatched house and nuclear family. She stays with her two childrens, husband and her occupation is as an agricultural labour. She is an illiterate and she has been participating in community activities in their village community festivals. Her husband was take care of the family financial responsibility. She was told that their village having separate street for each caste and told did found could not practiced untouchability in their village. Dalit women are allowed into the temples and she expressed that the inter caste marriages will bring changes in society. She is not carrying the profession of their own caste and she felt that Dalit women have not looked down as comparing to the women in the society. She expressed that there equal opportunities to Dalit women in comparing to the other caste women and she accepted that equal reorganisation is been getting to Dalit women in comparing with other women. She did not find discrimination on the name of the caste in their village. She has been earning her family livelihood through daily wages. She has been encouraging their family member for education and also to their relatives, neighbours and their community people. She has been exercising her right to vote in every election.

She joined in Self-Help Group (SHG) and expressed the reason for join in SHGs for promoting savings and getting loans. Her SHG group consists of 10 members. She did not know an idea about banking before joining SHG members and saving Rs. 50/- per every month. She informed that her group did not take any revolving fund. Their group was taken loan an amount Rs. 1,50,000/-. Her groups is maintaining attendance register, minutes books, group meetings are conducting meetings for every month and monthly savings are collecting in group meeting. The installments for payment have fixed in between 10 to 20 months for repayment of loan amount. She has been using money withdrawing from SHG for her childerns educations.

She was aware about MGNREGS and having MGNREGS job card in her family. She knows about family planning and she was undergone family planning. She was aware about Rajivee Arogyasri Scheme. Her family was having Rajivee Arogyasri card and her family members did not treated under Rejivee Arogyasri Card as there was no need. She was awareness about the help rendering by Government to pregnant women until the delivery in the Government Hospitals and she was aware about 108, 104 medical services in their villages provided by the government. These services have been providing by the Government of Andhra Pradesh for emergencies in every village. The patient will be picked up by just telephone call to the nearest primary health centre. She revealed that they could overcome from the social backwardness and reported that the high per cent of the poorest in the poor in society could be found in the scheduled caste people. According to her hat the reasons may be lot of suppression to these caste people since generation together, though the constitution has provided equal rights and opportunities they could not come up financially as their poverty make them very poor again. Poverty is a viscerally to become poor and very backward incomparing other sections of people in the society.

10 CONCLUDING OBSERVATIONS AND SUGGESTIONS

This chapter presented overview of the findings of the study and examines their implications for social policy formulation.

The present study on the Status of Dalit Women in Andhra Pradesh – A Case Study in Guntur District is take up in Six Villages in Tenali Mandal. The major objectives of the study are:

1. To study the Socio-Economic and Political conditions of the Dalit Women in Rural Areas.
2. To study the Educational and Health aspects of the Dalit Women in Rural Areas.
3. To study the Impact of Developmental Programmes on the Dalit Women in Rural Areas.
4 To make necessary suggestions for effective implementation of developmental programmes for the Empowerment of Dalit Women in Rural Areas.

Sample of the Study

The sample of the study consists of the socio-economic and political status, education, health aspects and impact of development programmes of the Dalit women. A sample of 300 Dalit women from six villages in Tenali Mandal; Guntur district of Andhra Pradesh had been selected by using simple random sampling method. In this present study an interview scheduled was used to conduct this study.

Findings of the Study

Social Status of Dalit Women

- According to this study majority respondents have found from Madiga Dalit sub-section and very few respondents are from other community of Dalit sub-section. In this study area majority of Dalit population are residing in this study area are belongs to Madiga Dalits sub-section.
- Age is an important factor in understanding the role and status of an individual in the society (Persons - 1942, Benedier - 1938). Society differentiates human beings into children, adults and old on the basis of their age. Age composition of the respondents reveals whether the sample is young, adult or old through interview schedule by drawing the information on their age composition. The study also revealed that most of the them have found in between 31-40 years of age group and very meager had found from less than 20 years of age group of the respondents.
- In this study it is noticed that the most of them are belongs to Hindu religion and 0.7 per cent respondents belongs to Christian as of the their religion.
- Marriage is an important event in the life of an individual. This is more so in the case of women. It redefines one's role and status in the society. In India married women have been respected and honoured. Marital status also indicates whether one is settled in life or not. It shows one's desire for family and kinship. It provides for a bigger and a broader vision of life. It also indicates a will power to know face life. It enables a broader view. The majority of respondents were married, 7.7 per cent have Unmarried and 1.7 per cent were Widows.
- Education as an important in schools and collages has came to be accepted as an agent of social change and modernization. It develops the skill of reading, writing, and numeracy. It also develops the capacity of reasoning, thinking and comprehension. It introduces dynamic

elements of one's personality. Education in the form of degrees, is intimately linked with modern occupation. The educated find better Employment opportunities. According to this study majority have found the illiterate there by there is a need to create facilities to educate all the Dalit-Women both by Government programmes and through also encouraging Non-Governmental Organizations (NGO).

- The study revealed that 66.3 per cent of the respondents had awareness of reservation of the seats in educational institutions, majority 99.0 per cent of the respondents are encouraging for education to their family members, relatives and neighbours.
- Majority percentage of the respondents have noticed that their status is increased, equal status of dalit women with other women and personality development through education.
- Majority per cent of the respondents reported that they did not get jobs through education because majority of them are illiterates. Only 6.0 per cent of the respondents had got job through reservation facilities.
- The study revealed that 12.6 per cent of the respondents noticed that they had been taken free coaching for *i.e.* APPSC, DSC, SSC, RRB and Other exams of the sample respondents.

Economic Status of Dalit Women

- The study also revealed that most of them earning more than above Rs. 20,000/- of annual income.
- In this study noticed, majority of the Heads of the family annual income is in between Rs. 20,000-30,000.
- In this study it is expressed that they have earning less income and residing in RCC and Thatched houses. Though Government is constructing houses for weaker sections, it is not sufficient to all Dalits and segregating them by constructing faraway places of the village. It may be possible to bring them into the main stream by

construction of an integrated housing scheme, so that they can establish relations with other caste groups and to some extent they can improve their social status.

- The study revealed that majority did not have sanitary facilities and most of them have reported their family is consists of nuclear family. Around 90 per cent of the respondents had their own houses, 92.0 per cent of the respondents houses have had electrification facility and majority of sample respondents are having television.
- Occupation interms of gainful employment is a crucial factor in deciding one's position and status in the society. A study of occupational status of the respondents explains their power position and income. According to this study majority have found agricultural labour. The majority of the respondents have revealed that they did not have milk animals.

Health Conditions of Dalit Women

- Regarding awareness of the health facilities in the village, high percentage of the respondents reported that their village have a primary health centre but did not have a qualified MBBS doctors.
- Majority percentage of the respondents have revealed that they have satisfied with the medical services rendering in their villages provided by the Government. In the study, majority percentage of the respondents have noticed the awareness about the help rendering by Government to pregnant women until the delivery in the Government hospitals. Majority of the respondents have expressed that they have undergone family planning, most of the respondents had aware about the nutritious food and cent percentage of the respondents have reported that they had knowledge about 108 medical services, 104 medical mobile services of their villages. 99.0 per cent of the respondents got awareness about the HIV/ AIDS.

- The study noticed that the high per cent of the respondents have reported that they had awareness about the Rajeev Arogyasree Scheme, 88.7 per cent of the respondents families had been Rajeev Arogyasree Cards. Only 9.0 per cent of the respondents have got treated under the Rajeev Arogyasree Scheme.
- In this study 90.0 per cent of the respondents informed that they did not have agri-land holding. Majority 83.7 per cent of the respondents have revealed that the husband and wife are taking care of financial responsibility in their family.
- The majority of the sample 47.3 per cent of the respondents reported wages have been paying them for their per day work is in between Rs. 50-100 rupees. Whereas 27.0 per cent of the respondents informed that the wages in their village are in between Rs. 101-150 rupees per day. As regards 17.0 per cent of the respondents revealed that the wages are in their village in between Rs. 151-200 per day work. According to this study it is found that the wages paying for them are not uniform among the sample respondents. It varies from Rs. 50 to Rs. 200/-.

Political Status of Dalit Women

Of the total sample of respondents exercising their right to vote for local body elections (Gram Panchayat, MPTC, ZPTC) and Assemble and Parliamentary elections a majority 89.7 per cent of the respondents have exercised their right to vote for local body elections and also very insignificant *i.e.* 10.3 per cent have not exercise their right to in the local body elections. Another important finding is that 71.7 per cent of the respondents have exercised their right to vote and 28.3 per cent have informed that they could not able to use their vote for both Assemble and Parliamentary elections.

- According to this study very meager *i.e.* 2.3 per cent of the respondents informed that they had been elected in the local body elections (Gram Panchayat, MPTC, ZPTC).

- The majority 88.3 per cent of the respondents could not take membership of any political party, followed by 9.7 per cent, 2.0 per cent of the sample respondents informed that they had taken membership like Congress party, Telugu Desam party.
- Regarding awareness about reservation of seats for SCs, STs according to the 73rd constitutional amendment Act. Out of the total sample 80.3 per cent of the Dalit women revealed that they did not have awareness on 73rd constitutional amendment Act, remaining 19.6 per cent of the respondents noticed that they had awareness on 73rd constitutional amendment Act.
- The majority sample 85.7 per cent said that they got knowledge on Gram Panchayat activities for development of village, 14.3 per cent informed that they did not have knowledge on Gram Panchayat activities for the development of village.
- According to the study 82.0 per cent revealed that they had a knowledge about ward members role in development of village, 18.0 per cent reported that they could not have knowledge on ward members role in development village.
- Majority *i.e.* 97.3 per cent of sample respondents have informed that they had utilised the right to vote, where as 2.7 per cent reported that they could not utilised their of right to vote.
- In this study 98.5 per cent could not participation in co-operative society elections, only 1.7 per cent have participated in co-operative society elections.

Impact of Development Programmes

- The majority 82.6 per cent have joined in SHGs (Self-Help Groups) and 17.3 per cent respondents reported that they could not joined in SHGs. In this study, majority *i.e.* 47.2 per cent of the respondents are in the age groups in between 31-40 years of their age. Calculated the chi-squire table value *i.e.* was found to be significant, because it is more than table value. The results reveals that a significant association was found in between the age and joining in self-help groups (SHGs).

- Of the total sample 96.3 per cent of groups have confined to one caste and 3.6 per cent of groups have confined all castes. 52.8 per cent of the respondents are monthly saving in (SHGs) members Rs.50/-, 99.1 per cent respondents are maintaining group meetings regularly, 0.8 per cent could not maintaining group meetings regularly.
- According to this study 33.8 per cent are taking revolving fund, 66.1 per cent did not take revolving fund.
- In this study 82.3 per cent have taken loan from SHGs, 17.3 per cent did not take loan from SHGs.
- Majority *i.e.* 35.0 per cent of the respondents informed that they had taken loan amount *i.e.* Rs. 5000/-, 25.8 per cent of the respondents said that they had taken loan amount *i.e.* Rs. 20000/- and above.
- Of the total sample 48.38 per cent of the respondents have revealed that they had taken loan from the SHGs for the purpose of the children's education, 18.14 per cent have reported they have taken loan for house construction, 14.11 per cent have informed that they have invested on agriculture.
- In this study majority 35.4 per cent of the respondents have informed that their group had been taken loan amount Rs. 50000/- from bank and 25.8 per cent of the respondents informed that their group had been barrowing loan amount above Rs. 2,00,000.
- According to this study 92.6 per cent respondents reported that they had a knowledge on the DWCRA/MGNREGS programmes. 73.0 per cent of the Dalit women informed that they had MGNREGS job cards. About 27.0 per cent did not have MGNREGS job cards. The majority *i.e.* 26.4 per cent of respondents revealed that they have done work in one year for 26-50 days, 65.7 per cent of the respondents stated that they have been earning through MGNREGS works is in between Rs. 75-100 per day.

The socio-economic and cultural forces of the market came into operation in the early Nineties and have produced adverse effects on the weaker communities including Scheduled Castes. The problem has been compounded by the fact that the agrarian economy has not turned as under the feudal relationships and the market is dumping consumer goods and commodities on the social sector that are tied up with caste and feudal structure. The market is tearing apart the lives of the labouring Scheduled Caste as they are unable to cope up with the growing aspirations, on one hand and the increasing deprivation on other. Moreover, agrarian relations have not shown market changes in terms of land, human relationship and the wages system. A vast majority of Scheduled Castes who come under the agrarian labour economy, live below poverty line. The imposed cash crop, fish, prawn and owner production to feed the global markets is showing a trend of labour displacement which has a tremendous impact on the living conditions of these people. The problem is getting complicated with the state's withdrawal from welfare sector and contrarily, emphasising on liberalization and privatization. The economy is geared to meet the consumerist aspirations of the employed, the business and other class, and the poor are getting popularised more and more.

The government have in the past taken several intervention programmes in rural as well as urban areas including stimulation of commodity production to meet urban needs and exports, education and training of peasants, absorption of labour and reduce dissatisfaction as well as migration creation of infrastructure such as roads, water supply and sanitary systems provision of health, family planning and welfare services. Government intervention has affected rural societies both positively and negatively. Earlier SC household was attached to a particular land owning high caste household under jajmani system and used to get a fixed quantity of cereals at each harvest in lieu of the services rendered to the satisfaction of jajman (*i.e.* land owning household) throughout the year. Besides, the SC household also used to have benefits like free collection of grass for domestic animals, vegetable leaves grown in the field, collection of fire woods etc. The cereals and other benefits so received were quite adequate to sustain the SC household's nutritional needs. But with the coming of money economy in the villages, the system has now almost broken down and the life of a SC household in rural setting, particularly in terms of nutritional needs. But with the coming of money economy in the villages the system has now almost broken down and the life of a SC household in rural setting, particularly in terms of nutritional needs has got adversely affected. *Secondly*, the SC workers formally in exchange of their manual and also artisanal services had been remunerated in kind. Due to the fact that the well to do families in the village now prefer to buy goods and services in the nearby towns, many of the SC artisan families had to look for other jobs or fall back on their small land holdings. Several SC families have left the villages in the past several years and migrated to the cities. In the absence of working men the responsibilities of maintaining the household have in majority cases fallen largely on the shoulders of women. Development and empowerment of women is one of the most crucial issuès of today. It is universally accepted that not with standing considerable governmental efforts, one of the sections of women, namely Scheduled Caste women lag woefully behind others in development and they continue to be among the weakest and the exploited. Moreover, women in transition economies are finding that their specific skills are becoming absolute. In weaker sections, women play a major role, especially in economic field. In spite of the development taking place all around, it has to be conceded that bulk of the Scheduled Caste women will continue to live and earn livelihood on their own environment. Women empowerment focuses on:

1. Recognising women's contribution, women's knowledge.
2. Women fighting their own fears and feelings of inadequacy and inferiority.
3. Women enhancing their self-respect and self-dignity.

4. Women becoming their self-reliant and autonomous.
5. Women controlling own bodies.
6. Women controlling resources like: land and property.
7. Reducing women's burden of work specially with in the home.
8. Women participation in decision-making within the family and in the society.
9. Women sharing responsibilities and rights equally.

Recommendations for the Better Implementation of the Schemes of Dalit Women

1. Selection and identification of the talented Dalit girls needs to be done scientifically.
2. Competitive spirit should be instilled in the Dalit girls.
3. Selection of candidate to be done at college level itself for coaching.
4. Result oriented, teaching is essential.
5. Activities oriented towards confidence building needs to be chosen.
6. Loan facilities needs to be made available.
7. Financial aid to be given to the meritorious Dalit girl to compete for UPSC, SPSC.
8. Hostel facilities for dalit girls at all levels of education should be provided.
9. Reservation policy for Dalit girls should be made available in both admission and employment along with other girls but not as separately created.
10. Government has to be increased awareness among dalit women about their rights and privileges. This should be augmented by information technology, which should reach even to the remote rural citizen who form the large majority of Dalit women population in our country.

The special programmes for Scheduled Caste have been taken up from the very beginning in terms of their special situation – disabilities of caste on them by nefarious traditions. However, in retrospect it is clear that these programmes are notional and continued to be defunct with low level of participation and achievements of the objectives.

The Following Suggestions for Overall Empowerment of Dalit Women may be Considered

1. Removal of traditional disabilities suffered by different sections of population of various counts.
2. Elimination of exploitation in all forms and protection of women's rights and interests, with formulation of gender sensitization programmes.
3. Equity for and protection of those engaged in the traditional sectors of economy including artisans and traditional services.
4. The present inequity in the statutory wages should be removed. The minimum Wages Act should contain a provision to the effect that the daily wages of ordinary labourers in all economic activities shall be so determined the following principle that the earnings of one person in a family should be sufficient for the maintenance of the entire standard of the family.
5. Specific training programmes should be conducted and their recruitment of SC/ST women as an Extension Worker in agriculture, animal husbandry, technology transfer, environment, forestry, waste land development, horticulture, sericulture, herbiculture, small-scale industries, electronics' should be ensured.
6. Credit should be made available to SC and ST in all credit schemes. A certain percentage of SC/ST quota should be earmarked for the women.
7. Raw materials for sustaining economic activities should be made available on concessional rates through effective and efficient distribution channel.
8. Women's co-operations should be strengthened through extending them monetary incentives and sustained monitoring.
9. Skill up-gradation programmes especially entrepreneurship development programmes for women should be further

extended to the SC/ST women. In this connection the local NGO's, should be encouraged to cater and initiatives gaining skills through training.

10. Social Security schemes of crèches, health care, maternity benefits for SC/ST women who engaged in unorganized sector should be extended.
11. A group insurance scheme should be considered for the health insurance of women, particularly those employed in hazardous and difficult occupations. Group insurance can also be considered in the context of natural calamities.
12. The economic role of SC/ST women should be highlighted. They should be mobilized for taking initiatives for formation of 'Self-Help Group' and socio-economically viable project.
13. Special schemes should be formulated for eliminating scavenging and dry latrines, thus freeing SC women from the dirty and demeaning work. They should be provided with special health care coverage and hygiene education to make them aware of their occupational hazards. The women and children of this groups should be trained in other occupational areas to encourage diversification of their occupation and encourage social mobility. Training programmes for the children of persons engaged in cleaning/scavenging operations should be started in all major urban and rural centres to facilitate occupational diversification amongst this class.
14. The long-term objectives of development programmes for SC/ST women, would be to raise their economic and social status in order to bring them into the mainstream of national development. In the process, due recognition should be accorded to the role and contributions of women in various socio-economic, political and cultural activities.
15. There is a need for evolving a responsive personnel policy in the sphere of welfare and development of weaker sections. In all matters relating to the welfare of weaker

sections reputed NGO's are needed to render yeomen services. A system of social justice clearance for all personnel responsible for welfare and development of weaker sections, women, SC's ST's and OBC's etc., is suggested. The organizations leadership should also control within them.

16. Women's organizations working among weaker sections should be encouraged more. There should be a system of reorganising even men working for women of weaker sections and conferring honours on those who work for the development of women.
17. Socio-economic empowerment has been considered instrumental for holistic development. Women's empowerment is obviously essential for raising their socio-economic status in the society. Recently, women's empowerment has acquired an important place in government policy, non-government advocacy and academic research.
18. There has been a paradigm shift in development and governance. Democratic decentralization, partnership with NGO's, empowering community based organizations, participatory development, sustainable in people participation in development and governance as well as their empowerment.
19. There has been a paradigm shift in development and governance. Democratic decentralization, partnership with NGO's empowering community based organizations, participatory development, sustainable growth and equity etc., have proved to be instrumental in people participation in development and governance as well as their empowerment.
20. Socio-economic empowerment has been considered instrumental for holistic development. Women's empowerment is obviously essential for raising their socio-economic status in the society. Recently, women's empowerment has acquired an important place in government policy, non-government advocacy and academic research.

21. The models of micro-finance were evolved in Bangladesh, Indonesia, Philippines, Sri Lanka etc., and were adopted in India too. Financing through SHG's has been considered instrumental in people's empowerment, mobilizing thrift and extending credit. The concept of micro-finance in India was introduced sometimes in 1985, however, since 1996 it was widely accepted and implemented.
22. The main factor of motivation for savings is mainly securing future. The SHG's face problem regarding income generation activities. They have also initiated community development. However, only 48 per cent of them have initiated income generating activities. Further, only some members of the SHG's initiated income-generation activities.
23. Most of the beneficiaries are belonging to the age group of 31-40 years. They were found either illiterate or educationally backward. They are mostly married and belongs to nuclear families. Their housing conditions are not so good where they face problems of electricity, safe drinking water and sanitation.
24. The land holding size of respondent's families has been reported to be small and one third of them were landless. The beneficiaries were mainly self-employed and housewives. The respondent's husbands were mostly either unemployed or self-employed. The household income of majority of respondents families has been reported to be low, however, the contribution of beneficiaries of the family income has been recorded to be significant.
25. Women groups with a bondage of true sisterhood and the spirit of global kinship, should yoke together and battle against these corroding evils of caste system which might, other-wise, dangerously weaken them if they stand divided into Dalit and Non-Dalit women. This will enable women to challenge sexual determinism and biological essentialism simultaneously.

26. Education plays a crucial role in the empowerment process, Education facilities should be geared to special needs like the employment oriented education and diversified vocational training. They can be trained in small-scale and cottage industries, village crafts and other occupations.
27. Educational facilities should keep in view the specific needs of the Dalits. Special measures should be taken to improve the enrolment/retention rates as school drop-outs continue to be high. The poor students of Dalit families should continue to be assisted through scholarships, financial assistance, free books, free uniforms.
28. Education should evolve a rationalistic attitude that all human beings are born free and equal and that the caste system is man made hierarchy to facilitate his own well-being. Untouchability as a social norm, should be completely eradicated. The Dalit children in schools and colleges should be treated on equal footings as the other children.
29. Their income earning should be raised by providing access to crucial inputs like: land and credit.
30. The rural Dalit women working on land should have right to claim equal facilities available to all other workers.
31. Women can be mobilized by promoting 'Self-Help Women's Groups', which help them to gain self-esteem and self-worth.
32. Informal education should be imparted to Dalit women.
33. Women should be trained in learning to organize them-selves into groups, so that a platform for voicing out their grievances and to demand better utility services and inputs can be established.
34. Considering the number and magnitude of the problems of Dalit women, voluntary agencies must be encouraged in the spheres.
35. Right values and ethics have to be inculcated in the minds of young Dalit children. Human Rights education should

be a compulsory component of the school and college curriculum that is respecting every human, whatever be the caste, race, creed or sex, each belong to.

36. An Integrative Approach should be followed in developing housing schemes for Dalit. It gives scope to all the different caste people living at one place will have an interaction with other caste people and also exchange their socio-economic and political development among them. The present system of construction of rehabilitation colonies to weaker sections on the name of SC/ST and BC colonies will be more widening the relationships among them and creating a long gap within them. So Integrative Approach to all the schemes may properly be suitable for equal development to all caste groups and to create a casteless society through Integrative Housing Approach. It also gives good scope for the people those who are interested to looking for casteless society.

37. The Government and NGOs should take initiatives to forming of Dalit Women Forums which can deal the problems and solutions specially for Dalit Women. So that the NGOs and Government can work effectively for their problems. The forums can also interact among themselves and can find the solutions of their own for their empowerment and development.

38. One of the most important observation through interacting with the Dalit women may not included in the schedule that majority of them reported that their husbands used to spend more money everyday for taking alcohol drinking which leads to so many problems in their development and unhappiness in the family. Dalit women informed that their husbands some time may forcibly taking money from their savings and earnings for drinking of alcohol. In this context the scholar would like to suggest that those NGO who are working for De-addiction should be encouraged by providing financial supports to establish De-Addiction centres at Dalit colonies.

39. It is also Observed while interacting with the Dalit women that they have to struggle to lead the family everyday by putting lot of efforts and they reported that they could not get support from their partners in procuring fire-wood, all food items and at least to fetching of drinking for their domestic needs. Women has to put all the efforts in all aspects of the development and daily maintains of their family. Women organizations working for women empowerment should arrange meetings with the Dalit women partners and involve them in the development activities of the family. If the women collective approach is there automatically the patriarchic ideology will be dissolve in the mind of men.
40. It is also noticed that they have less freedom when comparing with the general women, Dalit men, inspite of all their bad habits, they will not allow women in decision-making and at least they do not have a control over the money they are earning. Still today there is a pathetic situation among the Dalit women. Women groups working for Dalits and women should initiate dialague with them which gives support to the Dalit women at least to question their partners.
41. Dalit-Women Forums along with SHG group should be promoted and encouraged which gives them space for discussing their problems, getting support to overcome for their individual problems and helps them in development of their families, socially, economically, and politically.

BIBLIOGRAPHY

Dr. Allu Gowri Sankar Rao and G. Samba Siva Rao (2010). Social Issues – Problems and Perspective: Article *'Status of Under Privileged (Dalit) Women – Role of Social Work'*. Sonali Publications 4228/1, Ansari Road, Darya Ganj, New Delhi - 110002 (India) p. 148, August 2010.

Asian Age 21st June 2006.

Ambedkar, B. R. (1945). Annuhilation of Caste. Bangalore: Dalit Sahitya Academy. – 1945b. What Congress and Gandhi have Done to the Untouchables. Bombay: Thacker Publication.

Andre Beteill, "The Futute of the Backward Class:" The Competing Demand of Status and Power" in Philip Masan (ed) India and (Ceylone: Unity and Diversity, London 1967), p. 93.

Asian Age 24th Sept. 2006.

Annual Report of University Grant Commission for 1999-2000.

Bhupendra Yada (2011). Much to Worry about Violence on Dalit – Article The Hindu July 19, 2011.

Babb, Lawrence, A. (1975). The Divine Hierarchy: Popular Hinduism in Central India. New York: Columbia University Press.

Bhagvan Das, "Untouchability Scheduled Caste and National Building", Reading on Scheduled Castes, National Institute of Rural Development, Hyderabad, p. 97.

Bidyut Mohanti, "Panchayati Raj, the 73rd Constitutional Amendment Act and Women". Economic and Political Weekly, *op. cit.*

Baxi, Uppendra, (1994). 'Emancipation as Justice: Babasaheb Ambedkar's Legacy and Vision', in Ambedkar and Social Justice, Vol. 1. Edited by Ministry of Information and Broadcasting, Government of India, Delhi.

Bandhu, P. (2003). *Dalit Women's Cry for Liberation: My Rights Are Rising like the Sun will you Deny this Sunrise"?* Edited in Rao (2003) *Caste and Gender*, Kali For Women, New Delhi.

Barbara, S., and Mahanta, R. (2001). Micro-Finance through Self-Help Groups and It's Saving Programme in Assam, *Indian Journal of Agricultural Economics*, Vol. 56 (3) July-Sept. 2001.

Bhatia, N. and Bhatia, A. (2002). Lending to Groups, *Yojana*, Feb. 2002.

Bilgrami, A. (2003). 'Gandhi the Philosopher', *Economic and Political Weekly* (EPW), September 27.

Chattopadhyay. R. and Duflo, E (2004). 'Women as Policy-Makers: Evidence from a Randomized Policy Experiment in India', *Econometrica*, 72 (5): 1409-1443.

Chandra Ramesh, Mitra Sangh (2003). *Dalit Identity in the New Millennium*, Commonwealth, New Dalhi.

Chakravati, V. (2003). *Reconceptualising Gender; Phule, Brahmanisam and Brahminial Patriarchy,* Edited in Rao (2003) *Caste and Gender*, Kali for Women, New Delhi.

Chitnis, V. (2005). *Human Rights of the Vulnerable Groups*, Futuristic Digital, Pune.

Champa Lernaya, Women Power and Progress, BPRC (India 4th Edition, Delhi, 1999).

Clage. W. H. The American Women: Her Chaging Social, Economic and Political Roles, New York, Oxford University Press, 1972, pp. 46-47.

Das, Bhagwan and James Massey. (1995). Dalit Solidarity. Delhi: The Indian Society for Promoting Christain Institute for the Study of Religion and Society.

Devanandan, P. D. (1960) The Dravida Kazagham: A Revolt Against Brachmanism. Bangalore: Christain Institute for the Study of Religion and Society.

Dewan, R. P. How to Erase Untouchability, R. P. Bookwala, New Delhi, 1979, p. 66.

Desai, A. R. "Social Background of Indian Nationalism", Popular, Bombay, 1981, p. 263.

Dietrich, G. (2003). *Dalit Movement and Women's Movement, Edited in Rao (2003) Caste and Gender,* Kali for Women, New Delhi.

Dasupta, R. (2001). An Informal Journey Through SHG's *Indian Journal and Agricultural Economics,* Vol. 56 (3), July-Sept. 2001.

Dhital Binay (2003). Dalit Participation: *How Over How Much',* Accessed from Http://www.msnepal.org/reports_pubs/ekchini/2003_issue2/04.html

Gurumoorthy, T. R. (2000). Self-Help Groups Empower Rural Women, *Kurushetra,* Feb. 2000.

Government of India Report to The *Committee on the Elimination of All Forms of Discrimination against Women,* UN Doc. CEDAW/C/IN/1, 1 March 1999, para. 83.

Government of India, *National Policy for the Empowerment of Women 2001,* Policy Prescriptions: para. 7.1.

Gurumurthy, U. Panchayati Raj and the Weaker Section, New Delhi, Ashish, 1987, p. 24.

Ghurye, G. S. Caste and Race in India, Popular, Bombay, 1979, Reprinted, p. 166.

Ghurye, G. S. Caste and Race in India, *op. cit.,* pp. 312-313.

Ghosh, A. "The Seventh Indian", Seminar, No. 243, November 1979, p. 27.

Ghurye, G. S. Caste and Race in India. *Op. cit.,* p. 180.

Hutton, J. H. Caste in India, Oxford, Delhi, 1981, pp. 65-66.

Hardgrave, Jr. Robert. L. (1997). The Dravidian Movement, Bombay: Popular Prakashan.

Harrison, Seling. (1960). India: The Most Dangerous Decades. Princeton: Princetion University Press.

Hocar, A. M. A Comparative Study, New York, 1948 p. 47.

Hoshior Singh and Ajmer singh Malik, "Women's Participation in Pandchayati Raj" is R. P. Joshi (ed.) Constitutionalisation of Panchayati Raj. Delhi Rawat 199s pp. 136-137.

Human Watch Report (1998). Broken People, New York, Press.

The Hindu. 20th Oct. (2010). "Dalit Women Demand Funds for Welfare" *A State – Level Conference of the Centre for Dalit Rights at Dholpur in Rajasthan.*

The Hindu, 29 June, 2003.

Hindustan Times 18th Feb. 2006.

The Hindu 29th Jan. 2010.

The Hindustan Times 28th Feb 2006.

The Hindu 5th June 2006.

The Hindu 29th June 2003.

The Hindu News Paper 29-01-10.

The International Labour Organization (ILO) Report 2007.

The Indian Express, 26th March 2002.

Jose Kanannikil, "Marginalisation of Scheduled Caste: A Sociological Interpretation", Readings on Scheduled Castes, *op. cit.*, pp. 78-79.

Jogolanad. P. G. (ed), Dalit Women: Dalit Women: Issues and Prespective New Dlihi, Gyan Publishing House, p. 156.

Ibid., p. 7.

Jain, P. C. and Shashi Jain, Shudha Bhatnagar, Scheduled Caste Women, Rawat publication. Jaipur and Delhi, 1997, p. 97.

Jahan, R. "Women in South Asian Polities," Manistream, Vol. XXV. No. 48, August 1987, pp. 35-43.

Johnson Craig (2001). *Local Democracy, Democratic Decentralisation and Rural Development:* Theirues Challenges and Options for Policy', Development Policy Review, 19(4).

Jodhka, S. (2002). *Nation and Village Images of Rural India in Gandgi, Nehru and Ambedkar'*, EPW, August 10.

Jodhka, S. (2000). *Caste and Untouchability in Rural Punjab'*, EPW, 11th May 2000.

Jogdand, P (1999). *Dalit Women, Issues and Perspectives*, Gyan Publication, New Delhi.

Kumar, N. (2004). *Dalit Policies, Politics and Parliament, Shipra* Publication, New Delhi.

Kumar, N and Raj, M. (2006). *Dalit Leadership in Panchayats*, Institute of Dalit Studies, Rawat, New Delhi.

Kupuswamy, B. Social Change in India, Vikas, New Delhi, 1879, pp. 203-204.

Kamble, J. R. Rise and Awakening of Depressed Classes in India, National, New Delhi, 1979, pp. 21-23.

Keer, Dhananjay, (1964). Mahatma Jotirao Phooley, Father of Indian Social Revolution Bombay; Popular Prakashan.

Meera Velayndhan: *"Dalit Women,s Concerns about Social Acceptionce and Specific Forms of Discrimination Need a Nuanced Approach"* Frontiline Valume 27, Issue 07: Mar 27th April 09th 2010.

The Ministry of Women and Child Development – 2009.

Manimekalai, M. and Rajeshwari, (2001). *Nature And Preformance of Informal Self-Help Groups* – A Case From Tamil Nadu, *Indian Journal of Agricultural Economics*, Vol. 56 (3), July-Sept, 2001.

Meenakshi, J. Ray, R. and Gupta, S. (2000). *'Estimates of Poverty fro SC, ST and Femal Headed Households'*, EPW, Vol. 35(15).

Mungekar, B. L. (2000). State *Market and Dalit:* Analitics of New Economic Policy' in S. M. Michael (ed), Dalit in Modern India: Vision and Values, Vistaar Publications, New Delhi.

Michael, S. (1999). *Dalits in Modern India, Vision and Values*, Vistar Publication, New Delhi.

Mahipal, (1998). Women in Panchayats, Experience of Training Camp, *Economic and Political Weekly*, Vol. XXIII, No. 4, Jan (24-30) Unpublished Papers.

Michal Moffatt, An Untouchable Community in South India: Strucure and Consesus,." *Op. cit.*, p. 4.

Michael Moffatt, An Untouchable Community in South India: Structure and Consensus, Princetion, New Jersy, 1997, p. 34.

Max Weber, On Charisma and Institution Buildings, Chicago 1966, p. 143.

Marshall, P. J. (1970). The British Discovery of Hinduism in the Eighteenth Century, Cambridge: Cambridge University Press.

Massey, James. (1990). 'Christian Dalits in India: An Analysis', Religion and Society XXXVII(3), September: 40-52.

Naicker, Ramaswamy, E. V. (1959). The Ramayana: A True Reading, Madas: Rationalist Publications.

Nargolkar, V. S. "Removal of Untouchability", *The Indian Journal of Social Work*, October 1969, Vol. 30, No. 3, p. 189.

Nargolkar, V. S. "Removal of Untouchability", *op. cit.*, p. 193.

Nanivadekar, Medha (2005) 'Indian Experience of Women 's Quota in Local Government: Implications for Future Strategies', United Nations Department of Economic and Social Affairs (DESA), Division for the Advancement of Women (DAW), Inter-Parliamentary Union(IPU), Export Group Meeting on Equal Participation of Women and Men in Decision-Making Processes, with Particular Emphasis on Political Participation and Leadership 24th to 27th October 2005. www.iknowpolitics.org/files.ep.8_rev.pdf (accessed on 13 April 2010)

National Commission for Women, *Women of Weaker Sections: Socio-Economic Development of Scheduled Caste Women*, New Delhi, 1996, p. 33.

National Human Rights Commission, *Report on Prevention of Atrocities against Scheduled Castes: Policy and Performance, Suggested Interventions and Initiatives for NHRC*, New Delhi, 2004, pp. 193-4.

National Federation of Dalit Women, *'Declaration of Dalit Women's Rights'*, Declared at 5th National Convention: Dalit Women's Assertions: Advancing their Socio-Economic Rights and Political Agenda, Chennai, 2002.

National Policy for the Empowerment of Women 2001.

The Navsarjan Trust and The Robert F. Kennedy. *Centre for Justice and Human Rights.*

Naggayya, D. (2000). Micro-Finance for Self-Help Group, *Kurukshetra*, August, 2000.

Narayanamoorthy and Kamble (2002). The Hindu, 20th November, 2002.

Opioneer, 30th Jun. 2000.

O' Hanlon, Rosalind. (1985). Caste, Fonflict and Ideology. Mahatma Jotirao Phule and Low Caste Protest in Ninteenth-Century Western India. Cambridge: Cambridge University Press.

Omvedt, Gall. (1976). Cultural Rvolt in a Colonial Society: The Non-Brahmin Movement in Western India, 1873 to 1930. Poona: Scientific Socialist Education Trust.

Pradhan, A. C. Emergence of Depressed Classes, *op.cit.*, p. 180.

Pradhan, A. C. The Emergence of the Depressed Classes, Bookland International, Bhuaneswar, 1986, p. 2.

Prasad, R. R. "Profile of the Scheduled Castes", in Readings on Scheduled Caste, National Institute of Rural Development, Hyderabad, p. 2.

Prabhakar, M. E. (1990). 'Developing A Common Ideology for Dalits of Christian and Other Faiths', Religion and Society XXXVII (3) September: 24-38.

Paswan, S and Jaidev. (2002). *Encyclopedia of Dalits in India* (Vol. No. 10 Education).

Puhazhendhi, V. and Satyasai, K J. S. (2001). Economic And Social Empowerment of Rural Poor through SHG's, *Indian Journal of Agricultural Economics*, Vol. 56 (36), July-Sept. 2001.

Parliamentary Committee on the Welfare of Scheduled Castes and Scheduled Tribes, Fourth Report on Ministry of Home Affairs, Ministry of Social Justice and Empowerment and Ministry of Tribal Affairs (14th Lok Sabha): *Atrocities on Scheduled Castes and Scheduled Tribes and Pattern of Social Crimes towards Them*, Government of India, 2004-05; see also news report in *The Pioneer*, 28 April 2005.

Pal, R. and Bhargav, G. (1999), *Human Rights of Dalits: Societal Violation*, Gyan, Publication, New Delhi.

Pandit, V (1995). Handbook on Prevention of Atrocities (SC/ST) Vidnayak Sansod Prakashan, Ujgaon, Maharashtra.

The Pioneer, 28th April 2005.

Rajasekhariah, A. M. (1971). B. R. Ambedkar: The Politics of Emoncipation, Bombay: Sindhu Publication.

Registrar General and Census Commissioner India, Primary Census Abstract – Scheduled Castes, Part IIB (ii), Series – I, Census of India, Controller of Publication, New Delhi, 1981.

Reddy, G. N. Unpublished Theses Submitted to Tata Institute of Social Science, Bombay, 1981 p. 307.

Reddy, G. N. Unpublished Thesis Submitted to Tata Institute of Social Science, *op. cit.*, pp. 313-315.

Rege, S. 'Dalit Women talk Differently: *A Critique of 'Difference' and towards a Dalit Feminist Standpoint Position'*, 6(2) Vikalp Alternatives, Vikas Adhyayan Kendra, Mumbai, 1998.

Report of the Special Rapporteur on Violence against Women, its Causes and Consequences, Radhika Coomaraswamy, Addendum 1: International, Regional and National Developments in the Area of Violence Against Women 1994-2003, UN Doc. E/CN.4/2003/75/Add.1, 27 February 2003.

Rao, A. 2003. *Gender and Caste,* Kali for Women, New Delhi.

Rakesh Malhotra (2000). *Access to Rural Women to Institutional Credit:* Issues And Alternatives, BIRD, Lucknow, 2000.

V. M., Rao (2002). *Women Self-Help Groups:* Profiles from Andhra Pradesh and Karnataka, *Kurukshetra,* April, 2002.

Singh, M. P. "Political Ariva", Seminar, No. 243, November 1979, pp. 13-19.

Shah, Ghanshyan. (1995). 'Dalit Movements and Search for Identity', in Manorama Savur and Indra Munshi (eds), Contradictions in Indian Society. Jaipur: Rawat Publications, pp. 23-43.

Shashi, S. S. (ed) (1992). Ambedkar and Social Justice. New Delhi: Government of India.

Sushila Kaushik "Women's Issue and Ninth General Election," Teaching Polities, Vol. XV. No. 3 and 4 1989 p. 113.

Sudha Pai, "Pradhanis is New Panchayat" *Economic and Political Weekly*, Vol. XXXII, No. 18 May 1998 pp. 1009-III.

Sridhar. V. (2011). "Deprivation among Dalits Remains High" by Article The Hindu News Paper 9th Jan 2011.

Satish. P. (2001). Some "Issues in the Formational of SHGs. *Indian Journal of Agricultural Economics*, Vol. 56 (3) July-Sept. 2001.

Sudha Umashanker (2011): *A Relentless Crusader* - by Article The Hindu News Paper 26th July 2011. p. 21.

Sainath, P. (2003). *Unmusical Chairs* Edited in Rao (2003) *Gender and Caste*, Kali for Women, New Delhi.

Sharma, K. C. (2001). Micro Financing through SHG's, *Indian Journal of Agricultural Economic*, Vol. 56 (3), July-Sept, 2001.

Sainath, P. (1999). Dalit and Human Rights: 'The Battles Ahead', PUCL Bulletin, June 15 p. 2001. *Some Issues in the Formational of SHG's. Indian Journal of Agricultural Economics*, Vol. 56 (3), July-Sept. 2001.

S. Viswanthan 1st Nov 2010 The Hindu News Paper.

Singh, Bhupendra and Menon, P. S. K., Report On Development of Female Education, Women Tribal Communities, National Commission for Women, Delhi, 1994.

Thorat, S and Umakant. (2004). *Caste, Role and Discrimination, Discourses in International Context*, Rawat Publication, New Delhi.

Tirmare, P. (2004). *Violation of Human Right of Dalit Women*, Issues and Facts, Paper Presented in the Seminar on ' Gender and Human Right' Organized by College of Social Work, Nanded, Maharashtra. News Paper Article.

Times of India, 26th March 2002.

Viswanthan, V. 1st November, 2010 The Hindu News Paper.

Venkitesh Ramakrishna and Ajoy Ashirwad Mahaprashasta: Vicitms Always *"The SC and ST (Prevention of Atrocities) Act has Failed to Make Dalits any Safer"* Frontline Volume 26-Issue 24: Nov. 21-Dec.04, 2009.

Waghmiore, S. (2002). *Rural Development in India: Putting the Caste Last,* Radical Humanist, August 2002.

Weber, Max. (1958). The Religion of India. Hans H. Gerth and Martindale, eds. and Trans, New York: Free Press.

Zelliot, Eleanor. (1992). From Untouchable to Dalit: Essays on the Ambedkar Movement. Delhi: Manohar. (1996). 'The Dalit Movement' Dalit International Newsletter 1 (1): 1 and 4.

INDEX

D

S

T

U

V

W

Z